The Writing of Guillaume Apollinaire

The Wesleyan Centennial Edition
of the Complete Critical Writings of Louis Zukofsky

Volume I
A Test of Poetry

Volume II
Prepositions +

Volume III and IV
Bottom: On Shakespeare

Volume V
The Writing of Guillaume Apollinaire/Le Style Apollinaire

The Writing of Guillaume Apollinaire

Le Style Apollinaire

Louis Zukofsky

Foreword by Jean Daive

Introduction by Serge Gavronsky

French Translation of Louis Zukofsky's Text by René Taupin

English Translation of Apollinaire in René Taupin's Text by Sasha Watson

Wesleyan University Press
Middletown, Connecticut

Published by Wesleyan University Press, Middletown, CT 06459

Printed in the United States of America
Library of Congress Cataloging-in-Publication Datas
Zukofsky, Louis, 1904–1978.
    [Writing of Guillaume Apollinaire. French & English]
    The writing of Guillaume Apollinaire : Le style Apollinaire / Louis
Zukofsky ; French translation by René Taupin ; English translation by Sasha
Watson ; foreword by Jean Daive ; introduction by Serge Gavronsky.
      p. cm.—(The Wesleyan centennial edition of the complete critical
writings of Louis Zukofsky ; v. 5) (Wesleyan Centennial edition of the
complete critical writings of Louis Zukofsky)
    ISBN 0-8195-6619-5 (cloth : alk. paper)—ISBN 0-8195-6620-9 (pbk. : alk.
paper)
    1. Apollinaire, Guillaume, 1880–1918—Technique.   I. Taupin, René.
II. Watson, Sasha.   III. Title.   IV. Series.
PQ2601.P6Z99913   2003
841'.912—dc21   2003010102

CONTENTS

FOREWORD

Louis Zukofsky et le style autobiographique

JEAN DAIVE

J'AI LONGTEMPS PENSÉ que le sens seul détermine la forme. Mon premier voyage aux Etats-Unis m'a persuadé du contraire. La forme, en premier, destine le sens.

L'agitation chez un auteur tel que Guillaume Apollinaire, sa complexité et son équivoque simplicité ou encore son écriture convulsive ont une puissance de contagion et d'itinérance formelles qui ne s'obtient qu'avec la souplesse inventive d'une forme nécessairement recommencée, c'est-à-dire qui relève de l'épidémie. Je m'explique.

Chaque poème, chaque vers, chaque prose est l'expérience d'un affrontement, parce que chez Guillaume Apollinaire une recherche permanente, une curiosité universelle, une règle esthétique fondée sur le principe de la nouveauté le tiennent en état de disponibilité, donc de frayeur, de panique et d'hospitalité continuelles. Il est partout. Il écrit. Il publie. Il lit tous les livres. Il émerveille. Il amuse. Il a un rire énorme. Il impose le Douanier Rousseau, il intronise le cubisme, il révèle l'art nègre, il redécouvre le marquis de Sade. Il dort dans l'atelier de Robert Delaunay. Blaise Cendrars lui donne à lire une version de ce qui devient très vite les "Pâques à New York." Il est l'ami de Picasso, Max Jacob, André Salmon. Il pleure les déceptions amoureuses. Il chante les obus et les tranchées.

Guillaume Apollinaire introduit dans le vers toutes les conquêtes de la vie et de l'art. Il y poursuit l'aventure de la simultanéité aussi bien que les niveaux de conscience au travail dans les conversations qu'il entend et capte au passage en marchant dans la ville et dont il transmet le parfait mouvement sonore, je veux dire une surimpression de sens, de voix, d'images qui résonnent. Cette attention-là se trouve tout entière dans "Zone" (1912) et annonce la mesure de l'œuvre de Louis Zukofsky, dont l'ordre est ainsi formulé par Louis Zukofsky lui-même en 1948 dans *A Test of Poetry*: sight, sound and intellection.

Je reprends. Guillaume Apollinaire chine. Il est bousculade. Il est transfert et qui-vive. Et j'imagine son aisance, (grâce à l'art du masque), à s'adresser à l'autre, à écouter l'autre. Il possède une intuition de l'autre très aiguë, évidemment jusque dans le langage. Il vit à la perfection une sorte de pénétration des manières, de la pensée de l'autre: il veut aller plus loin que la compréhension et le transfert spontané lui permet d'éviter ce qui contrarie l'interlocuteur. Lorsqu'il écrit, il naturalise ce qu'il trouve en le rendant exceptionnel.

A ces changements organiques de ton correspondent les changements de forme, dont Guillaume Apollinaire explore en magicien la nature, le rêve intérieur, les limites, la séduction, sans jamais perdre de vue l'effet même de l'opération poétique qui touche à tout: contes, nouvelles, romans, conférences, poèmes, chroniques, essais, lettres, calligrammes, études critiques, théâtre. La métamorphose est là: il y a toujours ce que la forme distribue en protocoles de ce qu'il faut comprendre comme le cours du temps, de la douleur, de la nostalgie et d'une délinquance même grammairienne qui n'épargne rien, ni jamais.

Une possession contagieuse, à la manière des danses de Saint-Guy, autorise une sorte d'expansion dont les strophes ou les paragraphes, par exemple, s'offrent en paniques, en sacrifices et en horizons voyageurs, ce que la technique des épidémies met en œuvre, parfaitement.

Une question: qui habite les épidémies? Une réponse: l'Etranger. Celui qui communément formalise sa parole sauvage. Autre réponse: l'Homme, dont l'évidente réalité est celle du masque. Et je pense aussi que l'artiste qui vit le babil habite en même temps la langue de l'épidémie. J'ai en mémoire ce passage de Louis Zukofsky écrit en 1946, "Poésie— Pour mon fils quand il saura lire"-dans *Prepositions (1967)*, à propos de son fils Paul alors âgé de 19 mois et babillant à toute vitesse *Go billy go billy go billy go ba:* «Le langage commun est ce à quoi les enfants sont habitués par ceux qui les entourent lorsqu'ils commencent à distinguer les mots . . . en sachant par ailleurs que l'exercice du discernement à l'égard des mots ne suppose nullement un effort de notre raison.» J'y reviens.

Comment affronter la question de l'équivoque simplicité qui exprime un état d'équilibre grâce entre autres au langage commun qu'il s'agit de faire résonner? Cette question de l'extrême simplicité (elle n'exclut pas une grande habileté, une fantaisie extrême, jeux de mots et jeux avec les mots, fragments d'entretiens, poèmes-conversations, toutes les difficultés et toutes les facilités, passages incessants du monde des objets au monde du langage en tant que sons, un sens inouï du mystère poétique où le vrai se dissout en vrai rêvé et merveilleusement en vers «ronds comme des âmes») ressemble beaucoup à l'expérience de la sincérité et son esprit en devance l'objet.

Deux images me viennent en mémoire, presque deux photographies. D'une agilité manuelle surprenante, Guillaume Apollinaire exécute le calligramme le plus compliqué avec une facilité déconcertante, comme il tient un aviron en équilibre sur son menton. Louis Zukofsky est la fragilité extrême et un document le représente en pierrot lunaire, gourmand et facétieux. A une sorte d'absence à soi-même s'ajoute l'errance chez Louis Zukofsky ou l'exil intérieur comme construction et forme déambulatoires, composées d'allées et venues, détours, silences, répétitions, ouverture. Et par absence à soi-même, j'entends associer le témoignage de Robert Creeley me confiant le 5 janvier 1995: «Il était si léger qu'il fallait l'attacher au balcon, de peur qu'il ne s'envole.»[1] J'y reviens. Maintenant, quelle est la construction de son absence (ou solitude) et de sa déambulation (ou solitude)? Le yiddish (la première langue de Louis Zukofsky, avant l'anglais, et la première langue des parents). L'économie. L'Histoire. La Politique, c'est-à-dire ce qu'un peuple fut et ce qu'il devrait être. Spinoza et Marx dans un parfait équilibre avec Jean-Sébastien Bach et la structure de la fugue. Le chiffre trois. Par exemple, le chiffre trois construit le premier livre de Louis Zukofsky, *An «objectivists» Anthology*. Le chiffre trois construit le deuxième livre: *A Test of Poetry*. Il confie par ailleurs à Ezra Pound que son Grand Œuvre est un triptyque et devrait se composer de *Poem beginning «The»* (article défini: le) et s'achevant avec *«An»* (article indéfini précédant une voyelle). Il confie aussi à Ezra Pound dans une lettre du 12 décembre 1930 que *Poem beginning «The»* est une réponse directe à *The Waste Land* de T. S. Eliot et que l'intention de *«A»* est de faire que la promesse s'accomplisse. J'en étais là de mes réflexions à propos de Louis Zukofsky et Guillaume Apollinaire quand un jour les deux poètes vinrent à ma rencontre.

Dans ma main, par un bel après-midi de printemps, chez un libraire de la rue de Seine à Paris, glisse, tombé de la lettre A comme Apollinaire, un livre introuvable de Louis Zukofsky publié en 1934. La couverture est ocre doré et le titre, *Le Style Apollinaire,* se détache, composé en caractère dit «françaises-légères». Très vite, je remarque deux choses: le mot Style et la table des matières, qui m'indique une construction en trois parties:

---

1. In *La Fin* de Robert Creeley : choix de poèmes, traduction et présentation de Jean Daive, Gallimard Éditeur, 1997.

I. «Il y a» — II. «Le poète ressuscité» — III. «Et Cⁱᵉ» —précédées d'une Préface: «Le flâneur». Je laisse défiler en moi quelques définitions du mot Style: manière de parler, formule de procédure, aspect de l'expression, le style est l'homme même. Toujours la question de la forme.

Dès la première phrase, Louis Zukofsky censé parler de Guillaume Apollinaire dévoile son projet résolument autobiographique: le monde de la rue dont la saveur est un véritable feu d'artifice ressemble à une immense bibliothèque pour le flâneur qui prête l'oreille à la promesse des mots dont sont chargées les conversations de hasard et ainsi s'isole parmi les autres, parmi les choses. L'écriture doit révéler aussi bien les formes de son époque qu'une littérature transplantée prenant en compte le sens du changement comme valeur constante, les accélérations et les ralentissements de l'Histoire, l'instinct de la simultanéité, un sens du mouvement attiré par l'espace, par l'art et par les airs qu'il faut mettre en scène au même titre que la page qui ne doit pas ignorer le lyrisme typographique ou visuel, enfin la synthèse littéraire de la musique, la peinture ou la poésie.

Louis Zukofsky ne passe pas sous silence ce que Guillaume Apollinaire attend du cinéma, du phonographe qui doit supplanter la littérature actuelle et donner aux poètes la liberté: «Le livre vu et entendu de l'avenir.» La matière est celle du quotidien. Les machines, le téléphone, la T.S.F., l'avion, la prophétie, l'Esprit nouveau envahissent la vie. Il observe chez Guillaume Apollinaire tous ces points d'ouverture—le poème «A» retiendra l'idée de structure ouverte—comme il a observé plus jeune dans un quartier de New York où il est né en 1904, le Lower East Side, Chrystie Street, l'arrivée en masse des Juifs russes déçus par la Révolution et j'imagine l'enfant Zukofsky entendre les voix et regarder tout un inventaire d'objets portés à dos d'homme émigrant, par exemple cet édredon rouge et par-dessus les toits, comme dans *les Mamelles de Tirésias,* les seins de la femme transformés en ballons s'envoler dans les airs. Il regarde. Il entend. Sight, sound and intellection. C'est la bibliothèque de Babel qui passe devant lui et ce sont aussi une structure, une innovation vivantes et un ordre qu'il a sous les yeux, dont il se souviendra en écrivant le poème «A» où le vécu biographique trame l'Histoire sociale, où les idées politiques radicales exprimées en russe, en yiddish, en polonais, en allemand trament naturellement une forme d'essence musicale sur le modèle de la fugue de Jean-Sébastien Bach et de la *Passion selon saint Matthieu.* Une genèse en marche, une genèse dans la rue mieux qu'une bibliothèque haute en couleur. Les conversations entendues, les différents niveaux de conscience du langage parlé offrent déjà une transcription de la réalité qui identifie les nombreuses couches sociales présentes à New York et venues de tous horizons. J'imagine aussi le jeune Zukofsky rentrer à la maison le soir et servir d'interprète ou de traducteur à la demande des parents, qui ne parlent que le yiddish, et des voisins, qui prolongent indéfiniment débats politiques, syndicalistes, révolutionnaires et refont l'Histoire. Et de ce point de vue, le chapitre II est directement autobiographique, où Louis Zukofsky reprend à son compte ce passage de "Zone" qu'il transforme en prose: «Tu regardes les yeux pleins de larmes ces pauvres émigrants / Ils croient en Dieu ils prient des femmes allaitant les enfants / Ils emplissent de leur odeur le hall de la gare Saint-Lazare / Ils ont foi dans leur étoile comme les rois-mages / Ils espèrent gagner de l'argent dans l'Argentine / Et revenir dans leur pays après avoir fait fortune / Une famille transporte un édredon rouge comme vous transportez votre cœur / Cet édredon et nos rêves sont aussi irréels." Venu d'ailleurs, ce cortège d'hommes, de femmes, d'enfants et d'objets entre dans la mémoire comme plaisir sonore aussi bien que visuel et nourrit la fonction d'une ode considérée sous le triple aspect du grammairien, du rhétoricien et du musicien. Le plaisir sonore et visuel est plaisir unique comme construction et sonorité de la construction dans le développement moderne de la critique. Il y a du reste quelque chose du défilé (de textes), dans la deuxième partie, «le Poète ressuscité», où Louis Zukofsky fabrique une œuvre de Guillaume Apollinaire en mettant bout à bout des extraits de proses ou de vers qu'il faut lire comme un autre *Test of Poetry*. C'est à la fois une traversée du monde apollinairien du point de vue de l'Etranger qui éprouverait la nécessité d'expliquer à sa famille, dont la langue est le yiddish, qui est Apollinaire et une projection du Grand Œuvre de Louis Zukofsky à venir: «*A*». Et je ne résiste pas à recopier le titre des sept premières citations: Palais, Alcools — Le Passant de Prague, L'Hérésiarque et Cie — Le Juif latin, L'Hérésiarque et Cie — La Synagogue, Alcools — La Serviette des Poètes, L'Hérésiarque et Cie — Que Vlo-ve? — L'Hérésiarque et Cie — Marie, Alcools . . . Je peux même me demander qui est le vrai poète ressuscité: Apollinaire ou plus réellement Louis Zukofsky qui écrit dans «*A*»-2 — "This is my face / This is my form?"

Mais Louis Zukofsky va plus loin. Un premier ordre de composition-action opposé à la composition des mots s'impose chez Guillaume Apollinaire: le dessin graphique où le calligramme participe à la poésie, parce qu'il participe à un ordre de l'intelligence véhémente qui est la nature. Le dessin graphique est poésie. Le projet du poème «*A*» est inscrit là — en partie.

Jean Daive

Sans y penser
 Je disais:
   Peut-on
   Transposer
   Le dessin
   D'une fugue
   En poème?
    «*A*»-6

L'avant-dernier mot de ce livre essentiel à la compréhension de la pensée de Louis Zukofsky et de la genèse de son œuvre incomparable est le mot «guerre». Et là encore je reviens au cortège d'émigrants, qui n'est pas sans évoquer un climat d'émeute ou de grève générale avec panneaux, valises, slogans, cris, sirènes, paniques, mouvement de foule et silence inquiétant ou mélange des langues. Seuls deux événements existent: la guerre et les mots, insiste Louis Zukofsky. Et le vrai dernier mot est celui de «simplicité», que Guillaume Apollinaire—poète, guerrier et trépané— réincarne au nom d'une enfance et d'une nostalgie sans fin transfigurées et sublimées de façon géniale dans «*A*».

INTRODUCTION

Guillaume Apollinaire Subsumed Under Louis Zukofsky's Gaze: ". . . listening receptively . . ."

SERGE GAVRONSKY

On an original unique written copy with the initials "G.A. & L.Z." continued by "The Writing of Guillaume Apollinaire," one can read the following: "This collaboration was written entirely by L.Z. and the French quotations are also his arrangement. It was subsequently translated by R.T. [René Taupin] into French, and the French version was published by Les Presses modernes, Paris, France, 1934." The copy is signed "Louis Zukofsky." As a result it's quite simple to discover at least one origin of *The Writing of Guillaume Apollinaire* as well as the way it got to Paris: via René Taupin, a friend of Louis Zukofsky and teacher of French at Columbia College.[1]

---

1. René Taupin (1905–81) earned the degree of *docteur-es-lettres* from the University of Paris, and received a Gold Medal from the *Académie française* in 1929 for his groundbreaking study *L'Influence du symbolisme français sur la poésie américaine (1910–1920)*, which was published by the *Bibliothèque de la Revue de littérature comparée*, vol. 62 (Paris: Librairie Ancienne Honoré Champion, 1929). This collection was coedited by two distinguished Sorbonne comparatists, Ferdinand Baldensperger and Paul Hazard. This dissertation was later translated in the United States by William Pratt and Ann Rich Pratt, revised, and edited with an introduction and a conclusion by William Pratt: *The Influence of French Symbolism on Modern American Poetry* (New York: AMS Press, 1985). Taupin's other scholarly works include *L'Interprétation américaine de la poésie française contemporaine: Quatre Essais sur une esthétique de l'Inspiration* and, with his Hunter College colleague, Professor Henri Dupont, *La France au XVIIIᵉ siècle*.

On the other hand there's no information that might inform us as to how precisely Zukofsky discovered Apollinaire.[2] What is beyond doubt is the result: a fascinating reading of a major twentieth-century French poet's work by an American poet whose poetics so closely resembled that of Apollinaire's that a near perfect match was in the making. (Could one repeat Baudelaire's comment that, when reading a poem by Edgar Allan Poe, the American had literally taken the poem out of the French poet's imagination?) Among the elements shared by Apollinaire and Zukofsky one would have to include the place accorded to linguistic registers, switches in tone and pacing, versification, syntactical innovations as well

---

René Taupin's familiarity with the United States goes back to the year he spent at Haverford College as a student in 1925–26. In a June 30, 1931, letter, Zukofsky writes to Pound and states explicitly that it is Columbia that is giving Taupin a leave of absence beginning February 1932 at full pay. He later returned to teach at Haverford in 1932–34. He later taught at Cornell and Hunter College, where, after 1934 and through to his retirement in 1966, he was professor of French and often chair of the Department of Romance Languages (alternating as chair with Henri Dupont).

Concerning Taupin's participation in *Le Style Apollinaire* (his French translation of Louis Zukofsky's *The Writing of Guillaume Apollinaire*), Professor Hanna K. Charney of Hunter College, a long-time admirer of Taupin's work, wrote: "La nature de la collaboration . . . restera sans doute un mystère" (René Taupin, *Essais Indifférents: Pour une esthétique de l'Inspiration*, ed. Hanna K. Charney and Bettina L. Knapp [New York: Peter Lang, 1989], 13). It is indeed a mystery, given Louis Zukofsky's formal disavowal of any help in either the writing of the text or the selection of the Apollinaire quotes. Perhaps a stylistic analysis might partially answer this question: were one to compare Taupin's polished, academic style with Zukofsky's idiosyncratic syntax and his inimitable use of language, little doubt would remain—unless, applying at least one theory of translation, Taupin had "Frenchified" the American text. The URL from the Zukofsky Collection at the Kansas State University Library includes a detailed locator for the Taupin-Zukofsky letters: *http://www.lib.ksu.edu/depts/spec/findaids/pc1994-07.html*. I thank Professor Mark Scroggins for this source.

2. Another unanswered question is the actual place of Apollinaire on the U.S. scene before Zukofsky undertook his critical essay. In the Columbia University Library there exists only one translation: Mathew Josephson's *The Assassinated Poet* (New York: Broome, 1923). The question remains open as Zukofsky had more than a reading knowledge of French, and Taupin of course was familiar with contemporary French poetry—though, in his study *The Influence of French Symbolism*, Apollinaire only appears five times (in the French, he had appeared six times!). Barry Ahearn, a close reader of Zukofsky's work, writes: "The Frenchman he most admired in his early years was someone who championed the work of Picasso and Braque— Guillaume Apollinaire." (Barry Ahearn, *"A": An Introduction* [Berkeley and Los

as typographical ones, the use of citations, and the practice of simultaneity. Finally I suspect that Louis Zukofsky sympathized with Guillaume Apollinaire's status as an "outsider." These are some of the questions the following pages hope to address.

In the opening paragraph of *The Writing of Guillaume Apollinaire*, Zukofsky expeditiously describes, if only partially, one of his own penchants of poetic definitions. He isolates the auditive faculty of Apollinaire's *Le Flâneur des deux rives* and in that text discovers a kindred spirit where, in line with an American tendency to "listen" to language and thereafter have the poem filter that quality, Apollinaire had refash-

---

Angeles: University of California Press, 1983], 28). Ahearn adds: "That century produced Apollinaire who taught Zukofsky to let go of the all-pervading ego in favor of the intermittent self" (ibid., 187). A number of years after *The Writing of Guillaume Apollinaire*, Zukofsky was to quote passages from Apollinaire's *Calligrammes* in his *Bottom: On Shakespeare* (Berkeley and Los Angeles: University of California Press, 1987, 235, 236; ©1963).

Ezra Pound, in a single letter written in French to René Taupin, did not mention Apollinaire even though he observed: "presque *toute* l'experimentation technique en poésie de 1830—jusqu'à moi—était faite en France." In that same letter he did declare: "Gautier j'ai étudié et je le révère," (*The Selected Letters of Ezra Pound, 1907–1941*, ed. D. D. Paige [New York: A New Directions, 1971], 216–17. This work is a reprint of *The Letters of Ezra Pound, 1907–41* [New York: Harcourt Brace Jovanovich, 1950]). (I am grateful to Professor Richard Sieburth of New York University for this lead.) In "Date Line," written on January 28, 1942, Pound mentioned Taupin who "took the trouble to look up a good many [criticisms, reviews] that I had forgotten" (ibid., 11). In Pound's February 1918 essay on "French Poets," which appeared in the *Little Review* (repr. in *Make It New, Essays by Ezra Pound* [London: Faber and Faber, 1934] 159–247), Pound does not mention Apollinaire even once although he wrote at length on Laforgue, Corbière, Rimbaud, Rémy de Gourmont, Emile Verhaeren, Stuart Merril, Laurent Tailhade, Francis James, Moréas, Spire, and Jules Romain (no Mallarmé and no Apollinaire). And lastly, not a peep on Apollinaire in Pound's letter to the review *Dial* (1920–23). See *Lettres de Paris,* trans. Marie Milesi, Jean-Michel Rabaté, and François Dominique (Dijon: Ulysse Fin de siècle, 1988).

Although Pound does not mention Apollinaire, Taupin mentions him in passing: for example, the influence of Apollinaire's *Marzibill* on T. S. Eliot (*L'Influence*, 221). Zukofsky's work, on the other hand, was appreciated by his friend William Carlos Williams who, in a letter dated March 28, 1934, wrote: "Let me, in a small way, express my thanks to both you and Taupin for the valuable and interesting work you have done in your thesis (Taupin's you'll say) on the work of Apollinaire"; see the *Williams-Zukofsky Correspondance, 1928–62*, ed. Barry Ahearn. I consulted the typescript given to me by Paul Zukofsky.

ioned a persistent French classical tradition going back to the sixteenth-century Pléiade school of poets, which favored the sublime alexandrine in its most writerly presence. Similarly, the Pléiade insisted on classical themes inspired by Greek, Roman, and Italian models. In contradistinction to those precepts, Apollinaire wedged open the door to orality in poetry. Of course he was not the first poet to do so; the brilliant Tristan Corbière should be mentioned here with his linguistic shifts and his transcriptions of the oral ("La Balancelle") still, in his day, Apollinaire was undoubtedly the poet who most thoroughly exploited the transcription of the oral into poetry.

In the past a poet was most frequently compared to a jeweler or a sculptor; that is, one who honed down the text. Apollinaire founded his poetics on an apparent rejection of those principles. I say "apparent" rejection: a most gifted practitioner, Apollinaire was equally able to exploit everything that had been done before him. Nevertheless, his work stands out in opposition to Théophile Gautier's practice, succinctly stated in his 1857 poem, "L'Art:"

> Sculpte, lime, cisèle;
> Que ton rêve flottant
> Se scelle
> Dans le bloc résistant!

Perhaps the most visible sign of Zukofsky's preoccupation with orality was the length of the Apollinaire quote on the first page of *The Writing of Guillaume Apollinaire*, as if Zukofsky had understood that the best way of demonstrating his affection for reading and listening to language per se was to quote it to a degree we would find impossible today (and, remembering authors' rights and all of that business, very expensive to duplicate). After all, how much can a poet expropriate of another's work without running into difficulty with the law?

Orality, then, is a guiding principle: that is, "listening" to the voice and thereafter making sure that on paper, in the poem, such a voice reigns indisputable. Apollinaire's 1899 "Stavelot" love poems are the earliest signs of this disposition where orality and traditional scriptural narrativity commingle; where evocation of place, sentiment, and poetic form seize the moment and, in so doing, hark back to a playfulness already readable in the fifteenth-century French poet Charles d'Orléans's work where sounds, puns, and visual transcription on the page of such effects were all rendered harmoniously.

In the 1888 poem "Le Teint," Zukofsky must have been touched to see in upper case the founding letter of his own epic poem-in-the-making: the grandiloquent *A*—in French, the dedicatory preposition "to" and, in this case, "to Linda," who becomes an excuse for an extended musical and visual variation on the letters composing her name going from Linda, Ilinda, to Ildan, twenty-two names later. Sing the poem! See the poem structured in three uneven columns on the page!

All of a sudden the poem becomes itself, wholly defined by its internal machinations, freed of a classical restriction that condemned such oral liberties—liberalities—as violations of a Cartesian injunction imposed on the text by an insistence on storytelling, on what Boileau, the 17th century poet and theoretician, underscored in his "Art poétique," when he emphasized meaning in poetry, rendered elegant by rhetorical ornaments. In the last century, the poet and playwright Paul Claudel, in his *La Cantate à trois voix*, echoed a similar sentiment when he wrote: "Il faut que le son s'éteigne afin que le sens demeure."

Zukofsky listens and he sees. But anyone even slightly familiar with "*A*" knows that, as well as orality and textuality, Zukofsky also insisted on powerful themes. After all, both the writing of poetry and a critical enterprise such as *The Writing of Guillaume Apollinaire* are founded on what Ezra Pound, a close friend of Zukofsky's, described as the coequal partners of the epic: History on the one hand and the travels of the "I" on the other (to which Zukofsky would humorously yet in utter seriousness, add the "eye," thereby objectifying the audible in the text). Thus Le Flâneur's initial impressions deal with a Borgesian interlocking, interwoven, closed universe of books, as Le Flâneur finds himself in the public library on Forty-Second Street, where books in Yiddish were copied to be sent to the local branch on Fourteenth Street, in a working-class neighborhood. It is difficult to read this passage without remembering Zukofsky's endless hours spent reading in the public library, and therefore his immediate identification with Le Flâneur's bibliophilic activities.

Here, then, in the inaugural pacing of the work, one finds two themes dear to Zukofsky. First, the preeminent signs that books contain and the extraordinary passion Zukofsky had for them—all of them, ranging from histories to poetry and philosophy. Second, as the biographical "I" in part revealed, his own familiarity with the Jewish neighborhood Le Flâneur frequented.

Apollinaire was indeed one of those rare poets to situate Jews in his poetry and prose. See for instance (and Zukofsky quotes the story), Apollinaire's "Le Passant de Prague" (The Wandering Jew), which first appeared in *La Revue Blanche* (June 1902) and then, slightly modified, in his *L'Hérésiarque et Cⁱᵉ* (1910). In its first version, the story alludes to the Dreyfus Affair where the narrator (The Wandering Jew) says to a certain Isaac Laquedem, about the ill-fated captain, "Votre légende . . . symbolisait votre race, que j'aime de s'être conservée si pure à travers les temps, car j'aime les Juifs." In the final version, the traveler says to Isaac Laquedem as they tour the city of Prague: "votre légende . . . symbolisait votre race errante. . . . J'aime les Juifs." (Is it a coincidence? Corbière's poem "Laisser-Courre" is to be accompanied by a musical composition written by Isaac Laquedem . . .)

In "Le Juif latin," another story in that same collection (which first appeared in *La Revue Blanche* on March 1, 1903), Gabriel Fernisour, a Jew from Avignon, who has read "Le Passant de Prague" (what a structuralist theory-dropping moment!), says to the narrator: "Vous ne me connaissez pas, mais vous aimez les Juifs, donc vous m'aimez, car je suis juif, monsieur!" And the same, in a pro-Sephardic statement, continues: "Ce ne sont pas les Juifs que vous aimez, ce sont les Latins . . . je vous ai dit que j'étais juif, monsieur, mais je parlais au point de vue confessionnel, à tous autres égards, je suis latin. . . . Vous nous aimez parce que, Portugais et Comtadins, nous ne sommes pas maudits."

Writing about Apollinaire, Zukofsky says: "Himself, like old Isaac Laquedem, he has to absorb, in several ways, all the life which had been." And commenting on "Le Départ de l'ombre," Zukofsky adds: "The magic hold, on Apollinaire, of Hebraic superstition . . ." One could just as well have applied that appreciation to Zukofsky himself.

In the poem "Rhénanes," Apollinaire (as Zukofsky quotes him) writes: "Nous transportâmes le *Festin* à Neuilly. Non sans faire halte à la synagogue de la rue Jacques-Dulud." Let's not forget that Zukofsky does not hesitate in "*A*" to recapitulate his own father's history, his religion as well as his friends' on the Lower East Side.

But another theme also emerges, as the title "Le Flâneur" indicates: the wanderer, the stroller through time and space—a consecrated theme, at least for those who have read Jean-Jacques Rousseau's *Promenades*, or Baudelaire's voyages. Zukofsky is explicit on this point: "The stroller, living thru the times he did, must have often appeared an isolated phenomenon to himself." This understanding is garnered from a reading of Apollinaire's self-observations as a solitary (soliloquizing) figure. The poem "Zone" is an exemplary demonstration of this feeling: Apollinaire wanders through his life from childhood to adult consciousness, wanders, too, through geographies both visited and read about—the *zones* of his poem.

But if the particular, as always, fascinated Zukofsky, the condition he ascribes to Apollinaire fits both Zukofsky and the French poet; indeed, without being over romantic about it, the status of the poet himself. The poet is not only an isolated figure but, in a grandiose way, a "phenomenon," something tragic and heroic—comical, too, resembling that eccentric Mallarmé so well described as "le spirituel histrion" (Stéphane Mallarmé, *Œuvres complètes*, texte établi et annoté par Henri Mondor et G. Jean-Aubry [Paris: Bibliothèque de la Pléiade, 1945], 307).

I would then say that Zukofsky translates himself into the *Writing of Guillaume Apollinaire*: the passages he lifts from the French poet's work are indicative of this mirror analysis of his own poetics, of his own "identity" as a poet. Let me first quote the French and then paraphrase it in English:

> Je me disais Guillaume il est temps que tu viennes
> Pour que je sache enfin celui-là que je suis
> Moi qui connais les autres.
> ("Cortège," in *Alcools*)
> I was telling myself Louis it's time you came around
> So that I may finally know who I am
> I who know the others.

Zukofsky is tenacious, a characteristic that well serves the epic poem. He finds in Apollinaire other self-identification passages in three calligrams that offer humor and pathos, a touch of melancholy, a touch of self-deprecation. They could have been written by Zukofsky, who easily switched language registers, going from the sublime to the most ordinary modes of speaking:

> I'm fed up
> I'm going to piss.

Or perhaps that may have been too frank for a rather prudish Zukofsky.

But Why Guillaume Apollinaire?

The principal question remains: why was Zukofsky attracted to this particular poet? Might it have been Apollinaire's reputation? After all he was, in the footsteps of Baudelaire and Rimbaud, and especially Mallarmé (who would figure so prominently later on in Zukofsky's

"*A*"-19), the very incarnation of the avant-garde at a time when both Tristan Tzara and André Breton were holding forth. Further, in a tradition going back to Diderot's eighteenth-century *Salons*, Apollinaire was a forward-looking art critic who fully defended his Cubist painter friends, including Picasso.

Apollinaire had also coined two terms closely associated with his epoch: one, *L'Esprit nouveau*, has fallen by the wayside but the other, *surréalisme*,[3] has had a long life. In 1924, André Breton, in his *Manifeste du surréalisme* (which Zukofsky quotes in his study), acknowledged if not the spirit at least the letter of that neologism which Apollinaire used to describe his play *Les Mamelles de Tirésias*, rejecting *surnaturalisme* which, for Apollinaire, had already outlived its usefulness. Apollinaire had his own definition of what was to become, after his death in 1918, a major literary-philosophic-artistic movement: "Quand l'homme a voulu imiter la marche, il a créé la roue qui ne ressemble pas à une jambe. Il a fait ainsi du surréalisme sans le savoir." (A humorous but useless definition in light of what was to come!) And Apollinaire added: "Surréalisme n'existe pas encore dans les dictionnaires et il sera plus commode à manier." In that he was perfectly correct.

In the concluding section of *The Writing of Guillaume Apollinaire*, Zukofsky quotes Apollinaire's preface to his play where he not only pointed out the difference between life and art (the theater) but equally defined the type of verse best suited to a play: "un vers souple, fondé sur le rythme, le sujet, le souffle." Would Zukofsky have proposed a better quadratic solution?

Especially as a poet, Zukofsky would have been attracted to Apollinaire. In "La Jolie rousse," Apollinaire voiced his desire to unite tradition with innovation. This ambition had already been a topos in French poetry; for instance, in Baudelaire's "Le Voyage" written in perfect alexan-

---

3. If in the poem, " 'Mantis,' an Interpretation," Zukofsky did not mention Apollinaire, he did, in the French spelling, indirectly acknowledge Apollinaire's neologism:

Dante's rubric
  Incipit
Surrealiste
  Re-collection

(Quoted in *Complete Short Poetry, Louis Zukofsky*, with a foreword by Robert Creeley [Baltimore: Johns Hopkins University Press, 1997], 69.) The poem is dated November 4, 1939, New York. What is certain is that Zukofsky could handle French to the extent of translating Guillaume Machaut's "Ballade: Ploures, dames" (ibid., 86).

drines, where the poet incited other poets to go "au fond de l'Inconnu pour trouver du *nouveau.*"

Zukofsky had a similar vision, combining old and new as he simultaneously played on a modern language scale and rendered homage to the Shakespearian sonnet in "*A*"-7 and "*A*"-9, to a *Midsummer Night's Dream* as well as to its hero in his own critical study, *Bottom: On Shakespeare*. A glance at "*A*" 's Index is sufficient testimony to warrant a rapprochement between Zukofsky and Apollinaire in the way both desired to make the old new, whether in rewriting a few lines from Shakespeare's *Pericles, Prince of Tyre* (see "*A*"-19), or in a book-length translation of Catullus's poetry that Zukofsky translated with his wife, Celia. It's one thing to render homage to the past via a system of collaging quotes or winks in the proper direction; it's quite another to rethink the past, to shape it in such a way as to have it participate in a most innovative poetic experiment.

Zukofsky surely appreciated the traces of tradition in Apollinaire's work: outright citations as well as textual inferences. Zukofsky will approvingly quote Apollinaire quoting Madame de Staël: "La littérature des anciens est chez les modernes une littérature transplantée, la littérature romantique ou chevaleresque est chez nous indigène et c'est notre religion et nos institutions qui l'ont fait éclore." The first lines in Ezra Pound's *Cantos* assume a reader's familiarity with Homer's *Odyssey*. Apollinaire, without going back that far, counted on his own readers' familiarity with some of the masterpieces of European literature; for example, *Robinson Crusoe* when he wrote "Le Robinson de la gare Saint-Lazare," *Le Poète assassiné*, or his transformative allusions to Arthurian legends in "Arthur Roi Passé Futur" in that same collection. Zukofsky will return to "Arthur Roi Passé Futur" later on and note that "the present tense of the telling dispenses with extra explanation of the mysteries of ressurection and immortality. Arthur is part of the future, because the 'story' is being told." The fact that Apollinaire had dedicated this story to Blaise Cendrars, one of his friends, for whom he had gotten the job of editing Chrétien de Troyes's thirteenth-century romance, *Perceval ou le Conte du Graal*, in a sixteenth-century version (a text that ultimately came out in 1918), is indicative of the contemporaneity of the Arthurian cycle. And who has not heard of Apollinaire's borrowing the narrative structure of Cendrars's "Pâques à New York" (1912) in order to work through his own "flâneur" in "Zone?"

Literary critics today consider such borrowings as indubitable evidence of intertextuality: then, it may simply have been an indication of a shared culture or an automatic memory reflex. Let us not forget that when Louis Zukofsky entered Columbia College in January 1920, and took courses with the recently appointed Mark van Doren, the humanities were still heavily represented by the classics, by a Greek and Roman literature implicitly defined as the foundation of our present civilization—a past "present" that today again has to be deciphered. Let us also remember the "Contemporary Civilization" course John Erskine had begun at that time, which included large doses of the classics.

Apollinaire conjoined tradition with innovation and that formula could not have escaped Zukofsky's attention. Especially in the American vein, Shakespeare and the King James Bible have nourished innovative attempts such as Walt Whitman's *Leaves of Grass*. I said Apollinaire *was* the avant-garde of his day; discussing his culture, Zukofsky writes that Apollinaire "made incumbent his constant heresies with respect to this past." In Apollinaire's poetry, this continuity/discontinuity with the past becomes clearer in his continuation of Mallarmé's nonpunctuation practice in poetry together with a much more daring *mise en page* of the poems in *calligrammes* where, on the page, what is thematically described is seen as well, and thus a calligram of the Eiffel Tower takes on the shape of that ultimate indicator of modernity.

Playfulness? Of course! *Homo ludens*, as Ortega y Gasset observed it and whose work was read and commented upon in Columbia College right through to my own student days there in the early 1950s. This visualization of the poem exemplifies Apollinaire's continued questioning not only of the language of poetry but also, in an era following *Un coup de dés jamais n'abolira le hasard*, its shape on the page. Could this audacity have had something to do with Apollinaire not being a true-blooded Frenchman but an interloper, a foreigner who had mastered the language of "culture" itself? Could one perhaps say the same thing about Louis Zukofsky, son of Russian Jewish immigrants and the first son to be born in the United States? The history of literature is dotted with such examples ranging most recently from Julien Green, Virginia-born French writer and member of the *Académie française*, to one of the founders of the *Nouveau roman*, Nathalie Sarraute, born in Russia. Or to Joseph Conrad or Vladimir Nabokov. The status of the "outsider" often spurs ambition as indeed it did for Apollinaire who, as foreign-born, enlisted in the French army to prove his patriotism and wrote what André Breton, in his pacifist moments after World War I, considered intolerably patriotic works.

What comes through from Apollinaire's experimentation with form, content, and language are preoccupations that both break with the historic tradition of verbal elegance (which consigned poetry to a sublime status) and inaugurate a totally new adventure in poetry, as "Zone" defined it most propitiously. The first two lines of that majesterial poem are fine examples. The first line is a perfect alexandrine:

"A la fin tu es las de ce monde ancien." The second line,

"Bergère ô tour Eiffel le troupeau des ponts bèle ce matin,"

has a handsome six-syllable hemistiche, followed by a daring break with tradition; the second half of the line contains nine syllables, reminding a reader of Walt Whitman's long line and what was to become Claudel's signature in *Les Cinq grandes odes* (not to forget Blaise Cendrars's own inventiveness in *La Prose du Transsibérien et de la petite Jehanne de France*).

Thematically the two lines quoted above are equally indicative of a departure from classical themes: "lassitude" does not figure at all in either Horace or Pindar; it is, most probably, sui generis of a nineteenth-century malaise that Mallarmé found when he translated Tennyson's "Mariana," whose heroine sighed (in French!): "Ma vie est morne. . . . Je suis lasse, lasse . . ." (Mallarmé, *Œuvres complètes*, 703). Apollinaire's second line is even more indicative of a disjunctive poetics: a combination of "bergère" (shepherdess) and "troupeau" (flock) with the Eiffel Tower and Parisian bridges. One might consider this binary and antithetical couple as the most illustrative representation of the essence Apollinaire is pointing to so provocatively: an acknowledgment of a bucolic past (a cliché ever since Marie Antoinette's "farming" days at Versailles) and an admiration for the Eiffel Tower, recently erected and standing there as a metonym for modernity. Then, to reconstruct a rhyming unit, as demanded by classical versification, Apollinaire puns on "ancien" and "matin," in fact, polar opposites if one considers "ancien" as the night of the past and "matin" as the clearest indication of the present. But there's more, if one wants to play the game of versification: "ancien" and "matin" constitute a weak rhyme; the two terms form a masculine scheme and both lines contain an even number of syllables—unlike Verlaine's suggestion that a certain (symbolist) aura would be attained were the poem to work on a series of uneven numbered lines.

"Zone" presents many other elements that must have attracted Zukofsky's taste; for example, the camera-like movement (which Cendrars had initially titled *Kodaks* until that company forced him to change it, leading the poet to rename the poems *Instantanés*) where the poet shifts his verbal gaze from one topos to another without providing the reader any advance notice of such moves. One might consider this sort of "surprise" a stylistic effect. Such shifts in language code from the spoken to the "written," are signs indeed of "modernity" as Rimbaud noted in his criticism of Baudelaire's admirable contents—which he faulted on the level of form, Baudelaire having been too servile in his exploitation of the sonnet.

What Rimbaud believed (including in his prose poems) could just as easily be applied to Zukofsky who, by 1933, had already (as of 1928) begun "*A*," which he would not conclude until 1974, four years before his death (and in fact did not "conclude" as "*A*"-24 is Celia's work, taking lines from Zukofsky's poems, his prose works, fiction, and dramas, and setting them to music). In that epic poem, and as of the incipit in "*A*"-1, the letter A stands by itself (legs akimbo) on the first line, thereafter to be succeeded by an evocation of Bach's *Saint Matthew Passion*, that is, going from "A" to "B" for Bach, thereby acknowledging a majestic musical tradition and immediately modifying it with a spoken sequence where the women in Bach's time chatter away on a churchgoing Sunday. Reading Zukofsky, like reading Guillaume Apollinaire, is an invitation to listen to a way of reading poetry: a demanding pedagogy, playing on the organ of language where a fugue of language attempts to rival its musical counterpart. Part of that complexity can be ascribed to Zukofsky's syntax, which I consider to be his fundamental identity.

Perhaps what most clearly distinguishes Apollinaire's writing from Zukofsky's is the very syntactical transparency in the works of the French poet and the often opaque (some might say Mallarmé-like) quality of the American poet's work. Zukofsky, analyzing Apollinaire's versification writes: "The syntax is nearly always popular, never troubling the reader." As for Apollinaire's use of the alexandrine, that is implicitly worked into one of his own poems:

> Mes tournoiments exprimaient les béatitudes
> Qui toutes ne sont rien qu'un pur effet de l'Art

As he does so frequently, Zukofsky lightly defines what later critics will ponderously exploit. When Roland Barthes typified the *passé simple* as the symptomatic sign of Literature (with a capital "L") he was—unknowingly, of course—repeating what Zukofsky had earlier concluded, via Apollinaire's own distich (quoted above): the alexandrine, all by itself, was *the* sign of Art (See Jacques Roubaud's chapter on Apollinaire in *La vieillesse d'Alexandre* [Paris: François Maspéro, 1978]).

I suspect that what may initially repel the so-called common reader from Zukofsky's "*A*" is not at all a lexical question, the trees described, but the forest itself; that is, what may be the underlying cause for the cantankerous reaction of a first reading: the Latin undertow in the phrasing that had also made Mallarmé's later poetry partially inaccessible in his own day. *Un coup de dés jamais n'abolira le hasard*, to many contemporary critics, seemed the work of a madman in its "incomprehensible" disposition of language on a page (a double page, as Mallarmé wrote *across* two pages, thereby breaking the sanctity of a Western habit of reading). That was true especially when *Un coup de dés* is compared to Mallarmé's earlier Lamartinian verses, which most anthologies still favor.

Apollinaire wanted to distance himself from that particular Mallarmé definition of poetry as an hermetic exercise, that syntactically demanding, un-"popular" form. Victor Hugo had proclaimed the need to "twist the neck" of the classical alexandrine, making it suppler, less boom boom boom. Apollinaire also engaged alexandrines but, as Zukofsky noted, when he does it, it "never shocks the traditional metric and has its own metric. Le vers libre." Still, when Zukofsky quotes four lines from "L'Hermite," it is obvious that Apollinaire was elegantly able to combine classical ABBA rhymes, adhering, furthermore, to a strict alternance between masculine and feminine rhymes (characteristic of the Petrachian sonnet) while playing with a description of his own erection:

> . . . mon sexe est innocent
> D'être anxieux seul debout et devant comme une borne

Zukofsky found an erotic lightness in Catullus's poetry similarly engaging; Apollinaire, on the other hand, had a well-established reputation as a prose writer of erotico-pornographic material, having not only researched that field, writing *L'Enfer de la Bibliothèque nationale* (1913) but also having penned pornographic novels including *Les Onze Mille Verges ou les Amours d'un hospodar* and *Les exploits d'un jeune Don Juan* (both published in 1907). Two years later, he would write a preface to *L'Œuvre du Marquis de Sade* as well as to other libertine texts. In 1910, he did the same favor for *Mémoires de Fanny Hill*. In fact, there would be few forms of *writing* Apollinaire did not try, even writing under a transvestite nom de plume: Louise Lalanne. Under that signature he wrote malicious reviews of contemporary feminine literature for the magazine *Les Marges* (in 1957 a limited edition of fifty-one copies was reprinted in Liège by Editions Dynamo). One is here reminded of Mallarmé, who also wrote his articles in *La Dernière mode* under a female pseudonym, not to mention the more outrageous Rrose Sélavy, Marcel Duchamp's female half and her verbal travesties. I am tempted to suggest that the *Ur*-model for this "crossing over" is Rimbaud's "Je est un autre."

When Zukofsky titled his essay *The Writing of Guillaume Apollinaire*, he knew full well that the singular "writing" would cover the totality of Apollinaire's production, that is, acknowledge the primacy of the signifier, of the *écriture*—or put another way, of Apollinaire's poetics. Zukofsky thus rejected analyzing all of Apollinaire's works. (One may also wonder to what extent Zukofsky actually knew of these erotico-pornographic texts. I presume René Taupin would have been familiar with them, sixteen years after Apollinaire's death.)

What must have caught Zukofsky's attention was how the French poet dealt with versification in some of his major poems. Zukofsky writes: "The dialectic, like versification *shuttles* [my emphasis] between contemporary and the classic." And Zukofsky concludes: "The poem is a series of modulations of an absorbed personal ritual become impersonal—presented as periphery." Obviously the same would apply to all Apollinaire works, including his art criticism, love poems, novels, prefaces, and speeches.

Is there a more perspicacious introduction to Zukofsky's exploration of autobiographical elements in his own work? Zukofsky garners from Apollinaire's "translations" of his life into poetry the evidence of an "emotive-intelligence"—what judiciously qualifies a poetics too often embalmed with the juices of an objectivist fruit. No doubt Zukofsky wished to expel the more facile romantico-lyrical from his poetry, but that never stopped him from combining (as in "*A*"-9, for instance) the most recondite poetic adaptation of Marx's theory of labor with a magnificent—emotive!—declaration of love for his wife, Celia (as he would, in "*A*"-12 and in "*A*"-19 later declare his paternal affection for Paul, his virtuoso violinist son). I am here reminded of what Yeats said to Pound: "I have spent the whole of my life trying to get rid of rhetoric. . . . I have got rid of one kind of rhetoric and have merely set up another" (*Make it New, Essays by Ezra Pound* [London: Faber and Faber, 1934], 245). Zukofsky's particular genius, as I see it, consists of a perfect lucidity as he examined a bouquet of topics and equivalent choices of rhetoric, thereby avoiding Yeats's dilemma.

Revelation and Concealment

To reveal *and* to conceal: there's always something to be claimed and something to be deflected, such as a birthday. Is it any wonder, then, that Zukofsky enjoyed reading not only Apollinaire's informative and "difficult" autobiographical poems, but also appreciated the cloud of doubt hanging over both Apollinaire's date of birth and his own? Zukofsky had two birth certificates, one composed by a midwife and another one, an official document. The double registration of his birth may have egged him on to develop a numerological interest that found its way in the numbers he enjoyed in poetry. It might further explain his fascination with Baruch Spinoza's axioms, propositions and demonstrations: "My Spinoza I take often / to the country" (*A*-12). Let me suggest a pattern in "*A*" parallel to Spinoza's mode of arguing; that is, the rhetoric employed, the way of defining, illustrating, and concluding (or not) an argument. I take the word *argument* as the equivalent of the Scholastic *disputatio*, which Apollinaire had learned to wield during his *lycée* years.

On this question of birth, not only the date, but the paternity of the French poet, Zukofsky writes: "Amusingly secretive to the point of emanating a superstition . . . the poet's father was either a Polish general or a Roman cardinal." Much like Zukofsky's own history, Apollinaire's birth on August 26, 1880, was registered five days later by a midwife, the mother wishing to remain anonymous and only "coming out" for his baptism on September 29 when he was then officially dubbed Wilhelm Apollinaris de Kostrowitsky. His friends were to call him "Kostro." As late as 1914, Picasso, in a portrait, called him "Guillaume de Kostrowitsky, artilleur, 1914." Zukofsky was familiar with all those patronymic peregrinations, having read André Billy's *Apollinaire vivant* (1923), and using that same work in his footnotes. Zukofsky futhermore was acquainted with Apollinaire's portraits painted by Marcoussis (somewhat parallel to Apollinaire's own *Calligramme* technique) and Jean Metzinger.

In writing about the other's writing, Zukofsky reveals his own spectral form in the shadow of Apollinaire's presence—indeed, generated by the French poet's work. As a result Zukofsky can "objectively" sketch out what usually remains in the wings: a poet's self-understanding. Zukofsky: "Writing becomes the work of making art of an intelligence of a life, of using an era as an illustration of an emotion, of isolating the mutations and historic metamorphoses of an era to record them." This observation is indistinguishable, in its application, from either Zukofsky's

poetics or Apollinaire's as the metaphorical terms Zukofsky uses—
mutation and *metamorphosis*—are both borrowed from the natural sci-
ences, thereby enveloping poetry in a scientific or objectivist habit. But
Zukofsky's terms also reveal a sort of micropoetics: such terms act as rev-
elatory metaphoric veils, at once concealing and revealing hidden truths
that, in this case, indicate the figures of both the poet and his times.

As a consequence Zukofsky discovers in Apollinaire's prose and poetry not only subjects of interests but what he calls "the logic of writing
which is the logic of intelligence," both of which are filtered through non-
lyrical rhetorical tropes: mutation and metamorphosis. The temptation
is great to consider such comments as precursors to our own theoretical
postulates (as jargonized by structuralist theoreticians). But why not recognize in this combination of "the logic of writing" with intelligence, a
Zukofsky find, arrived at because of his own perceptions of the matter
at hand? Anterior to Philippe Sollers's *Tel Quel*'s position on the primacy of *écriture* as the sign of a critical and autonomous attention to
the text (in the footsteps of Derrida's *Grammatology*), Zukofsky had, in
his own criticism and in his poetry as well, foreshadowed such formulas.
But in the intellectual gyrations of Parisian circles the contributions of
poets count less (and American poets especially, with Poe as the notable
exception, given his French godfathers, Baudelaire and Mallarmé).

So Zukofsky discovers a principle of the autonomy of writing: "imagery has its own logic, the logic of writing . . . separate from, though
connected to, History itself." And now the twist: "the inclusive sense of
its intelligence is historical only in the immediate sense of ubiquity . . .
with always the proviso that the poet's passions do not surpass his destiny." As he shuttles from one to the other—the game of polyvalen-
cies and ambiguities—the poet may or may not become the captive of
his fate. Everything rests on the question of the passions (a surprising
evocation for a poet principally known for doubts cast upon that romantic quality). And yet, there's no doubt for any reader of *"A"* that
this is not an eighteenth-century grammarian's poem; I'm thinking here
of poets such as Voltaire, Delille, and Chénier where "passions" are
hemmed in by logic, by sparkling wit or a show of scientific knowledge. To the contrary, one could without hesitation say of Zukofsky's
poetics that which holds true for Apollinaire: there is no poetic creation
without passion. But add the proviso that such passions do not over-
shadow the poet's destiny (an apparently odd choice of words for a mod-
ernist poet).

One can perceive in the above definition the very core of Zukofsky's poetics, where each word reveals the heart of a poetic practice beginning with an assumption: *homo faber,* "writing becomes the work of making [*faber*]." And then, even as the metaphor clarifies it, Zukofsky evokes the principle of translation (digestion) of reality into the real of the text— the metamorphosis without which (and syntax would properly fit here) there would be no art but only the raw material constituting it.

Zukofsky further engages the reader in what can only be seen as a postmodern exploration of the aesthetic endeavor when he suggests a shift from History (epoch) to its equivalent, evident in "an illustration of an emotion" or what can be called a simulacrum of reality, here understood not as a virtual "take" on the present, but as its aesthetic objectification. André Breton's double definition of Surrealism in the *Manifesto* (one for the dictionary and the other for the encyclopedia) is here amply quoted by Zukofsky. The definition unfolds not as founded on a dream mechanism but on "an art of familiarity"; that is, a duplication of the staging of one's life in a text, *as* text. There, in a poem, "intimacy [has] achieved distance and space with emotion."

The scientific metaphors often favored by Zukofsky (including the aforementioned mutation and metamorphosis), spice "*A*" with references to physics as well as to astronomy; they reinforce a complex thought he attributes to Apollinaire but which, in effect, corresponds to his own endeavors. Zukofsky again: "The writing is a period of vibration off the ring of intelligence which is an object." He rejects an intimist poetics, which Apollinaire calls a lakeside poetics (a reminder of Lamartine's "Le Lac?"); that is, one centered on the self. Such poetics will give way to "intelligence," which Zukofsky equates with "the fact and a life" that is objectively in harmony ("vibrations off the ring") with Apollinaire's own time. This interpretation thereby succeeds in reinscribing a Marxist reading into a literary order, somewhat reminiscent of Francis Ponge's virulent rejection of anthropomorphism which, he claimed, had caused the downfall of Romantic poetics. In alluding to "facts" and a parallel preoccupation with "life," Zukofsky rejected a Carlylean vision of a heroic individual determining the course of history. For Zukofsky, the *form* is not of one's creation yet it "pervade[s] the writer involved in fostering it." Let us not forget that this was written nearly thirty years before Roland Barthes's *Zero Degree Writing* where the French semiotician insisted that the so-called hyperbolic style of Revolutionary journalism (he was thinking of Marat's newspaper, *L'Ami du peuple*) was dictated by events, that style itself was shaped and determined by historical events.

There is indeed an equation between forms the poet utilizes and the historical period, although the poet may not be aware of that interference. "Sharp tho unconscious as a tool" (Zukofsky). And Zukofsky translates a passage from Tristan Tzara's *Manifeste de Monsieur Antypirine* that reinforces the point: "Life . . . within the frame of European weaknesses." If the "frame" metaphor switches from Marx to a yet-to-be Derrida, the upshot is the same: Man is not a freewheeling agent. So spoke Marx, so echoed Zukofsky.

Zukofsky spares no subject from his analytical grid, so it is no wonder that even a universal platitude such as love (perhaps *because* such a platitude!) is scrutinized through "scientific" lenses, through metaphors that occupy a privileged place in Zukofsky's work. Writing about the nature of love, Zukofsky suggests: "ceasing to attract it would be merely enervated of its radiation (the medieval image is circuitous in these lines)." He then adds, about that favored topos: "But it is there, too, to be emitted, to shift its quantum and form new energy, new substance."

Apollinaire wrote voluminous love poetry, to women he (momentarily) adored. Zukofsky rarely indulged in that sort of testimonial venture; when he did, it was to transcribe the "event" into its scientific equivalent, thereby objectifying it, removing it from its habitual framework. In a sense, this was much like the undertaking of Parnassian poets or more specifically of Mallarmé himself, who was to write about the perfection of poetry that could only be attained by the removal of the poet. "Les mots eux-mêmes, s'exaltent" (Mallarmé, *Œuvres complètes*, 386).

This positivist and ideological transformation is founded both on a personal rejection of a poetry laden with emotions (poetry is now re-viewed as a non-Byronic space) and on contemporary discoveries in physics, such as that science defined matter and its continuum, its transformation of matter without matter disappearing. In this process, Apollinaire's "Zone" becomes "Apollinaire's image"; that is, the "objective" representation of an evolving "I." That autobiographical leitmotif in the poem, which dictates its movement, is born of Apollinaire's present and the result of an interplay between the individual's intelligence and the epoch's impositions. The alchemical exchange between a poet's volition and the "present" he inhabits lead Zukofsky to note Apollinaire's "intelligence as writing which to the concerned or the observant never becomes an attitude, the subjective grease in the cracks of brilliance." The shifting metaphorical range—from quantum to grease—testifies to a singular struggle of the poet to multiply ways of escaping what otherwise, as the Romans understood it, would be determined by Fate. An easy quote: "His emotions . . . never surpassing his destiny always included the past. Transformed, but it had preceded him."

Another precautionary maneuver, a way of evading the dictates of *fatum*, gives rise to yet another by-product: "The effect of intelligence is inevitable plasticity." I see Zukofsky's statement as his equivalent to *Calligrammes*: plasticity in its less obvious manifestations, that is, the unpredictable variations of lines and their disposition, ranging from packed sonnets to columnar stretches as in "*A*"-10. Numerous options allow the poet to play with plasticity. In reading Apollinaire's first *calligramme*, Zukofsky described the layout: "The verses are childlike, single words of shaded calligraphy or arabesque frills waveringly tangent to the right side of a childlike clock." And so the poet constitutes his own critical appreciation.

Zukofsky's composite style in "*A*" is yet another proof of similarity: the way, without opening or closing quotes, or when Zukofsky situates lines by Apollinaire within his own phrasing in *The Writing of Guillaume Apollinaire*. This practice calls for comment. In so doing, Zukofsky does a number of things, successively. First, he centers the marginal text so that it "figures" within his own English composition; second, he heightens the audibility of language as the reader goes from French to English and then back again to the French, as if almost nothing had happened when, in fact, an audible plasticity had been dramatically put in place.

I was speaking about Zukofsky's scientific bent; as a student at Columbia, he witnessed the auspicious presence of that university's commitment to anthropology. Franz Boas was hired at Columbia in 1896 and became the first professor of anthropology in 1899. In the concluding section of *The Writing of Guillaume Apollinaire*, Zukofsky will quote Boas's *Primitive Art* (1927) in order to distinguish between modern and primitive productions and art appreciation: "It is the quality of their experience, not a difference in mental make-up." In a para-Marxist analysis, Zukofsky ends up by writing: "every cultural phenomenon [is] the result of historic process."

Given this cultural-scientific ideology, why wouldn't Zukofsky project onto Apollinaire a similar interest? "Working with the ardor of a good anthropologist, Apollinaire recognized the effect of historical process in every cultural phenomenon and the fundamental sameness of mental processes in all racial and cultural forms as embraced by the intelligence in the present day." Zukofsky recognized the similarities between "us" and "them" when he put quotes around "primitive," much as Claude Lévi-Strauss, the founder of structural anthropology, would do on the first page of his 1962 *La Pensée sauvage.* In "*& Cie,*" the final chapter of *The Writing of Guillaume Apollinaire,* Zukofsky recognized that: "Apollinaire was a historian (or more specifically an anthropologist) in the sense that the American Henry Adams was a poet." Zukofsky will return to that same characterization a few pages later when he refers to Apollinaire as "a good anthropologist" and writes: "The poet studied his race as tho it were 'primitive.' "

In this fashion yet another coat of similarity was placed on Apollinaire's shoulders. When Zukofsky compared Apollinaire's stories of Cyprienne, Que Vlo-ve [Que voulez-vous, in Wallon] to Flaubert's Salomé in *Trois contes,* he saw a telling difference: "The gravity of acceleration in Flaubert's narrative is in each sense history veiling a myth; the surprise or mystic complicity of Apollinaire's is in each case data inciting ethnic comparisons." More than a positivist interpretation, Apollinaire's insistence on racial approximations demonstrated an aspect of his intelligence that usually has been limited to an understanding of *Calligrammes*: the visual effects of simultaneity. "Apollinaire's artistic instinct for the natural simultaneity (rather than unity) of intelligence is a constant in his work."

I wonder if for Zukofsky Apollinaire's penchant for anthropology may not, at least in part, have had something to do with his own status as an "outsider"? The French literary critic, Urbain Gohier, writing in the December 1911 issue of *L'Œuvre* (a xenophobic *Action française* literary magazine) called Apollinaire a pornographer and a *métèque,* a highly pejorative term used to finger foreigners and, by the end of the nineteenth century (the time of the Dreyfus Affair), Jews, in particular.

Apollinaire a pornographer? Zukofsky—was it out of a rather moral (Russian?) disposition?—does not include that form of writing in his analyses (perhaps repressing it). But Apollinaire a *métèque?* That's a whole other kettle of fish and one with which Zukofsky could personally identify, he a Jew living on the Lower East Side and then going uptown to Columbia at a time when there were no Jews on the faculty. (Nonetheless, while Columbia had quotas for Jewish students, its student body was still 20 percent Jewish, a far higher proportion than in the other Ivies.) This said, would Zukofsky have been attracted to the writing of, let's say, foreign-born Isidore Ducasse, count of Lautréamont, or Rimbaud who had fled (on numerous occasions) his town of Charleville which he mockingly referred to as Charlestown? Apart from the poetics

Zukofsky shared with Apollinaire, such a hypothesis—an encounter between two *mètèques*—appears to justify Zukofsky's selecting Apollinaire as his principal object of study.

A less debatable connection was their relation to language itself. Edouard Drumont in his *La France juive* ruefully noted that Jewish authors tended to write an even better French than your ordinary (*France profonde*) Frenchman. The relation, especially for a poet, between his affirmation of self-via-text, and the Other (using that Heideggerian term) is here quite believable. Indeed, Zukofsky and Apollinaire do not immediately belong either to a traditional American vein or to a French one.

Would the application of simultaneity have something to do with the effort to provide oneself with an identity unlike that of others? Or to distance oneself from the canon? The concept of simultaneity, signaled by the absence of a temporal progression in verb tenses, insisting on the present (as in "Zone," for instance) is a basic concept for both poets, especially in Zukofsky's "hearing" the text, of assuming that the existence of a multiplicity of voices and times acting together add up to "sense"—or, to use one of Zukofsky's own terms, to "intelligence." (Virginia Woolf did exactly the same in her overheard and simultaneous dinner-table conversations in *To the Lighthouse*.) What may haunt some poets is a musical model that allows a polyphony to exist in lieu of the conventional understanding of the isolation of units of words on a line (which obviously reinforce linearity).

Poets have traditionally had their ways of contravening this canonical grammatical / syntactical stricture. First, intratextual echoes when, within the same work (let's say a sonnet), the reader is not only a forward-reading machine, but a discerning recorder of repetitive sounds that, as a consequence, create a significant motif, sonorously enhancing the meaning of the text (what James Joyce called "sound sense" in *Finnegans Wake* and Zukofsky, "intelligence"). Apart from signaling yet another musical element in language, rhymes also assure the same intratextual effects, highlighted by syntactical breaches in the form of caesuras or enjambments. The result for Zukofsky is a language akin to a harmonic composition, the whole always greater than any of its parts. Thus, there would appear to be a logic of structure in both music and poetry, what Zukofsky found in "Apollinaire's instinct of the natural simultaneity of intelligence." For Zukofsky, the surrealist play *Les Mamelles de Tirésias* was a perfect demonstration of the "simultaneity of intelligence . . . [that] rockets at a tangent from the theme of Aristophanes' *Lysistrata*." Zukofsky then goes on a quoting binge, constituting

a veritable Noah's Ark, as he recovers animals from Apollinaire's *Le Bestiaire ou Cortège d'Orphée*: the horse, the goat, the serpent, the cat, the
lion, the hare, the rabbit, the dromedary, the elephant, the fly, the dolphin, the octopus, the jellyfish, the shrimp, the carp and, finally, sirens
themselves.

One may ask, why quote so many pages in French?

> . . . J'achète ma gloire
> Au prix des mots mélodieux

"I buy my glory / At the price of melodious words," says Apollinaire,
evoking the elephant. That micropoetics couplet, insisting on the harmonic essence of poetry, is found in the nature of words: that is a true
beginning, that is what poets do when they wish to rival Orpheus (an
emblematic figure for Apollinaire, who had wished to call modernism
in painting "Orphic"). For such poets, glory is equated with an understanding that there is, fundamentally, no difference between music and
words. Zukofsky is aware of this charm cast upon the reader as his own
poetry functioned on multiple levels of auditive perception; that is, a
simultaneity of effects, where the poet exercises language, forcing it to
work its way through all possibilities, including the rampant system of
internal rhymes and alliterations that all conform to Apollinaire's "mots
mélodieux."

Zukofsky may still have had another project in mind when he so
abundantly quoted Apollinaire's verses. It may have been an homage to
poetry itself, to language itself, to that French model defined by Arthur
Symmons in his influential *Symbolist Poetry* (1899), demarcating the
French model from Anglo-Saxon practices. In Mallarmé's "L'Après-
midi d'un faune," Pan's hypnotic playing of the flute is both an image and a sound, indicative of Mallarmé's certitude that the language
of poetry *was* musical, the "visible et serein souffle artificiel / Des inspirations" or again, "La Poésie . . . est Musique" (Mallarmé, *Œuvres
complètes*, 381).

Finally for Zukofsky, this lengthy sequence of miniatures from *Le
Bestiaire* conformed to "the epic of Apollinaire's early intelligence," and
thus Zukofsky, with that single word, epic, recognized the possibility
of a *tangential* epic, constituted no longer by a Homer-Pound tradition but what, on the surface, appears to be a far more modest enterprise: the bestiary, a medieval topos that would continue through Francis
Ponge's interpretation in his *Préface à un Bestiaire*. These bestiaries are,

of course, of a Hellenic and Roman origin, as Zukofsky well knew, but they were equally "French, subsuming the classic; they lived in the Paris of his time."

Zukofsky's use of the word "subsuming" may once more be a verbal mutation of the metamorphosis paradigm, transformation, in effect, of the concept of translation itself. What is *there* to see are several cloaks where "each unfolds in the inside of the other." As simple as these verses quoted by Zukofsky may be, on closer look, what is concealed is revealed: "The sadness of the verses incised in allegory—art's worness, art's renewal—is their essential self-contradictory life."

How intuitive Zukofsky's comments are as he inscribed within the tradition of the bestiary a range of intimate creations, "a sentiment given flare by personal hurt become art." This passage of life into art is indeed a key to Zukofsky's appreciation of poetry—as it is to Guillaume Apollinaire's.

A New Poetics

When Zukofsky applied himself to *The Writing of Guillaume Apollinaire*, he did not only limit himself to an implicit parallelism between his own work and Apollinaire's. In an extensive quote pertaining to Apollinaire's research in the "Enfer" [Hell] section of the *Bibliothèque nationale*, Zukofsky reproduced Apollinaire's reading of Baudelaire's neoteric aspects as well as Baudelaire's commenting on the more recent rejection of a poetics founded on a moral stance. But for Apollinaire (as with Rimbaud before him): "La liberté qui règne dans ce recueil [*Les Fleurs du mal*] ne l'a pas empêché de dominer sans conteste la poésie universelle à la fin du XIXe siècle." There are less obvious links between poets, and Baudelaire remains one of those links; witness the impact of his poetics on the latter half of the nineteenth century, on Pound's work as well as on T.S. Eliot's.

I would then recall my earlier image of Zukofsky's (Borgesian) library where the reader (in this instance, the poet himself) is every time implicated in works of the past, in a sort of closed circuit universe, out of time, where Literature exists and feeds upon itself. (There's an obvious linguistic pun when one compares Louis Zukofsky's initials to the German LZ, standing for *Literatur* and *Zukunft*, "the future of literature.")

Zukofsky "subsumes:" he does not obliterate those links with the past. That may be a working definition of a literary culture. The idea of "subsuming" may be as applicable to Zukofsky when again, and at length, he quotes Apollinaire on modern painting and concludes that "it would be easy to show the resemblance of the literature of his paintings to the literature of his *Calligrammes*." A synesthetic pronouncement that will be clarified in the following lines by Apollinaire:

> Sans lien apparent comme dans la vie
> Les sons les gestes les couleurs les cris les bruits
> La musique la danse l'acrobatie la poésie la peinture

Take note of two elements: first, the absence of punctuation (a post-Mallarmé necessity denoting innovation); second, something that (knowing Zukofsky's own mode of composition, primarily in "*A*") can be called the effect of fragmentation—fundamental to modernism in poetry and painting. Zukofsky writes: "Fragments, often showing amazing completeness in themselves . . ." One can say that, as of Cubism (so admired by Apollinaire), fragmentation is a dislocation of poetic narrativity. Whether in Khlebnikov's Saint Petersburg or in the New York of the 1913 Armory Show, featuring works by two Dada poets, Francis Picabia and Marcel Duchamp, things "sans lien apparent" closely resembled life itself. Fragmentation thus becomes, at least in our time, a witness to both the war Apollinaire would live through and the *Esprit nouveau* he saw in the making.

Read again Zukofsky's "*A*" (or, for that matter, *Bottom: On Shakespeare*), and it's apparent that in adhering to a theory of simultaneity (even though the examples provided are chronologically and nationally identified), Zukofsky combined a thematic analysis with what Burroughs would later call his "cut-ups"; that is, a fragmentation of the linear continuum into multiple texts from a vast variety of poets answering the question of the "eye" in the text. For *L'Esprit nouveau*, old forms had to be discarded in the name of authenticity and truth-in-representation, in the hope of reflecting what Apollinaire had called the *Couleur du temps* or what he saw as a perfect oxymoron: "chaos harmonieux," a description that became reality in his wartime experiences that so coincidentally duplicated Alfred Jarry's *Ubu roi* in their mix of the comic and the tragical.

L'Esprit nouveau: for Apollinaire as in his pithy definition of his poetics in his poem-manifesto "La Jolie rousse," that expression was founded on the union of "heritage" and a "Romantic curiosity." Under "heritage" he enumerated: "classic good sense, assured critical spirit, restraint of sentiment." Under "Romantic curiosity" he signaled: "The exploration of truth in ethnic, as well as in imaginary, sense." Zukofsky's reading of Apollinaire's work corresponded to his own practice: "Vers libre; researches into form; assonances; alliteration; typographical or visual lyricism; the literary synthesis of music, painting, and poetry."

I don't believe that one could identify a more perfect Zukofskian poetics. The preceding list contains much that is readily known; what may not be so evident are the resemblances between Apollinaire's "typographical or visual lyricism" and Zukofsky's *mise en page*. Scattered throughout "*A*" are shapes like a Valentine heart, a circle, a handwritten musical clef, a graph, as well as two terms connected by an oversized integer. *A*-16 is examplary of Zukofsky's Apollinaire-like page. There on a single page the reader finds:

An

inequality

wind flower

A Japanese resonance? In any case, such illustrations secure a place for Zukofsky in the field of Apollinaire's technical brilliance—as it does for Zukofsky's poetry, which is to be "seen and heard." Zukofsky implicitly referred to the great nineteenth-century French literary critic and historian, Hippolyte Taine, when he declared: "Wagner and Rousseau were rejected. Art would more and more be the expression of a country, since it has always been the expression of a milieu, of a nation, a race." (Taine had coined his own triadic approach to the literary text via "race, milieu, and moment.")

Zukofsky could not escape the temptation of analogy (what Mallarmé had called "Le Démon de l'Analogie," as he would, later on, write about "Le Démon de la Perversité," [Mallarmé, *Œuvres complètes*, 297]) when he compared Apollinaire's "destiny of . . . writing" to "love as Cavalcanti defined it." This comparison will segue into a lengthy Zukofskian insertion of Cavalcanti's "Donn mi Prega" in *The Writing of Guillaume Apollinaire*. Both Pound and Zukofsky had translated a passage from that Italian *canzone*, the first with decorum, the second in Brooklynese as "A Foin Lass Bodders." This unexpected appearance of one of Zukofsky's preferred poets, first in Italian and then in English, may indicate Zukofsky's desire to provide a degree of equilibrium to his otherwise hagiographic focus on Apollinaire.[4]

4. In comparing a scholarly edition of Cavalcanti's *canzone* (see Guido Cavalcanti, *Rime*, ed. Marcello Ciccuto, introd. Maria Corti [Milan: Biblioteca universale

Le Poète ressuscité

(The temptation is too great: even before considering this section, we cannot help reading into Apollinaire's title *The Poet Resuscitated* a possible and double Zukofsky project. First, obviously, to "resuscitate" Apollinaire, apparently little known in the United States, judging by the feeble representation of his work in translation. Second, and I would suspect much more telling, to see poetry itself fully appreciated, somehow brought back from the ashes of public detritus and simultaneously, a possible desire to assure himself some sort of posterity as he, Zukofsky, was assuring it for Apollinaire in praising his writing. If the title of the present section is explicit so is *The Writing of Guillaume Apollinaire* which, as I have said repeatedly, functions in a similar manner.

Zukofsky subdivided his reading (writing) of Guillaume Apollinaire into three sections (much as Gaul had been in Roman times!): (1) *Il y a* (discussed previously); (2) *Le Poète ressuscité*; and (3) *& Cie*. Each section indicates Zukofsky's particular interest in the writing of his French (Polish? Roman?) counterpart. Furthermore the footnotes in *The Writing of Guillaume Apollinaire* are all indicative of a wish to appear as scholarly as possible (a sign of objectivity) even though he did not rigorously follow what we would now consider the *Chicago Manual of Style* rules for a manuscript. Zukofsky often dispensed with italicizing book titles; he often left out the place of publication and, more important for us, pagination. Yet heedful of the need to back up his material, Zukofsky diverts his reader's eye to the bottom of the page, where anyone could check his sources, and conclude that he was indeed well informed, especially as to primary sources. Further, he lets the reader appreciate his ample use of quotes, all of which demonstrate just how close a reader he was of Apollinaire's writing.

Let me illustrate this point with the prolegomenon to *Le Poète ressuscité* which takes the form (the intelligence) of yet another extended (prose) quotation. In fact, the thirty-six pages in the manuscript are all in French; that is, the prolegomenon *is* the critical text. Zukofsky allows

---

Rizzoli], 1996), with Zukofsky's Italian entry, there's a near perfect unmatch. That is, Zukofsky most probably referred to a 1926 edition of Ezra Pound's own translation of that poem as he would, later on, in *The First Half of "A"-9* (privately printed in 1940). Rather than correcting this disparity, I have chosen to respect Zukofsky's Italian, which matches Pound's; see *Ezra Pound: Translations* (New York: New Directions, 1963), 134–38.

the writing of Guillaume Apollinaire to supersede his own: there's not a single word in English here; that is to say, not a single word in this section II that belongs to "our" author. Without necessarily invoking structuralist arguments concerning the identity of the author (following the theories of such luminaries as Lacan, and especially Foucault), we may nonetheless conclude that, in the mid-1930s, such preoccupations were already common practice.

Upon beginning this section, one would find oneself in that *unheimlich* (unfamiliar) condition that the Russian theoretician Roman Jakobson defined as the very sign of literariness: the irreducible specificity of *écriture*, a presence apart from thematics. As a result the author is and is not the one we presume he is: shortly after the beginning of this section, Apollinaire is quoted as writing: "Oi! oi, ce qui signifie 'hélas' en hébreu." Besides the Hebrew (one of the threads in Apollinaire's tapestry), Zukofsky might have playfully heard "œil! œil" (eye) or "I" in that double exclamation. In any case, as Ionesco puts it in the *Bald Soprano*, in matters coincidental, what a curious recollection of Zukofsky's experiences on the Lower East Side where Hebrew was very much the lingua franca. Here then is a renowned French poet, consecrated by the time Zukofsky deals with him, yet whose life at times paralleled his own. Unlike contemporary French admirers of Apollinaire's writing, Zukofsky goes straight for the Hebrew: humor and reminiscences, acting at a second degree of reality. In his own home, Yiddish was spoken perfectly, though both Celia and Louis's mother found Louis's Yiddish quite lacking.

Zukofsky continues his reading, undoubtedly surprised by what was to follow: "L'hébreu? c'est-à-peine si la plupart d'entre nous le savent lire au moment de la Barmitzva." Apollinaire then mocks the French translation of the Talmud: "qui est au dire des Juifs allemands ou polonais, un monument de l'ignorance des rabins de France." We are no longer in a topic-dropping stage: Apollinaire, as we know it and as Zukofsky read him, is not merely concerned with Jews whether in Prague or in Paris. They represent for him a true interest, one that pops up at unpredictable moments, much like a musical phrase. The rest of the passage is marked by anecdotes told in synagogue during Succoth (in French, "la fête des cabanes"), with the presence of four convivial Jewish poets, all of whom were to die (with their faces impressed in a dirty napkin—reminiscent of St. Veronica's napkin). Then all of a sudden, Apollinaire switches gears and the Hebraic overture disappears to make way for another topic, introduced by a Wallon expression: "Que Vlo-ve?" (Que voulez-vous?). Besides making us aware of the themes that fascinated Apollinaire, this move from Hebrew to Wallon is yet another sign of writing, properly identified as a presence in and of itself, totally apart from what we would call "content."

The centrality of writing: dissemination of a classical insistence, making room for a pure and unpredictable invention in both prose and poetry. Indeed, the genres become interchangeable when only numbers count, syllables. Or, as Baudelaire exclaimed: "L'ivresse est un nombre." (Today's Oulipians, Jacques Roubaud, for example, and Raymond Queneau before him, would have followed Baudelaire's analysis.)[5] As genres change so does the language: from French to Hebrew, to Yiddish, to a sort of medievalized French, to a Wallon dialect—undecipherable, claims Apollinaire, to those who have three testicles. "*V'n en savez nin comme ça, vous qu'avez* trois couilles." Then, unexpectedly, Apollinaire recenters those "pauvres émigrants," those Jews who gather in the waiting room of the Saint-Lazare railroad station (Lazarus, of course, is identified with resurrection.) "Ils ont foi dans leur étoile. . . . Quelques-uns . . . se logent rue des Rosiers ou rue des Ecouffes." To make it quite clear whom he is describing, Apollinaire adds: "Il y a surtout des Juifs, leurs

---

5. The question, or one might say, the passion for numbers and for numerology that are so present in Zukofsky's work (and are, coincidentally, also found in Baudelaire's work) warrants an explanation here. Baudelaire wrote: "Tout *est* nombre. Le nombre est dans *tout*. Le nombre est dans l'individu. L'ivresse est un nombre." See Charles Baudelaire, *Œuvres complètes*, ed. and annotated by Y-G. Le Dantec (Paris: Bibliothèque de la Pléiade, 1951), 1181). The final observation was put into English as "Ecstasy is a Number," in *The Intimate Journals of Charles Baudelaire*, trans. Christopher Isherwood, introd. W. H. Auden (Boston: Beacon, 1957), 3. Given Zukofsky's interest in numbers and in translation (in all of its manifestations), Isherwood's switch of paradigms, from "drunkenness" to "ecstasy"—especially considering Baudelaire's emphatic interest both in wine and in inebriation—constitutes a very particular reading of the original. Indeed, the French corresponds rather well to a traditional Chinese image of the philosopher. (The eighth-century Chinese anthology of eight poets—including Li Po—is marked by their Taoist interest in drunkenness.) Moreover, the paradigm switch bespeaks a future Oulipo consecration of numbers in its method of writing. (Baudelaire was also aware of Swedenborg's interest in drunkenness.) Presumably then, Isherwood's choice would be more in line with a translated Saint Theresa and her "Ecstasy"; that is, more sexual and religious than the original. And yet, the shadows of Chinese poets and Swedenborg might also justify his decision in favor of ecstasy. In their translation of Catullus, Louis and Celia Zukofsky paved the way for an adventurous reading of the original, but both were scrupulously "listening" to the Latin. The same can be said of Zukofsky's translations of the Book of Job ("Iyyob") in "*A*"-15 where the sounds reverberate as a plaint. Both "translations" were done during the same time period: Catullus (1958–69) and "*A*"-15 (1964).

femmes portent perruque." Later on, Apollinaire will remember Tycho Brahe who made love to "une jolie juive qui lui disait tout le temps *chazer*, ce qui signifie cochon en jargon," (it wasn't "jargon" but Yiddish). Apollinaire's translational pleasures go on: he will show that the Hebrew letters composing the first man, Adam, are founded on Aleph, Daleph and Meme.

Such affinities for the Hebrew and for Jews are made even more evident when Apollinaire writes: "car je suis aussi poète comme tous les prophètes juifs." What a comparison to underscore the act of *writing*, whether in the hands of Jewish Prophets or in the poet's! If one can compare Mallarmé's project for *Le Livre* to its prodigious counterpart, the Bible, then there's no reason why a poet (the seer is Rimbaud's term) cannot himself aspire to duplicate, especially in a secular society, the function of the priest. Victor Hugo had framed the poet in just such a manner in one of his lesser significant poems, "Fonction du poète" (1839). It is not beyond imagining that Apollinaire might have memorized Hugo's lines:

> Il est l'homme des utopies
> . . . .
> C'est lui qui sur toutes les têtes
> En tout temps, pareil aux prophètes . . .

Once again, on Zukofsky's part, a break without warning. Now Zukofsky's narrative doubles the opening lines of "Zone" (previously quoted), a perfect reminder of the dialectics of simultaneity, where an autobiographical demonstration reconciles opposites (a precept dear to André Breton's definition of Surrealism). As a result "Zone" embraces not only antiquity and modernity (in their symbolic representation) but heralds Pope Pius X as "L'Européen le plus moderne." If that were not enough, Apollinaire adds: "C'est le Christ qui monte au ciel mieux que les aviateurs," thereby uniting what might have appeared to be two antithetical representations: religion and aviation or again tradition and innovation. In *La Prose du Transsibérien*, Blaise Cendrars wrote:

> Pardonnez-moi de ne plus connaître l'ancien jeu des vers
> Comme dit Guillaume Apollinaire[6]

6. A great deal has been written on the relation between Blaise Cendrars and Guillaume Apollinaire; see Marc Poupon, *Apollinaire et Cendrars* (Paris: Editions Paul Minard, 1969).

Apollinaire's "confession," that is, his having forgotten the rules of versification, should be taken with a large grain of salt as he was past master
of both classical verse and *vers libre*. He was also beyond comparison in
highlighting *writing* itself, as he moved from prose to verse, from language to language, with a Jabberwocky-like invention. Some examples:
"Ma Ma ramaho nia nia," "MAHEVIDANOMI RENANAOCALIPNODITOC,"
and "oeaoiiiioktin." (Was he a pseudolinguist on an anthropological expedition, a sort of Henri Michaux on one of his fabled travels?) What
is obvious is that Apollinaire enjoyed flaunting language whether a recognized one or a fictitious one. Proper names do not escape: Apollinaire
named some of his characters Croniamantal, Tograth, or Tristouse Ballerinette (Marie Laurencin did her portrait). One final and comical example is offered to us by Apollinaire when he launches into a pseudo–
Spanish-accented French. Here, the lover speaks to his beloved, Elvire:
"Elbirre, je te jourre que je raconte . . . l'amour c'est la paix, et je souis
l'amour puisque je souis neuttre?"[7]

The explanation for such linguistic inventiveness is found in the text
itself where Apollinaire writes, in *Le Poète assassiné*: "Il se peut que
cette mode de mêler au français des termes étrangers soit un moyen de
renouveler le langage, de lui infuser une vertu nouvelle." (In his poem
"Ça?" Corbière, reading himself as a poet, exclaims: "—Bon, ce n'est
pas classique?—A peine est-ce français!" Aimé Césaire, the Martinican
poet, agreed with that observation when he said: "I wanted to make . . .
a Black French.")[8] I find it difficult to overestimate this particular effort to conjoin foreign tongues with French in order to enrich it, to
"infuse it with a new virtue." ("Virtue" taken here in its Latin etymology, meaning courage or wisdom, and certainly not as an indicator of
moral conduct.) Today we might consider this proposal as evidence of
a linguistic *métissage*. In fact, such mixing of dialects and tongues, diachronically speaking, constitutes the evolution of any given language;
French, clearly, has incorporated over centuries expressions from Latin,
German, English, and more recently, Arabic. As of this (subversive,

7. The question of the proliferation of languages in Apollinaire's writing was
the topic of one of Michel Decaudin's conferences in Stavelot. The papers may be
consulted in *Apollinaire, inventeur de langages*, ed. Michel Decaudin (Paris: Editions
Paul Minard, 1973).

8. In an interview, Aimé Césaire declared that he "wanted to make an Antillean
French, a Black French"; see "An Interview with Aimé Césaire, Translated with an
Introduction by Dale Tomich," *Radical America* 5, no. 3, (May–June 1971): 32.

métèque) enterprise, Apollinaire finds himself sharing the platform with the Pléiade poet Joachim du Bellay, whose *Défense et Illustration de la langue française* (1549) proposed imitating Italian via mimicry and translation as modes of enriching the French language, in order to get as far away as possible from the corrupted (debased, vulgar) language of Clément Marot's French; this ambition, initially voiced by Cardinal Bembo in Italy, and wholly translated into French, became Du Bellay's longest chapter in his manifesto. What may provide a single-word résumé of Apollinaire's proposal is MUTATION, with its illustration so analytically observed: "La guerre éclata donc, brisant comme erre cette vie adorable et légère." Nevertheless, the poet was encouraged in his work: "La guerre même a augmenté le pouvoir que la poésie exerce sur moi et c'est grâce à l'un et l'autre que le ciel désormais se confond avec la tête-étoilée." Such parallelisms—topical mutations—did not stop Apollinaire from entertaining other thoughts, usually of an amorous kind; for example (and way before Simone de Beauvoir), the idea of a "mormonisme féministe, des femmes ayant plusieurs maris." This thought engendered a long passage on the Mormons, their origins, their connection to Israel, their polygamous practices (which had long fascinated the European imagination). As one of the Mormon women exclaimed: "Et quel bonheur est semblable à celui de la chair satisfaite quand l'esprit ne peut plus connaître la jalousie?" Or, on a more sinister note, Apollinaire recalling how four white Mormons lynched a black man from Missouri.

Language shifts, topic shifts, genre shifts from prose to poetry: the whole being a fireworks display offered to the modern reader.

Keeping Company

The longest sequence over, *The Writing of Guillaume Apollinaire* then enters on its final run: *& Cie*, with an astonishing reaffirmation of Louis Zukofsky's analysis of writing based on Dante's *De Vulgari Eloquentia* (a text he was going to quote again in "*A*"): "Writing—the choice of words—(1) the composition as action—of the process—(2) the composition as passion felt." In this conjuration of Dante's text—the poet responsible for the creation of modern Italian—Zukofsky discovers eternal verities leading to an evaluation of Apollinaire's own writing that "reads its implicit self-criticism." Again: "therefore the best language is only suitable in those whom knowledge and genius are found." One might consider such explicit restatements of Dante's thought (as Zukofsky had previously done with Cavalcanti's poetry) as evidence of knowledge, evidence too of the heritage of judgment, which "may go under the name of a dialectic, an esthetic, a criticism." Was it necessary to pull Dante off the shelf to support such banalities? Clearly, yes: in so doing, Zukofsky further demonstrated what was as keenly felt by Apollinaire; that is, the legitimate weight of tradition. There may have been an additional and veiled justification: "Apollinaire's criticism of painting and of literature other than his own is self-criticism as expression." And thus Zukofsky's criticism of Apollinaire's self-criticism becomes a part of Apollinaire's argument; another light shed on writing, on "composition as action." Analogically one could compare this strategy of criticizing criticism to a *mise en abîme*, once again a Borgesian or Barthian mode of intratextuality that never precludes whatever remains on the "outside" from being recuperated in the body of the text.

Zukofsky reads Apollinaire reading a Picasso painting and, thus thrice removed, observes how "Apollinaire has done an approximation in words of the objects of painting." In a most self-revelatory statement, via Apollinaire's prose, and very close to Francis Ponge's formula, "Le parti pris des choses égal le compte tenu des mots," the American poet writes: "An art of criticism being in all senses . . . an advertisement of another object." Because art, in this instance, is verbally expressed, the choice of words becomes the art of writing. At this juncture it is Longinus's turn, that Greek rhetorician who is falsely attributed authorship of *On the Sublime*. Longinus shall illustrate the purport of images: "Weight, grandeur and energy of writing." Such a dwelling on writing underscores the proximity between classical rhetoricians (as Barthes had shown it in his article "L'ancienne rhétorique, Aide-mémoire," in *Communications*, vol. 16) and our own contemporary theories of *écriture* as Derrida, Foucault, and Co., have so incisively adumbrated them.

What immediately strikes the reader, entering this final section, is a *musical* change, the way in which words-in-composition (syntax) approximate a play on music. I could thus imagine *The Writing of Guillaume Apollinaire* as a composition defined in three movements, where the power of the concluding section is amplified by the reappearance of Zukofsky's own writing, this time even more specifically preoccupied by the poetics of verbal constructs. The middle section—all in French—whatever the variations in meaning, linguistically speaking, maintains the unitary harmony of the French language. The middle section is then the interlude, an andante preceded by a powerful overture, an allegro, with a conclusion that can only be heard as a presto.

Zukofsky's signature is everywhere apparent in this "composition," as his choice of Apollinaire's texts had been in the long middle passage acting as a bridge. To each his autonomy; together, however, the writing becomes *writing* in all of its mutations, its metamorphoses, in all of its constructs. Zukofsky: "If by construction is meant the arranged sentences, and by the utterance of construction of their grammatical and typographical morphology by the voice."

Zukofsky's argument insists that Apollinaire's chapter on the Mormons in "La Femme assise," "if sounded aloud or read in the ear, would indicate: that there is no preestablished law by which internal rhymes . . . destroy the movement of prose, but that there is an actual law . . . showing that internal rhymes may enhance the arrangements of prose and 'hide' to reveal its singular movement." A Zukofsky lesson: Hear my lines! Listen to the acceleration and order of my words! Once more quoting the second treatise, chapter 12 of Dante's *Convivio*, Zukofsky delineates the three constitutive elements of meaning of the ode and concludes that "in the modern extension of verbal expression evolving out of criticism [they] become as one banquet: grammar, rhetoric and music subsumed under a single absolute of all three, which early natural critical synthesis also knew as construction and the utterance of construction."

To prove his assertions, Zukofsky picks an apparently negligible text borrowed by Apollinaire from a popular children's ditty:

> J'ai du bon tabac
> Dans ma tabatière
> J'ai du bon tabac
> Tu n'en auras pas

As Zukofsky writes: "A grammatical negative future has been subsumed as music under the absolute construction." So much for grammar. Now for rhetoric:

> Mets y pour deux sous de tabac mais du fin

"The simplicity of conversation has become rhetoric, a simple naïve ordering of discourse by mouth." Lastly, as the classics themselves would have it, is music or what Zukofsky sees (hears) as "the presence of the musical adornment of the initial rhyme making for the parallelism of rhetoric." Let us not forget that tropes or rhetorical turns were part of what Roland Barthes called the "adornments" adjoined to a Boileau-like prose turned into poetry by this costume jewelry addition. Thus closes the circle of music equaling rhetoric.

I now, parenthetically, call attention to the term *subsumed,* which Zukofsky will use over and over again in his description of Apollinaire's writing. I have already noted that "subsume" does not imply disappearance of one element in favor of another; here it is indicative of a classical concept, defined by the *Académie des Beaux Arts* in the seventeenth century, where an aesthetic hierarchy exists. For example, poetry is considered "superior" to prose as portraits are to landscapes and especially to sculpture. Paragons then and now existed.

Under that hierarchical concept Zukofsky also envisaged the double visibility or audibility of the text: "subsume," never—according to its dictionary meaning—implies other than ranking in simultaneity. It is the mechanism of composition that best illustrates the seduction of the particular as it too contains a multitude of signs, all revealing, in Zukofsky's expression: "an ubiquitous intelligence." A passage is then relegated without destruction or, to quote Dante (as Zukofsky did), it is a mode of movement: "This fusing aspect of construction . . . 'curial' . . . because 'curiality' is nothing else but the justly balanced rule of things." In other words, *subsumed.* Borrowing the word "dominant," perhaps from a Marxist analytical paradigm, Zukofsky writes: "Apollinaire infused the contemporary principles of a dominant (if not *the* dominant) industry of the arts—painting—into the implicit judgment of his compositions as action—poetry and prose being so-called."

The question persists: is there a need to differentiate the theory of simultaneity from the concept of subsumation? Apollinaire proposed an answer, repeating the French painter Robert Delaunay's aesthetic formula: "le *contraste simultané,*" which is "le moyen le plus fort d'*expression de la réalité.*" Still referring to Delaunay, Apollinaire maintained that "la simultanéité des couleurs . . . voilà la seule réalité pour construire en peinture." Painting as an equivalent to music (a Baudelairian example of synesthesia): Zukofsky is attracted to such passages where Apollinaire waxes eloquently on the specific aspects of painting that make it "modern," that is, postimpressionist. Such considerations are doubly applicable to Zukofsky. First, those considerations could equally apply to music, a running leitmotif in Zukofsky's poetry, and a corollary to poetry itself. Second, and with even greater applicability, such a joining of painting with music illustrates Zukofsky's ongoing unfolding of his own poetics via other artistic endeavors.

When Zukofsky approvingly quotes Apollinaire quoting Delaunay's theory of "simultaneous contrasts" as "the most powerful expression of reality," isn't Zukofsky, once again, providing us with a key to his own poetics? A poetics that never excludes a fundamental anchoring of the poetic in reality. And that reality is multiform and multifaced to the point that one could—should—approach *"A"* with the expectation of a translation of reality where no element is left out, either elements pertaining to the "outside world" (what we call "reality") or elements pertaining to that filtering device, that is, to language itself. In the 1930s Francis Ponge was equally convinced of the intricate if metaphorical connection between the material world and language itself—or at least that language and rhetoric he was refashioning in order to close the gap between seeing and writing. If this overcharge on the reality connection between language and the world smacks of Plato's *Cratylus,* it may be that, for Ponge as well as for Louis Zukofsky, such an interlinking may have been the only felt philological-philosophic justification for writing poetry. Apollinaire's daring cross-fertilization of French poetic language, with intrusions from "reality" (street posters, for example), is a true precursor of Zukofsky's own objections to the academic establishment's proclamation on what poetry means and is.

I take as one example those half-literate letters sent to Louis Zukofsky by Jackie, son of the Connecticut farmer whose cottage Zukofsky rented two years in a row. *"A"*-12 allows considerable space to these letters sent by a U.S. soldier stationed in California and later in Japan. These letters can be compared to Apollinaire's own dialect intrusions in his French, or to his much-admired letter-poems from the war. Zukofsky quotes Apollinaire and then goes on to quote Delaunay, who declared: "C'est dans nos yeux que se passe le *présent*." Such a declaration might be translated as "the present passes through our eyes," thereby lending a further degree of credence to Zukofsky's 1930s objectivist formulation. Zukofsky's rejection of a strictly intellectual (mental) or metaphoric ordering of the world found its correlation in the mechanics of the camera's eye as well as in a more subtle homonymic substitution where *I* and *eye* were to become inextricable.

What did painting do in Delaunay's day that it hadn't done before? Simply this: at the dawn of painting, a single line encircled man's shadow on the ground whereas today, Delaunay claims (before Baudrillard), we are at a distance from our present, solely confronted by simulacra. That precarious distance can be overcome, however. Delaunay believed that, with all the colors (words) at their disposition, painters (poets) could finally, actually, possess light, that is, the material world.

Such theories of distantiation, of a split between what we believe we observe and translate verbally or pictographically and what actually exists, appear to diverge from Zukofsky's appreciation of the anthropological "oneness" of human nature. It would appear then that Delaunay's oneness of light conflicts with Zukofsky's double belief in simultaneity and his justification of subsuming elements therein.

In following Zukofsky's reading of Apollinaire's writing, I am struck by both the convergence with oft-stated positions and the concurrent introduction of ambivalence, or a duality. To reconcile this possible contradiction, Zukofsky insisted on a variety of stated or implicit "harmonies," a functional term in Delaunay's theory of art. In this musical analogy—but also going back to Greek theories of the harmony of the spheres as well as to Christian theological treatises on the harmonies of the soul—we may find a resolution of these apparently disparate elements. There would then be a sequence one could read through Zukofsky's appreciation of *The Writing of Guillaume Apollinaire*; that is, a series of substitutions when terms like simultaneity, integration, mutation, subsuming, harmonies, dialectic, and distillation would fit, where appropriate, in the scheme of intelligence much as Delaunay had recognized the array of colors at his disposition: "couleurs claires, couleurs foncées, leurs compléments, leurs intervalles et leurs simultanéités." In the final analysis, for both poet and painter, each in his own way applying rules of grammar, rhetoric, and music, what counted was a harmonic proportion—to borrow once again a term from the musical realm.

Delaunay insisted, and the terms are emphasized: "*le* sujet est 'éternel' dans l'œuvre d'art et doit apparaître à l'*initié* dans tout son *ordre* et dans toute sa *science*." As if Delaunay could—prescient as he was—foresee objectivist poetics in the making. Zukofsky might have borrowed such poetics from André Breton's definition of Surrealism, when Breton insisted on placing Surrealism under the encyclopedic sign of philosophy rather than the more expected literature or poetry entry, where a theory of de-subjectification (in line with Mallarmé's indictment of the personal) heralded what Breton called the "jeu désintéressé de la pensée." The ideal Breton had, an old and haunting one, was the resolution of the principal problems of life (a venture parallel to Freud's). Wouldn't this project equally apply to Zukofsky or to poets—Orphic ones—as well? Apollinaire's *Calligrammes*, as they resolved the difference between "the choice of words and the graphic mutual" would "reveal writing the composition as action." What was "resolution" for Breton becomes "simulation" for Apollinaire, who mimed rain or hair, the Eiffel Tower, or a tie via a graphic disposition of letters. On his side, Zukofsky nearly duplicated Francis Ponge's equation: "Parti pris des choses . . ." when he wrote: "repayment of a state of things into a choice of words."

The ranking is clear. From reality to poetry's reality—that was Apollinaire's major contribution according to Zukofsky: "the insistence on the constant display and play of language."

Speaking about Marinetti's Futurism, Zukofsky noted a correspondence between early twentieth-century theory and its application to painting as well as its adaptation into poetry: "the particular rhythm and interior force of the object projected . . . a synthesis recalling the dynamics of sight." Zukofsky will collate painting's theory with poetry's. Further, and quoting Leo Frobenius's *Paideuma* on African art (Frobenius was an illustrious German Africanist who influenced both Pound and Senghor), Zukofsky will write: "Apollinaire's time, a period of cities and manual crafts, seemed to have *radiated, in his writing*, the solar gods of velocity." A Futurist dogma that Zukofsky transferred to Apollinaire's way of writing poetry without punctuation: "natural after Mallarmé." (In a footnote Zukofsky claimed that not appreciating this constituted "a considerable loss to American scholarship, since it has often given the most careful attention to misprints of punctuation.")

Have I so far accorded to speech transferred into poetry its proper due? The French tradition (as I noted in the beginning of this essay) as of the sixteenth-century Pléiade, right through the Parnassian poets of the mid-nineteenth century, were nearly all convinced that writing poetry somehow placed the poet on the right(hand) side of God himself, or the gods themselves, according to a more ancient perspective. Poetry turned language into gold and Rimbaud's alchemical metaphor, even when that poet wrote prose poems, does not significantly alter a dearly held belief that prose, in Mallarmé's view, was but "silver." That is, prose was gross as *reportage* while poetry traveled to unexpected regions of difference, to those "vaste et . . . étranges domaines" Apollinaire wrote about in his "Jolie rousse."

Zukofsky, master intertwiner of the oral / aural, of the "shuttling" back and forth between high and low, and all of the intervening linguistic registers, was especially sensitive to Apollinaire's exploitation of this viewing of language in poetry. Writing about *La Chanson du Mal-Aimé*, where "the voice articulating is logical, hence the phrase must take on the logic of the voice," Zukofsky duplicated his own practice-in-theory; he too placed such emphasis on "the logic of the voice." He then added: "Diction (as in all the poems of *Alcools*—*Calligrammes* seems persistently close to actual speech): a fluent blend of the rare, aureoled word—'argyraspides,' 'chibriape'—and the resurrection of the common epithets." Could there be a more transparent description of Zukofsky's own way—or Shakespeare's for that matter? In reading "A," could one not equally conclude that "great poetry" is defined by "the vigor of the movement and the force of the sensible disposition and contiguity of the words?"

What Zukofsky says about Apollinaire, we as readers would unhesitatingly say about Zukofsky. Ethnographically speaking, two apparently different poets belonging to two different tribes are brought so close to each other that they merge one into the other: writing about writing is, after all, writing about oneself writing.

In conclusion, the complexity of the title Zukofsky chose might lead us to suspect that part of its interpretation might be to insist on Zukofsky writing Apollinaire. That fully justifies the title and the ambition of the work as it suggests, too, in other such endeavors, a similar duplication of approach where the center of attention is only superficially to be understood as a critical reading of the other. In fact, it is an analysis of oneself-in-the-other's writing or again, to quote John Cage, in the way Zukofsky "wrote [himself] through" Apollinaire. Or, as Roland Barthes put it: "Peut-on . . . commencer à écrire sans se prendre pour un autre?" (*Roland Barthes par Roland Barthes* [Paris: Editions du Seuil, 1975], 103).

HOW TO READ THE TEXT

The *original* Zukofsky text *The Writing of Guillaume Apollinaire* can be read by reading the left pages ONLY, alternating between the French and English as Zukofsky intended.

In order to read *Le Style Apollinaire* in its entirety, one should only read the French texts, crossing back and forth across pages as needed. For convience, the Apollinaire texts have all been translated into English by Sasha Watson.

Le Style Apollinaire

Le Flâneur

"Le flâneur des deux rives" who visited "le plus rarement possible dans les grandes bibliothèques" and liked "mieux (se) promener sur les quais, cette délicieuse bibliothèque publique" listened receptively and wrote down the words of a singularly mindful reader of his acquaintance:

"A New York, j'ai fait de longues séances à la Bibliothèque Carnegie, immense bâtiment en marbre blanc qui, d'après les dires de certains habitués, serait tous les jours lavé au savon noir. Les livres sont apportés par un ascenseur. Chaque lecteur a un numéro et quand son livre arrive, une lampe électrique s'allume, éclairant un numéro correspondant à celui que tient le lecteur. Bruit de gare continuel. Le livre met environ trois minutes à arriver et tout retard est signalé par une sonnerie. La salle de travail est immense, et, au plafond, trois caissons, destinés à recevoir des fresques contiennent, en attendant, des nuages en grisaille. Tout le monde est admis dans la bibliothèque. Avant la guerre tous les livres allemands étaient achetés. Par contre, les achats de livres français étaient restreints. On n'y achetait guère que les auteurs français célèbres. Quand M. Henri de Régnier fut élu à *l'Académie française*, on fit venir tous ses ouvrages, car la bibliothèque n'en possedait pas un seul. On y trouve un livre de Rachilde: *Le Meneur de Louves*, dans la traduction russe, avec la traduction en caractères latins suivis de trois points d'interrogation. Cependant, la bibliothèque est abonnée au *Mercure* depuis une dizaine d'années. Comme il n'y a aucun contrôle, on vole 444 volumes par mois, en moyenne. Les livres qui se volent le plus sont les romans populaires, aussi les communique-t-on copiés à la machine. Dans les succursales des quartiers ouvriers il n'y a guère que des copies polygraphiées. Toutefois, la succursale de la quatorzième rue (quartier juif) contient une riche collection d'ouvrages en yiddish. Outre la grande salle de travail dont j'ai parlé il y a une salle spéciale pour la musique, une salle pour les littératures sémitiques, une salle pour la technologie, une salle pour les patentes des Etats-Unis, une salle pour les aveugles, où j'ai vu une jeune fille lire du bout des doigts *Marie-Claire*, de Marguerite

The Stroller

"The stroller of both banks" qui n'allait "as rarely as possible to the great libraries" et aimait "mieux (se) promener" along the quays, that delightful public library," savait aussi prêter l'oreille: il a noté les paroles d'un lecteur de sa connaissance singulièrement observateur:

"In New York, I put in long hours in the Carnegie Library, an immense building of white marble that, according to certain regulars, was washed with black soap each day. The books are brought in an elevator. Each reader has a number and when his book arrives, an electric lamp switches on, lighting up a number corresponding to the reader's. Constant ruckus of a train station. The book takes about three minutes to arrive and a bell rings to signal every delay. The workroom is immense and each inlaid panel of the ceiling, meant to hold a fresco, meanwhile contains grayish clouds. Everyone is allowed entrance to the library. Before the war, the library purchased all of its German books. It was, however, limited in its buying of French books. The library purchased books by only the most famous French authors, and very few of those. When Henri de Régnier was elected to the *Académie française*, all of his works had to be ordered because the library did not possess even one. One of Rachilde's books could be found: *Le Meneur de Louves* in the Russian translation, with the translation in Roman characters followed by three question marks. However, the library has had a subscription to *Mercure* for a dozen years. As there is no stamping of tickets, an average of 444 volumes are stolen each month. The books that are stolen most often are popular novels, which is why machine-copied versions are distributed. Yet, the Fourteenth street branch (in the Jewish neighborhood) houses a rich collection of works in Yiddish. Beyond the large workroom that I spoke of, there is a special room for music; a room for Semitic literature; a room for technology; a room for United States patents; a room for the blind, where I saw a young girl reading *Marie-Claire*, by Marguerite

Audoux; une salle pour les journaux, une salle pour les machines à écrire à la disposition du public. A l'étage supérieur enfin se trouve une collection de Tableaux."[1]

Years after the War, following the shadow of the flâneur's seeming divagations, his three books *Il y a*, *L'Hérésiarque & Cie*, and *Calligrammes* disappeared from the "Bibliothèque Carnegie" for several months, and after that passage were again available for public use.

New York, March 14, 1932

---

1. *Le Flâneur des deux rives*, Paris, 1928, Librairie Gallimard, pp. 75–77. First published, Editions de la Sirène, 1928.

Adoux, with her fingertips; a room for newspapers; a room for typewriters for public use. Finally, there is a collection of paintings upstairs.[1]"

Bien des années après la Guerre, se laissant attirer par les prétendues divagations de l'ombre du flâneur, ses trois livres, *Il y a*, *L'Hérésiarque et Cie*, et *Calligrammes* disparurent de la "Carnegie Library" pour plusieurs mois. Après cet égarement, ils se trouvaient remis à la disposition du public.

New York, 14 mars 1932

---

1. *Le Flâneur des deux rives,* Paris 1928, Librairie Gallimard, pp. 75–77. First published, Editions de la Sirène, 1928.

Il Y A

The stroller, living thru the times he did, must have often appeared an isolated phenomenon to himself. He might have often said—Guillaume, what troubles you? What is it?—as he did say:

> Un jour
> Un jour je m'attendais moi-même
> Je me disais Guillaume il est temps que tu viennes
> Pour que je sache enfin celui-là que je suis
> Moi qui connais les autres[2]

As a phenomenon, that is not as a wonder but as a human entity, he thus isolated his time, literature as well as habit.[3]

There are, by way of self-, as well as, objective isolation, the three calligrammes:

> 1- Mon cœur pareil à une flamme renversée
>
> 2- Les Rois Qui Meurent Tour A Tour
>   Renaissent au cœur des poètes
>
> 3- Dans ce miroir je suis enclos
>   vivant et vrai comme on imagine
>   les anges et non comme sont
>   les reflets de Guillaume Apollinaire[4]

There are also the posthumous lines of "Chapeau-Tombeau:"[5]

2. "Cortège"—*Alcools*, Mercure de France, 1913

3. Cf. "Paul Dermée ou Le Flâneur des deux rives" in *L'Esprit nouveau*, #26, October 1924.

4. *Calligrammes*, Mercure de France, 1918.

5. "Reflets de L'incendie," edited by Philippe Soupault, *Les Cahiers du Sud*, 1927.

There Is . . .

Le flâneur, vivant à l'époque où il vivait, devait se regarder comme un phénomène isolé. Il aurait pu dire souvent: "Guillaume, qu'est-ce que tu as? Qu'est-ce qu'il y a?" de même qu'il a dit en fait:

> One day
> One day I was waiting for myself
> I said to myself Guillaume it's time you came
> so that I might finally know who I am
> I who know others[2]

Le poète, phénomène naturel, c'est-à-dire entité humaine et non être miraculeux, a ainsi isolé l'époque, sa littérature et ses moeurs.[3]

Il y a—comme exemples de double isolement: isolement de soi-même autant qu'isolement des choses, les trois calligrammes:

> 1- My heart like an overturned flame

> 2- The Kings Who Die Each In Turn
>   Are reborn in the hearts of poets

> 3- In this mirror I am held
>   living and real as angels
>   Might be and not as reflections of
>   Guillaume Apollinaire[4]

Il y a aussi les vers posthumes de "Chapeau-Tombeau:"[5]

2. "Cortège," *Alcools*, Mercure de France, 1913.

3. Cf. "Paul Dermée ou Le Flâneur des deux rives," *L'Esprit nouveau*, no. 26, October 1924.

4. *Calligrammes*, Mercure de France, 1918.

5. "Reflets de l'incendie," édité par Philippe Soupault, *Cahiers du Sud*, 1927.

On a niché
Dans son tombeau
L'oiseau perché
Sur ton chapeau

Il a vécu
En Amérique
Ce petit cul
          Or
Nithologique
          Or
J'en ai assez
Je vais pisser

As a pen-stroke, "Le Phoque"[6] (possibly a self-portrait) is as reliable:

J'ai les yeux d'un vrai veau marin
Et de Madame Ygrec l'allure
On me voit dans tous nos meetings
Je fais de la littérature
Je suis phoque de mon état
Et comme il faut qu'on se marie
Un beau jour j'épouserai Lota
Du matin au soir l'Otarie
          Papa Maman
Pipe et tabac crachoir caf' conc
          Laï Tou

In *La Femme assise*[7] in which the writing and the sense are often, of compunction, dry, there are the words of this notation:

"Dans le milieu de poètes et de peintres qu'ils fréquentaient, milieu où l'on n'est pas toujours enclin à la bonté, mais où l'on est toujours sensible, une anecdote émouvante remuait alors les cœurs . . ."[8]

6. "Reflets de l'incendie."
7. *Nouvelle Revue française*, 1920.
8. Page 189.

A nest was made
in his grave
the bird perched
On your hat

He lived
in America
This little
Ornithologi
cal ass
But
I've had enough
I'm going to piss

"The Seal,"[6] portrait, si l'on veut, de l'artiste par lui-même atteint dans le dessin à la plume, la même solidité:

I have true sea-calf's eyes
And Madame Y's allure
I attend our every meeting
I work in literature
I am the seal of my state
And since a man must wed
I'll marry Lota one fine day
The Sea-lion from morn' to night
        Daddy Mommy
Pipe and tobacco spittoon cabaret
        Laï Tou

Dans *La Femme assise*[7] où l'écriture et le sens deviennent souvent, par componction, secs, il y a pourtant les mots de cette remarque:

"In the circle of poets and painters that they frequented, circles whose members are not always inclined toward acts of kindness but where one is always sensitive, a touching anecdote stirred every heart . . ."[8]

6. "Reflets de l'incendie."
7. *Nouvelle Revue française*, 1920.
8. p. 189.

Never exactly given over to the times of Madame de Staël, and if there were less haste his kindness might have exceeded the use of the word "sensible," preferred "l'intelligent," or the composite "emotive-intelligent:" intelligence, emotive-intelligence of the stroller's writing dispenses with the mileposts of autobiography.[9]

The poet kept them for "L'Ermite:"[10]

> Seigneur que t'ai-je fait Vois je suis unicorne
> Pourtant malgré son bel effroi concupiscent
> Comme un poupon chéri mon sexe est innocent
> D'être anxieux seul et debout comme une borne

Amusingly secretive to the point of emanating a superstition, like Descartes who kept his birthday to himself so that no astrologer could cast his nativity, the poet's father according to biographers, was either a Polish general or a Roman cardinal (the reader has but a perfunctory choice); and the poet, a great friend of painters, found all portraits of himself strange to himself.[11]

Of these, to the poet, strange likenesses, there are by Picasso:[12]

The linear, somewhat cross-eyed turnip head and tuft of hair, the pipe and brief mustache indicating a mouth.

9. For what has been done, tho, in the way of biography see the complementary bibliographies of 1—Hector Talvert, *La Fiche bibliographique française,* 1931; 2—Hector Talvert et Joseph Place, *Bibliographie des auteurs Modernes, Langue française,"* 1929; 3—M. Elie Richard in *Les Images de Paris* and subsequently in *L'Esprit nouveau,* October 1924.

10. *Alcools.*

11. Cf. André Rouvèyre. *Souvenirs de mon commerce,* G. Crès et Cie 1921: "Je le savais monégasque, et il prétendait qu'il était né Romain. En tout cas il fut baptisé à Rome, le 29 sept. 1880 à la Sacrosanta Patriarcalis Basilica Santa Maria Majoris." Billy's date of Apollinaire's birth is Aug. 26, 1880 in Rome.

12. See André Billy, *Apollinaire vivant,* Editions de la Sirène 1923; the frontispiece to *Contemporains pittoresques,* 1929, *L'Esprit nouveau,* Oct. 1924.

Jamais précisément retenu par l'époque de Mme de Staël, il aurait pu, avec moins de hâte, permettre à sa bonté de contourner et dépasser le mot "sensible," pour lui préférer le mot "intelligent," ou le composé "intelligent-émotive." Du moins, l'intelligence émotive de l'écriture du Flâneur dépasse les bornes de l'autobiographe.[9]

Le poète les a gardé pour "l'Ermite:"[10]

> Lord what have I done for thee Look I am a unicorn
> Like a beloved child my sex is innocent
> In spite of its fine terror concupiscent
> Standing like a post upright anxious and alone

Se plaisant à ce mystère, peut-être par un sentiment qui touchait à la superstition, et en cela semblable à Descartes qui gardait secrète sa date de naissance pour qu'aucun astrologue ne pût faire son horoscope, il a laissé dire aux biographes que son père était soit un général polonais, soit un cardinal romain (on n'a pas l'embarras du choix); et le poète, grand ami des peintres regardait comme de parfaits étrangers tous les portraits qu'ils avaient faits de lui.[11]

Parmi ces figures étrangères, il y a les étranges images de Picasso.[12]

Des lignes qui s'arrangent pour former une tête en navet, des yeux qui louchent un peu, une touffe de cheveux, une pipe et une moustache courte qui indiquent une bouche.

9. For several biographical essays already completed, see the bibliographies of (1)Hector Talvert, *La Fiche bibliographique française*, 1931; (2)Hector Talvert et Joseph Place, *Bibliographie des auteurs modernes, Langue française*, 1929; and (3)Elie Richard in *Les Images de Paris* and later in *L'Esprit nouveau*, October 1924.

10. *Alcools.*

11. Cf. André Rouvèyre: *Souvenirs de mon commerce*, G. Crès et Cⁱᵉ, 1921:
"I knew that he was Monacan and he pretended he had been born Roman. In any case, he was baptised in Rome, September 29, 1880, at the Sacrosanta Patriarcalis Basilica Santa Maria Majoris." The date given by Billy for Apollinaire's birth is August 26, 1880, in Rome.

12. See André Billy: *Apollinaire vivant*, Editions de la Sirène, 1923; the frontispiece of *Contemporains pittoresques*, 1929; *L'Esprit nouveau*, October 1924.

A similar head with a plump, black-inked body attached, the black, glancing white, of formal and busy full dress, a fat seemingly small sensitive hand dragging the ruffled or feathered or laced chevalier (he was never of the Legion of Honor) hat, not so busy tho formal; the other hand holding a paper away from itself—all in all, an embarrassed pomp which seems to have inveigled humor and irony in action[13] seducing and traducing the scatter-brained, from the poet's appearance, evidently not there: remaining intact himself, if doubtful, the eyes squinting doubtful.

The unwieldy heresiarch, if he may be guessed, mysteriously weighed down by the bishop's petticoats and mitre, fingers beringed, watch on the wrist of the other hand. Equivocally turnip-faced, still squinting and smoking his pipe above the chain of the cross, above the cushion under his feet, the crozier, held slanting, taller than his seated height, than the tall back of the armchair.

Or meeker, the same, petticoats doffed, an overpowering Polish peasant, in uniform and smoking a pipe.

Or the soldier, bandaged head, Apollonic profile and youthful beard, to the poet probably a portrait which never suggested his lines: "Un grand manteau gris de crayon comme le ciel m'enveloppe jusqu'à l'oreille, Sans pitié chaste et l'œil sévère."[14]

And the brigadier, linear, considerable body but lithe, Spanish-Semitic beard and nose. He is seated in an armchair, one hand on the left knee, and looks on and out.

The eau-forte of Marcoussis:

Well-dressed business editor, smooth-shaven chin, eyes, lips, formed, geometrically outlined by planes, sectors and circles, intersected by the title pages of his books; his pipes and penholder, and from the fingers of a cleanly wooden sculptor's manikin, in calligraphy on a sheet of paper: "Un jour je m'attendais moi-*même*."

---

13. "Naturally, irony applied to writing is intolerable, but, naturally, humor and irony together make a pair." Jacques Vaché—*Littérature*, #6.

14. Gravé sur bois par R. Jaudon, see *Calligrammes*.

Semblable à celle-là, une tête où s'attache un corps enflé. Ce corps est fait à l'encre noire. Tout le noir d'un habit de cérémonie dans l'exercice de ses fonctions, sur lequel la lumière blanche éclate; une main grasse et qui paraît petite et très sensible traîne une coiffe non moins cérémonieuse, mais moins active qui porte des plumes, de la dentelle, ou autre chose; l'autre maintient un papier à l'écart d'elle-même—en somme une pompe embarrassée, qui semble avoir empêtré l'humour et l'ironie[13] dans l'action qui, séduction et traduction pour l'étourdi, laisse le poète lui-même intact, éloigné peut-être dans le doute, car les yeux louchent.

Hérésiarque corpulent, si toutefois on peuts approcher de lui, que les jupes et la mitre de l'évêque appesantissent mystérieusement, doigts bagués à une main, au poignet de l'autre une montre-bracelet. Equivoque, la tête navet louche toujours et fume la pipe par dessus les chaînes de la croix, le coussin de ses pieds, la crosse inclinée et plus haute que son grand corps assis, que le grand dossier du fauteuil.

Plus doux, dépouillé de ses jupes, c'est encore lui, paysan polonais, colosse en uniforme, fumant la pipe.

Ou soldat, la tête bandée, profile apollinien, barbe juvénile, probablement étranger au poète ce portrait qui n'a jamais évoqué pour lui les vers: "a great coat pencil-gray like the sky envelops me up to my ears, Pitilessly chaste and severe of eye."[14]

Et le brigadier, corps linéaire, puissant mais souple, nez et barbe hispano-sémite. Il est assis dans un fauteuil, une main sur le genou gauche, et laisse son regard fixé dans le lointain.

L'eau forte de Marcoussis:

L'éditeur chic, le menton bien rasé; les yeux, les lèvres formés par des combinaisons géométriques de droites et de courbes que les pages de garde de ses livres viennent intersecter; ses pipes et ses plumes, et sur un papier tracé par la main calligraphiante d'un mannequin articulé d'artiste, la phrase: "One day I was waiting for *myself.*"

13. "Naturally, irony applied to writing is intolerable, but, naturally, humor and irony together make a pair." Jacques Vaché, *Littérature,* 6.

14. Wood engraving by R. Jaudon, *Calligrammes.*

On the word of the sweet and somewhat asthmatic voice[15] of the poet, he did not recognize these portraits. But consistently skeptical, he realized, writing of one of his illustrators:[16] "Les portraits les moins ressemblants lui coûtent le plus de peine. Il met parfois plus d'une année à les achever. Et lorsqu'ils paraissent bien éloignés de la réalité, voilà notre dessinateur content. La cruauté de cette méthode a donné quelques portraits surprenants qui, loin de la réalité, s'approchent singulièrement de la vérité."

But the conditions of reality inscribed the plane of the poet's fact. ("Vendémiaire") "Je vivais à l'époque où finissaient les rois."[17] He lived also in the time "(du) commencement de la division du travail, en littérature." La nouvelle mode pour les écrivains, he wrote, c'est d'être très peu les auteurs de leurs livres. Ainsi, M. F— écrit volontiers d'après un canevas que lui apporte son éditeur. Il ne reste à l'éminent critique qu'à amplifier. C'est en cela qu'il excelle.

Je connais un éditeur qui vient d'apporter un plan à l'illustre amplificateur. "Le jeune auteur du canevas, m'a-t-il dit, attend avec curiosité l'issue de cette collaboration. Il n'attendra pas longtemps. Il faut à M. F— deux jours pour écrire un livre, il en faut quinze pour qu'on l'imprime. Dans vingt jours, mon jeune homme lira cet ouvrage qu'il a conçu et n'a point écrit."[18]

Feat which was an impossibility to one who wrote:

> La parole est soudaine et c'est un Dieu qui tremble
> Avance et soutiens-moi je regrette les mains
> De ceux qui les tendaient et m'adoraient ensemble
> Quelle oasis de bras m'accueillera demain
> Connais-tu cette joie de voir des choses neuves[19]

---

15. Alberto Savinio—*L'Esprit nouveau*, October 1924.

16. *Anecdotiques*, Librairie Stock, 1926 - a collection of *La Vie anecdotique*, articles which appeared in the *Mercure de France* from April 1, 1911 to November 1918 (he died November 9). The first three articles of *La Vie anecdotique* appeared under the signature of Montade.

17. *Alcools*.

18. *Anecdotiques*, 9.

19. *Calligrammes*—"La Victoire."

Selon l'affirmation du poète à la voix douce et légèrement asthma-
tique[15] il ne reconnaissait pas ces portraits. Mais sceptique avec méthode
il remarquait, parlant d'un de ces dessinateurs:[16] "The portraits that look
the least like him give him the most difficulty. Sometimes it takes him
more than a year to finish them. And when they seem quite far from
reality, only then is our illustrator satisfied. The cruelty of this method
produced several surprising portraits that, far from reality, come singularly closer to the truth."

Mais les conditions de la réalité circonscrivait le plan de la vérité
du poète ("Vendémiaire"). "I lived at the end of the reign of kings."[17]
Il vivait aussi à l'époque "of the beginning of the division of labor in
literature." The new style for writers is barely to be the authors of their
books. Thus Mr. F— is willing to write according to an outline that his
editor brings to him. All that remains for the eminent critic is to amplify.
It is in this that he excels.

I know an editor who recently brought a framework to the illustrious
amplifier. "He told me that the young author of the outline is waiting
with curiosity for the result of this collaboration. He won't have to wait
long. It takes Mr. F— two days to write a book, it takes fifteen to print
it. In twenty days my young man will read this work that he conceived
and not one word of which he wrote."[18]

Exploit impossible à celui qui écrivit:

> Speech is sudden a God is trembling
> Come hold me up I miss the hands
> That together tended and adored me
> What oasis of arms will welcome me tomorrow
> Do you know this joy of seeing new things[19]

---

15. Alberto Savinio, *l'Esprit nouveau*, October 1924.

16. *Anecdotiques*, Librairie Stock, 1926. Collection of articles in *La Vie anecdotique* which appeared in *Le Mercure de France* from April 1911 to November 1918
(he died on November 9). The first three articles of *La Vie anecdotique* appeared
under the name of Montade.

17. *Alcools.*

18. *Anecdotiques*, 9.

19. "La Victoire": *Calligrammes.*

If one does, writing cannot be a matter of setting down aesthetic principle by way of filling a sketch. Writing becomes the work of making art of an intelligence, of a life, of using an era as an illustration of an emotion, of isolating the mutations and implicit historic metamorphoses of an era to record them.

Such work does not innocently dispense with the writer by terming him a catalytic agent or a medium, the criticism of "l'esprit scientifique"[20] in aesthetics, the metaphorical chemistry of the man of letters, is a phase not too far staged from an "automatisme psychique" "la croyance à la réalité supérieure de certaines formes d'associations négligées, à la toute puissance du rêve, au jeu désintéressé de la pensée."[21] To make an art of familiarity rather "par les cinq sens et quelques autres."

> Un jour je m'attendais moi-même
> Je me disais Guillaume il est temps que tu viennes
> Et d'un lyrique pas s'avançaient ceux que j'aime
> Parmi lesquels je n'étais pas
> . . . .
> Et le langage qu'ils inventaient en chemin
> Je l'appris de leur bouche et je le parle encore
> Le cortège passait et j'y cherchais mon corps
> Tous ceux qui survenaient et n'étaient pas moi-même
> Amenaient un à un les morceaux de moi-même
> On me bâtit peu à peu comme on élève une tour
> Les peuples s'entassaient et je parus moi-même
> Qu'ont formé tous les corps et les choses humaines

Intimacy has achieved distance and space with emotion. There is no subject nor the pretense at an object. The writing is a period of vibration off the ring of intelligence which is an object. For the intimacy revealed is not Apollinaire's, a reflection, but that of an intelligence, the fact and a life. The writing down of this intimacy has become the cast of forms of his time. For another time may be imagined when no such intimacy will not or cannot be recorded, the cast of forms of that time so rigorous in its production as to pervade the writer involved in fostering it, become sharp tho unconscious as a tool.

20. "la vanité de l'esprit scientifique,"—André Breton, Préface, *Manifeste du surréalisme.*

21. André Breton, *Manifeste du surréalisme.*

L'écriture ne peut pas consister pour l'artiste à couvrir une page blanche de principes esthétiques. Il s'agit plutôt d'un travail qui fait de l'art avec une intelligence, une vie; il s'agit d'employer une période pour illustrer une émotion, d'isoler les changements et les métamorphoses historiques qu'implique la période, pour les enregistrer.

Un tel ouvrage n'escamote pas ingénument l'écrivain en le nommant agent catalytique ou intermédiaire, comme le fait la critique née de l'esprit scientifique[20] qui, chimie métaphorique de *l'homme de lettres*, est une phase assez proche du "psychic automatism . . ." "the belief in the superior reality of certain neglected forms of association, in the all-powerfulness of the dream, in the disinterested game of thought."[21] Faire plutôt un art de la familiarité "with all five senses and a few others."

> One day I was waiting for myself
> I said to myself Guillaume it's time for you to come
> As my loved ones approached with a lyrical step
> And I was not among them
> . . . .
> And the language they invented on their way
> I learned from their mouths and I speak it still
> I looked for my body in the passing retinue
> All those who happened by and were not I
> Brought bits of myself one by one
> They built me little by little as if I were a tower
> Peoples gathered and I appeared
> Who had formed all bodies and all human things

L'intimité a conquis la distance et l'espace par l'émotion. Il n'y a pas de sujet, ni de faux airs d'objets. L'écriture est un temps de vibration en dehors du cercle de l'intelligence qui est l'unique objet. Car l'intimité qui se révèle n'est pas celle d'Apollinaire, un reflet, mais celle d'une intelligence, le fait et une vie. L'écriture qui révèle cette intimité est devenue le moule des formes de son époque. Car on peut en imaginer une autre où telle intimité ne sera ou ne pourra être enregistrée, le moule à formes de cette époque-là sera si précis dans son fonctionnement qu'il attaquera l'écrivain dont le travail est de l'entretenir et qui est devenu sûr et inconscient comme un outil.

20. "La vanité de l'esprit scientifique"—André Breton, *Manifeste du surréalisme* (preface).

21. André Breton, *Manifeste du surréalisme*.

His work, the lyric pace of his time or the tripping up of it and its modes of love or movement and their recoil a necessity, is a choice and a return to this choice. Adventurer of invention, which takes cognizance of order but particularly of its vehemence, he left to that "vide avenir l'histoire de Guillaume Apollinaire," realizing at once the future's illimitability as well as its indeterminate present; realized also, pitiless for himself, that there were many things which he did not dare, or was obliged not to say, and asked at the same time for the present's pitying disdain and the uncolored future's indulgence.[22] "Life without slippers or parallel, which is against and for unity and decidedly against the future; we know wisely that our brains become downy cushions that our anti-dogmatism is as exclusivist as the functionary and that we are not free and go crying liberty . . . severe necessity without discipline or morality . . . within the frame of European weaknesses . . ."[23]

By the same necessity, Guillaume Apollinaire kept a close watch on his followers:

> demain est incolore
> Il est informe aussi près de ce qui parfait
> Présente tout ensemble et l'effort et l'effet

The biographer, follows through and comes in only as an axiomatic witness: "Quant à son œuvre, je considère qu'elle est à la fois remplie d'invention et du choix le plus intelligent. C'est un ami que je regrette profondément, il avait le charme incomparable de ne pas se compromettre pour être compromis."[24]

22. "Cortège," *Alcools*; "Merveille de la guerre," "La Jolie rousse," *Calligrammes*.

23. Tristan Tzara, *Manifeste de Monsieur Antipyrine*.

24. Francis Picabia, *L'Esprit nouveau*, October 1924.

Son œuvre, le cours lyrique de son temps ou ses sauts et sursauts amoureux et leurs retours fatidiques sur eux-mêmes, est un choix et un retour sur ce choix. Explorateur de l'inspiration, qui prend connaissance de l'ordre mais surtout de l'ardeur qui dirige l'ordre, il a laissé à son "empty future of the story of Guillaume Apollinaire," comprenant et l'illimitable du futur et de celui-ci l'indéterminé présent; et, sans pitié pour lui-même, se voyant bien désemparé devant tant de choses qu'il n'osait pas ne pas dire ou ne pouvait pas dire, il demandait le dédain apitoyé du présent et l'indulgence de l'avenir incolore.[22] "Life without slippers or parallel, which is against and for unity and decidedly against the future; we know perfectly well that our brains become downy cushions, that our anti-dogmatism is as exclusivist as the functionary and that we are not free and go crying liberty . . . severe necessity without discipline or morality . . . within the framework of European weaknesses. . . ."[23]

Poussé par la même fatalité, Guillaume Apollinaire suivit de près ses adeptes:

> tomorrow is colorless
> It is formless too next to that which perfects
> Presents together and the effort and the effect

Le biographe fait suite et n'intervient qu'en témoin axiomatique: "As for his work, I see it as being at once full of inventiveness and of the most intelligent choice. He is one friend whom I miss deeply, he had that incomparable charm of never compromising himself in order to be compromised."[24]

22. "Cortège," *Alcools*. "Merveille de la guerre," "La Jolie rousse," *Calligrammes*.

23. Tristan Tzara, *Manifeste de Monsieur Antipyrine*.

24. Francis Picabia, *L'Esprit nouveau*, October 1924.

Any example taken at random may serve: the "Soleil cou coupé" of the christian era and its farewell in the Parisian zone. The recoil of skepticism of "Zone"[25] strips turn by turn because it loves. *Je suis malade d'ouïr les paroles bienheureuses.* This scepticism also perpetually active, which is the nature of love—ceasing to attract it would be merely enervated of its radiation (the medieval image encircles these lines.) But it is there, too, to be emitted, to shift its quantum and form new energy, new substance. The transformation, the tiredness with being what it was, is natural, it will not be lost, but be a new substance—an entity; its natural affinities. His friends suffer its impatience;[26] if they do not tearfully linger to prove its honesty,[27] they grow impatient.[28] They do not move instinctively as it does with the same unconscious conscience. The *te* of "Zone" is thus Guillaume Apollinaire; the identification of the *te* by surname and familiar name[29] might as well have been dispensed with, yet Guillaume is known only thru the name of his familiar, the familiar's emotions set down are Apollinaire's morphology. The poem is Apollinaire's image. Even sentimentality is objectified as in a Mozart fantasia. For there can be either intelligence or an erased slate following subjection to a code of subversive ritual. With intelligence, there is the handling of, and absorption by, a matter and a time for a creation which moves: intelligence as writing which to the concerned or the observant never becomes an attitude, the subjective grease in the cracks of brilliance.

25. *Alcools.*

26. "L'arbitraire si, du long charmant, nul si peu que lui n'est enclin à se libérer"—André Breton, *Les Pas perdus.*

27. René Dalize.

28. Jacques Vaché, *Littérature #6*—Also Breton's edition of Vaché's *Lettres de guerre* (1919).

29. "Zone," *Alcools.*

N'importe quel exemple pris au hasard peut servir: le "soleil cou coupé" de l'ère chrétienne et ses adieux dans la zone parisienne. Le scepticisme qui se retourne contre soi de "Zone"[25] s'accentue graduellement par amour. *I am sick of hearing happy words.* Ce scepticisme est aussi constamment actif, car telle est la nature de l'amour qui, cessant d'attirer, serait simplement énervé de son rayonnement (l'image médiévale de l'amour encercle ces vers). Mais il doit encore ici se livrer, pour transformer sa puissance en une énergie nouvelle et une substance neuve—une entité; ses affinités naturelles. Les amis souffrent cette impatience[26] en souffrant d'impatience;[27] quand ils ne se lamentent en voulant prouver son honnêteté ils s'impatientent.[28] Eux ne s'agitent pas instinctivement comme lui dans sa conscience inconsciente. Lui, c'est la personne tutoyée de "Zone," c'est Guillaume Apollinaire; l'identification de la personne par un nom familier ou un surnom[29] eût pu être évitée, pourtant Guillaume n'est connu que par le nom de son familier; les émotions du familier, une fois fixées, sont la morphologie d'Apollinaire. Le poème est l'image d'Apollinaire. La sentimentalité est objectivée comme dans une fantaisie de Mozart. Car il peut y avoir soit intelligence, soit table rase après la soumission à un code de rituel subversif. Avec l'intelligence, il y a le traitement d'une matière et d'un temps et il y a leur action absorbante en vue d'une création en mouvement: l'intelligence considérée comme une écriture qui pour l'acteur ou l'observateur ne se résout jamais en une attitude, la graisse subjective dans les failles de la brillance.

25. *Alcools.*

26. "The arbitrary if, so long charming, nothing so little as him was inclined to liberate himself." André Breton, *Les Pas perdus.*

27. René Dalize.

28. Jacques Vaché, *Littérature*, no. 6; also the Vaché edition of *Lettres de guerre* (1919) by Breton.

29. "Zone," *Alcools.*

"We don't recognize Apollinaire any longer, for we suspect him of being a bit too canny in the matter of art, of patching up romanticism with a telephone wire and of not knowing his dynamos. The stars are unhooked—it's very tiresome."[30] The difference is in the order of the voice: his critic "preserving modernity likewise, and killed every night" and Apollinaire, "C'est toujours près de toi cette image qui passe."[31] Guillaume showed the same impatience, saying[32] he had never read Rimbaud. Perhaps because in writing "Seuls des bateaux d'enfants tremblaient à l'horizon" and the rest of *l'Emigrant de Landor Road*[33] he did not need to resort to Rimbaud's final decision in which thought no longer had its recoil and action was an enervation—not a passage to the cherished finality. Too skeptical to say that art was a stupidity, Guillaume found even the record of enervation not a stupidity.

"Ah, well, I can see two ways of putting up with all that. To shape the personal sensation through the aid of a blazing collusion of rare words—not often, eh, what?—or else to trade angles or cleancut squares of feeling. Those of the moment, naturally. We will leave to one side a logic probity—whose business it is to contract us—like everybody else."[34] A twofold exaction which the sponsor of cubism and the writer of *Méditations esthétiques*[35] did not fail to attain in the implicit ubiquity of these verses:

> L'orange dont la saveur est
> Un merveilleux feu d'artifice[36]

The affect of intelligence is inevitable plasticity. That is constant. It grows but it is the seed. The growth of its embrace summed up at a life's end by these verses heralded by the title of "Les Collines" was already present in Guillaume's earliest outgoings, the finished symbol as well as the liberated excursion which prompts it.

30. Billy, *Apollinaire vivant*.

31. *Alcools*.

32. *Ibid.* Vaché.

33. Paris, Figuière, 1912. See also *Anecdotiques*: "le plus de plasticité possible, les couleurs sont des symboles, la lumière est la réalité," p. 43.

34. "Les Collines," *Calligrammes*.

35. Written first, 1908, tho appended to the volume.

36. 1909.

"Nous ne reconnaissons plus Apollinaire, car nous le soupçonnons d'être un peu trop malin en matière d'art, de rapiécer le romantisme avec un fil téléphonique et de ne pas connaître ses dynamos. Les étoiles sont décrochées — cela est très fatigant."[30] La différence est dans le timbre de la voix. Le critique s'accuse "Equally saving modernity and killed each night" et Apollinaire dit: "This passing image is never very far from you."[31] Guillaume montrait la même impatience disant[32] qu'il n'avait jamais lu Rimbaud. Peut-être parce qu'en écrivant: "Only children's boats trembled on the horizon" et le reste de *L'Emigrant de Landor Road,*[33] il n'avait pas besoin d'en arriver à la décision finale de Rimbaud dans laquelle la pensée n'avait plus sa retenue et l'action était un énervement—non un passage à une finalité convoitée. Trop sceptique pour dire que l'art était une idiotie, Guillaume jugeait même que la notation d'un énervement n'était pas une idiotie.

"Eh bien, je vois deux moyens d'arranger tout ça. Façonner la sensation personnelle à l'aide d'une collusion de mots rares—pas souvent, hein, ou bien trafiquer avec des angles et des carrés de sentiment. Ceux du moment, bien sûr. Nous laisserons de côté une probité logique qui ne s'occupe que de nous contrarier comme tout le monde."[34] Double accomplissement que le protagoniste du cubisme et l'auteur des *Méditations esthétiques*[35] ne manqua pas d'atteindre dans l'implicite ubiquité des vers:

> The orange whose flavor is
> A marvelous firework[36]

Les émois de l'intelligence se résolvent inévitablement dans la plasticité. Ils sont constants. Ils se développent mais sont d'abord les germes. Ce développement se résume à la fin d'une vie par ces vers annoncés par le titre: "Les Collines," mais les premières aventures d'Apollinaire contenaient cet aboutissement le symbole achevé aussi bien que les évasions qui l'inspirent.

30. Billy, *Apollinaire vivant.*

31. *Alcools.*

32. *Ibid.* Vaché.

33. Paris, Figuière, 1912. See also *Anecdotiques*: "As much plasticity as possible, colors are symbols, light is reality," 43.

34. "Les Collines," *Calligrammes.*

35. Already written in 1908 and added to this volume.

36. 1909.

In the "Onirocritique"[37] to *L'Enchanteur pourrissant*[38] can be found:
"Le soleil n'était pas plus libre qu'un fruit mûr." In anticipation, "je
procréai cent enfants mâles dont les nourrices furent la lune et la colline,"
the theme of *Les Mamelles de Tirésias*, practically finished in 1903,[39]
resembles the ardor of some of the last verses of *Calligrammes*:

> Voici s'élever des prophètes
> Comme au loin des collines bleues

Of an earlier date than 1903, there exists the poet's first calligramme[40]
done at the age of 14 (1894). The verses are childlike, single words of
shaded calligraphy or arabesque frills waveringly tangent to the right
side of a childlike clock, the hours in roman numerals and the hands
at twelve suggesting heavy gold. The words, some above, some below
the clock, make oblique angles with the top and left side of the page,
seem to drop above stars with points of pyramidal faces. In the extreme
upper left corner of the page, hanging by a thread, a line, is the lamp,
its metal a jack-in-a-box, arms, a fleur-de-lys (flame sputters) decidedly
above the words which are above the chimney, showing up above itself
and the eaves and rafters of the slanting roof of an attic perhaps another
chimney, but it may be a reverberator, a reflecting lamp for the sky and
air thru which the words fall: "Minuit Dans L'ombre Sombre D'une Nuit
Sans Lune Sans Bruit L'heure Pleure." Under the attic roof, the young
subject, poet, dreams, "à l'école," other indistinguishable words mixed

---

37. Presented in 1916, published in 1918. "Apollinaire a fondu dans *Les Mamel-
les*, deux parades (notamment la scène du gendarme) dont il nous fit lecture à
l'Odéon, au dessert. Les deux pièces devaient être publiées sous ce titre unique:
Théâtre de Guillaume Apollinaire. Le même soir, Apollinaire nous a lu *Le Gim-
Gim-Gim des Capucins*, jamais édité et que, dans la suite, a constitué le chapître du
Poète assassiné intitulé *Dramaturgie*, mais sensiblement remanié.' " André Salmon,
La Nouvelle Revue française, November 1, 1920.

38. *Il y a*, 1925.

39. cf. Guillaume's improvement on it:
Oiseau tranquille au vol inverse oiseau
Qui nidifie en l'air
A la limite où notre sol brille déjà
Baisse ta deuxième paupière la terre t'éblouit
Quand tu lèves la tête ("Cortège," *Alcools*).

40. Essay on Jean Royère, 1908, reprinted in *Il y a*.

Dans "l'Onirocritique"[37] de *l'Enchanteur pourrissant*,[38] on trouve, "The sun was no freer than a ripened fruit," et aussi: "In anticipation, I procreated 100 male children whose nurses were the moon and the hill;" voilà le thème des *Mamelles de Tirésias* en somme achevé en 1903[39] et la ferveur de quelques-uns des derniers vers de *Calligrammes*:

> Now see the prophets rise
> Like blue hills in the distance

Avant même 1903, nous avons son premier calligramme[40] fait à l'âge de 14 ans (1894). Les vers sont "enfant," de simples mots, pleins et déliés bien marqués, une ondulante arabesque fixée au côté droit d'une pendule enfantine, les heures sont en chiffres romains, et les aiguilles sur le douze font croire à de l'or massif. Les mots, les uns au-dessus, les autres au-dessous de la pendule font des angles obliques avec le haut et le côté gauche de la page et semblent tomber au-dessus d'étoiles dont les pointes sont des pyramides. A l'angle gauche supérieur de la page, suspendue à un fil est la lampe—qui tient d'un diable noir, avec des armoiries, une fleur-de-lys (flamme crachée) placée bien au-dessus des mots qui sont au-dessus de la cheminée; et montrant encore au-dessus d'elle et des poutres et chevrons du toit penché d'une mansarde, ce qui est peut-être une deuxième cheminée, mais peut-être aussi un miroir réfléchissant ou un réflecteur pour le ciel et l'air au travers duquel les mots tombent: "Midnight In the Dark Shadow Of a Moonless Soundless Night The Hour Weeps." Sous le toit mansardé le jeune poète, le sujet rêve; "à l'école,"

---

37. Presented in 1916, published in 1918. "Apollinaire blended two spectacles in *Les Mamelles* (notably the scene with the gendarme) which he spoke to us about over dessert at Odéon. The two plays should have been published under the single title : *Théâtre de Guillaume Apollinaire*. The same night, Apollinaire read us *Le Gim-Gim-Gim des Capucins*, which was never produced and which, having been sensitively reworked, made up the chapter of *Poète assassiné* called *Dramaturgie*." André Salmon, *Nouvelle Revue française*, November 1, 1920.

38. *Il y a*, 1925.

39. See how Apollinaire perfected this technique:
Tranquil bird of inverted flight bird
Who nestles in the air
At the edge where our sun is already shining
Close your eye the earth blinds you
When you raise your head. ("Cortège," *Alcools.*)

40. Essai sur Jean Royère, 1908, reprinted in *Il y a*.

with the checkered pillow-case and pillow, dreams become an object, the horizontal of his body framed in a shaded rectangle which means the wood of the attic, which means sleep. A mother superior floats and prays in the air, her lectern back of her robes, under the lamp, to the left of the attic roof under which in a rectangle is the sleeper (on the right center of the page). The bottom of the page is filled with steeples, villages, a rolling country hiding a various inked penmanship. Ubiquity speaks for itself.

Later, Guillaume could explain himself more consciously. "On a trop souvent voulu nous faire croire que les Français n'aiment pas la beauté pour elle-même, mais surtout à titre de renseignement." Le goût français est autrement raisonnable. Nous ne voulons plus d'un lakisme[41] insensé. Sous couleur d'aimer la nature, la science et l'humanité, trop de jeunes gens ont gâté leur art par un enthousiasme écœurant. En France, plusieurs générations littéraires qui pouvaient s'approcher de la perfection en ont été écartées par l'influence de la littérature anglaise, si riche, si attrayante, mais pleine de vérités inutiles. Lessing rendit un mauvais service à l'Allemagne, lorsqu'il décréta qu'elle devait abandonner les modèles dramatiques proposés par la France et en demander à l'Angleterre. Il est responsable non seulement de la barbarie du théâtre, mais encore de l'état misérable dans lequel l'inféconde littérature allemande a toujours végété.—la nature et la science en ont assez qui nous portent malheur. La poésie—est aussi fausse que doit l'être une nouvelle création au regard de l'ancienne. Quelle fausseté enchanteresse! Rien qui nous ressemble et tout à notre image.—a rempli ainsi la première condition de l'art le plus pur et le moins stérile. La fausseté est une mère féconde. Les centaures étaient fils d'Ixion et d'un fantôme de nuées semblable à Junon. Et, sœur nue de Narcisse, créature certaine du poète, il ne se doutait pas de votre existence antérieure. Mais, triomphe de la fausseté, de l'erreur, de l'imagination—le poète (créé) à l'envie. . . . On croyait autrefois que les yeux de la chatte croissaient avec la lune et diminuaient avec elle; de même les facultés poétiques se trouvent toujours au niveau des passions du poète. Celles de ne dépassent pas sa destinée. . . .[42]

41. Letter of Alfred Jarry to Madame Rachilde, page 12 — *Ubu Roi* — Fasquelle, Paris, 1921.

42. Enoch.

d'autres mots inextricables mêlés à l'oreiller diapré, des rêves, deviennent l'objet; l'horizontal de son corps encadré d'un rectangle ombré signifie le bois de la mansarde qui signifie le sommeil. Une nonne flotte et prie dans l'air, un pupitre derrière ses robes, sous la lampe à la gauche de la mansarde où le dormeur est dans son rectangle (dans la moitié droite du centre de la page). Le bas de la page est rempli de clochers, de villages, un pays se déroule, dissimulant une calligraphie barbouillée d'encre. L'ubiquité se déclare.

Plus tard, Guillaume pouvait s'expliquer plus consciemment: "Too often we have been encouraged to believe that the French love beauty not for itself but primarily in the interest of information. French taste is otherwise reasonable. We don't want any more of an insane Lakism.[41] In the name of a love for nature, science, and humanity, too many young people have, with a sickening enthusiasm, wasted their art. In France, several literary generations that could have come close to perfection were kept from it by the influence of English literature, so rich, so attractive, but filled with useless truths. Lessing rendered a poor service to Germany when he decreed that she should abandon the dramatic models proposed by France and seek them in England. He is responsible not only for the barbarity of the theater but also for the miserable state in which Germany's barren literature has always stagnated—nature and science bring us enough bad luck. Poetry—is as false as any new creation must be in the eyes of the old. What enchanting falsehood! Nothing resembling us and all in our image—has thus filled the first condition of the purest and the least sterile art. Falsity is a fertile mother. The centaurs were the sons of Ixion and of a ghost cloud resembling Juno. And, naked sister of Narcissus, certain invention of the poet, he didn't suspect your former existence. But triumph of falsity, of error, of imagination—the poet creates as he wishes. . . . In past times we believed that the cat's eyes waxed and waned with the moon; so the poetic faculties are forever equal to the poet's passions. Those of . . . do not exceed his destiny."[42]

41. Letter from Alfred Jarry to Madame Rachilde, *Ubu Roi* (Fasquelle, Paris, 1921), 12.

42. Enoch.

Creatively, not exceeding the gage of his critical destiny, Guillaume must have by that time written, or thought of, the lines of his *L'Enchanteur pourrissant*: "Toi que j'aimais, je sais tout ce qui me ressemble et tu me ressembles, mais tout ce qui te ressemble ne me ressemble pas. . . . O toi que j'aimais et pour qui les vers depuis ma naissance, o temps de la moelle fœtale, patientèrent, dis-moi la vérité" . . . The lady who has put him under her spell and to whom the words are addressed stops only at the edge of the lake and does not answer the question. "Elle descendit lentement la pente que surbaigne l'onde silencieuse, et s'enfonçant sous les flots danseurs, gagna son beau palais dormant plein de lueurs de gemmes au fond du lac."

"Il croit que le cerveau dans la décomposition, fonctionne au-delà de la mort et que ce sont ses rêves qui sont le paradis."[43] Asked for an explanation, Guillaume, who was attracted by the presence of superstitions, might have chosen this sentence to define the limits of *L'Enchanteur pourrissant*. Dead for love, but living in the tomb, the enchanter in his questioning across history does not approach a state of Paradise, for he continues in his decay as on earth to ask for bread ("du pain pétri, du bon pain!") "Quand le fruit est mûr, il se détache et n'attend pas que le jardinier vienne le cueillir. Qu'ainsi fasse l'homme, le fruit qui mûrit librement sur l'arbre de la lumière. Mais, vous ne mourûtes pas, qui êtes six dans la forêt, comme les doigts de la main, et un poignard dans la main, que ne vous serrez-vous, que ne vous repliez-vous? O doigts qui pourriez fouiller; o poing qui pourrait poignarder! o main qui pourrait battre, qui pourrait indiquer, que pourrait ratter la pourriture. Antédiluvien![44] Hermaphrodite![45] Juif errant! Volcanique![46] Magicien![47] Puceau! Vous n'êtes pas mort, vous êtes six comme les doigts de la main et un poignard dans la main, que n'agissez-vous comme la main qui poignarde? Hélas! Il y a trop longtemps que vous n'êtes pas immortels." But the poet who ineluctably pursues the somatic reverie of the enchanter, in the onirocritique, attains the paradisical efflorescence of his own rêve: "Je maudissais les astres indignes dont la clarté coulait sur la terre. Nulle créature

43. Elie.

44. Empédocle.

45. Simon le Magicien.

46. Apollonius de Tyane.

47. Cf. his review of Delanie Mardus, under the pseudonym of Louise Lalanne. *Les Marges*, 1909.

Dans ses expériences créatrices, ne dépassant pas la capacité de sa destinée critique, Guillaume dut écrire à cette époque ou penser ces lignes de son *Enchanteur pourrissant*: "You that I loved, I know all that is like you is unlike me. . . . Oh you whom I loved, for you these verses since my birth, oh times of poetic marrow waited, tell me the truth . . ." La dame qui l'a placé sous son charme et à qui s'adressent ces mots ne s'arrête qu'au bord du lac et ne lui répond pas. "She slowly descended the slope of the swollen, silent wave, and sinking beneath the dancing tides, arrived at her beautiful sleeping palace, filled with gleaming gems at the bottom of the lake."

"He believes that the brain, in decomposing, functions after death and that these dreams are Paradise."[43] Asked to explain himself, Guillaume, who was attracted to superstitions, could have chosen this sentence to define *L'Enchanteur pourrissant*. Il est mort à l'amour mais vit dans la tombe; en scrutant l'histoire il n'approche pas de cet état paradisiaque, car il continue dans sa putréfaction à demander du pain comme sur la terre ("kneaded bread, good bread!") "When the fruit is ripe it falls without waiting for the gardener to come pick it. Thus does man, the fruit that ripens freely on the tree of light. But you do not die, you six in the forest, like fingers on the hand, and a dagger in hand, that you grasp, that you withdraw? Oh, fingers that can search; oh fist that can stab! oh hand that could beat, that could point, that could scratch the rottenness. Antediluvian![44] Hermaphrodite![45] Wandering Jew! Volcanic![46] Magician![47] Virgin! You are not dead, you are six like the fingers of the hand and a dagger in the hand, that you can't act like the hand that stabs? Alas! It was too long ago that you were not immortal." Mais le poète qui poursuit inéluctablement la rêverie somatique de l'enchanteur, atteint, dans l'onirocritique l'efflorescence paradisiaque de son propre rêve: "I cursed the unworthy stars whose light flowed upon the earth. No other

43. Elie.

44. Empedocles.

45. Simon the Magician.

46. Apollonius of Tyane.

47. Cf. his criticism of Delanie Mardus, under the pseudonym of Louise Lalanne. *Les Marges*, 1909.

vivante n'apparaissait plus. Mais des chants s'élevaient de toutes parts.
je visitai des villes vides et des chaumières abandonnées. Je ramassai les
couronnes de tous les rois et en fis le ministre immobile du monde lo-
quace. Des vaisseaux d'or sans matelots, passaient à l'horizon. Des ombres gigantesques se profilaient sur les voiles lointaines. Plusieurs siècles
me séparaient de ces ombres. Je me désespérai. Mais j'avais la conscience
des éternités différentes de l'homme et de la femme. Des ombres dissem-
blables assombrissaient de leur amour l'écarlate des voilures, tandis que
mes yeux se multipliaient dans les fleuves, dans les villes et dans la neige
des montagnes."

The imagery has its own logic, the logic of the writing, which is the
logic of the intelligence. Replete tho it is with the dialectic of a transition between paganism and christianity, the logic of other histories, and
the diction of the French symbolists, it never presents a double plane
of similitude and morality. None of the sentences makes a platitude, its
formative power never allowing for a chain of reasoning. The work bears
one date, in consequence, the date of its composition. The inclusive sense
of its intelligence is historical only in the immediate sense of ubiquity, in
the rejected ejections of faiths and histories by the present's immediate
plasticity, with always the proviso that the poet's passions do not surpass
his destiny.

Definitely, the writing of *L'Enchanteur pourrissant* is not meant for
exoticism of which—especially oriental (the poet found a saturation in
his time).[48] Apollinaire quoted Madame de Staël with approval: "La
littérature des anciens est chez les modernes une littérature transplantée,
la littérature romantique ou chevaleresque est chez nous indigène et c'est
notre religion et nos institutions qui l'ont fait éclore."[49] For the rest,
Apollinaire found it easy enough to follow this thought with a preference for "les œuvres d'art authentiques. Celles qui ont été conçues par
des âmes qu'on n'a point refaites."[50] In the same essay on a subject illustrating his preference, he says: "Il est un des premiers qui résistant
à l'antique instinct de l'espèce, à celui de la race, se soient livrés avec

48. Louise Lalanne: "La Littérature féminine," *Les Marges*, 1909. This history
of Apollinaire's pseudonym is given in *Les Marges*, December 15, 1918: "Lorsque
Louise Lalanne en eut assez de cette plaisanterie nous la fîmes enlever par un officier
de cavalerie."

49. *Les Peintres cubistes*: (Fernand Léger).

50. Vide *l'Enchanteur pourrissant*: "la Dame du Lac." *Le Poète assassiné*: Tristouse Ballerinette. *La Femme assise*: Elvire.

living creature would appear again. But songs rose up from all around. I visited empty cities and abandoned cottages. I gathered the crowns of all the kings and made of them the immobile minister of the talkative world. Golden ships without sailors passed on the horizon. Gigantic shadows cast profiles upon distant sails. Several centuries separated me from these shadows. I despaired. But I was conscious of the different eternities of man and woman. Dissimilar shadows darkened with their love and the scarlet of the sails, while my eyes multiplied in the rivers, in the cities, and in the mountain snow."

Cette imagerie a sa logique propre, logique de l'écriture qui est la logique de l'intelligence. Bien que saturée de la dialectique du stade transitoire entre le paganisme et la chrétienté, de la logique d'autres histoires et de la diction symboliste, elle ne présente jamais un double plan de comparaison ou de morale. Aucune phrase ne tombe dans la platitude; car ce n'est pas sur un fil de raisonnement que s'échappe le pouvoir inventif. L'œuvre porte une date par conséquent, la date de sa composition. L'intelligence combinatrice n'est historique que dans cette intelligence de l'ubiquité, que dans le rejet des rejets de croyances et d'histoires, grâce à la plasticité immédiate du présent et cette clause sous-entendue que les passions du poète ne dépasseront pas sa destinée.

Décidément, l'écriture de *l'Enchanteur pourrissant* ne flirte pas avec l'exotisme dont l'époque était saturée (selon la remarque d'Apollinaire qui visait plus particulièrement l'orientalisme).[48] Il citait en l'approuvant Mme de Staël: "The literature of the ancients is, in a modern setting, a transplanted literature; romantic or chivalric literature native to us, hatched by our religion and our institutions."[49] Par ailleurs, Apollinaire n'eût pas de mal à continuer cette pensée par une préférence pour "the authentic works of art. Those that were conceived by souls that have not been remade."[50] Dans le même essai, parlant d'un homme dont l'œuvre illustre cette préférence, il dit: "He is one of the first who, resisting the ancient instinct of the species, that of race, happily gave himself up to the

---

48. Louise Lalanne: "La Littérature féminine," *Les Marges*, 1909. The story of this pseudonym is given in *Les Marges*, December 15, 1918: "When Louise Lalanne had had enough of this joke, we had her removed by an officer of the cavalry."

49. *Les Peintres cubistes* (Fernand Léger).

50. Vide: *l'Enchanteur pourrissant*: "la Dame du Lac." *Le Poète assassiné*: Tristouse Ballerinette. *La Femme assise*: Elvire.

bonheur à l'instinct de la civilisation où il vit. C'est un instinct auquel restent beaucoup plus de gens qu'on ne croit. Chez d'autres il devient une frénésie grotesque, la frénésie de l'ignorance. Chez d'autres enfin, il consiste à tirer parti du tout ce qui nous vient par les cinq sens. . . . Il ne s'agit pas non plus d'une œuvre dont l'auteur a fait come tous ont voulu faire aujourd'hui. Il y en a tant qui veulent se refaire une âme, un métier comme au XVe ou au XVIe siècle. Il y en a de plus habiles encore qui nous forgent une âme du siècle d'Auguste ou de celui de Périclès, en moins de temps qu'il faut à un enfant pour apprendre à lire. Non, il ne s'agit point—d'un de ces hommes qui croient que l'humanité d'un siècle est différente de celle d'un autre siècle et qui confondent Dieu avec un costumier, en attendant de confondre leur costume avec leur âme."

Working with the ardor of a good anthropologist, Apollinaire recognized the effect of historical processes in every cultural phenomenon and the fundamental sameness of mental processes in all racial and cultural forms as embraced by the intelligence in the present day. This special ardor accounts for the feeling of ethnic primitivism pervading *L'Enchanteur pourrissant*, and much of his other work. His art revolves about qualities that may be found, for instance, in the subjoined descriptions dealing with "primitive" races:

"C'est de telles mœurs, de plus en plus raffinées que le sentiment de vie de la spiritualisation de la matière fait surgir une nouvelle conception, à savoir celle de l'honneur. La mise en jeu de l'honneur est tout pour les hommes de cette culture. Sous l'influence de cette idée, tout devient sport: la chasse, le vol du bétail, l'amour! Et nous en arrivons ainsi au dernier domaine où ce sentiment de vie prenne forme."

"Tous les auteurs de relations ayant pénétré la nature intime de ces peuples hamitiques du nord, trouvèrent qu'à cette idée de l'honneur, qu'à cette ivresse sanguinaire des hommes correspond également une singularité caractéristique des femmes. Elles sont si fortement attachées à leur parenté consanguine, à leurs pères et à leurs frères, que les époux ne prennent pour elles d'importance que dans les heures de désir et dans les instants d'abandon passionné.[51] La forme de famille est celle du clan

---

51. Vide *Les Mamelles de Tirésias*: Thérèse.

instinct of the civilization in which he lives. Many more people than you would think keep to this instinct. In others it becomes a grotesque frenzy, the frenzy of ignorance. In others again, benefitting from everything that comes to us through the five senses. . . . Nor does it have to do with a work whose author did as everyone would do today. So many would like to remake their souls, a trade as in the XV or XVI centuries. There are those who are still more skillful and forge souls for us from the centuries of Augustus or Pericles, in less time than it takes a child to learn how to read. It has nothing to do with . . . one of these men who believe that the humanity of one age is different from that of another age and who confuse God with a suit maker, as they wait to confuse their suit with their soul."

Travaillant avec la même ardeur qu'un bon anthropologiste, Apollinaire reconnût l'action des énergies historiques dans tout phénomène culturel et l'identité fondamentale des activités mentales dans toutes formes culturelles ou ethniques quand les encercle l'intelligence de cette époque. Cette ardeur particulière explique ce sens du primitivisme ethnique qui baigne *l'Enchanteur pourrissant* et une grande partie de son œuvre. Son art tourne autour de qualités qu'on peut retrouver par exemple dans ces descriptions complémentaires traitant des races "primitives:"

"It is from these more and more refined morals that the feeling of the life of matter made spiritual gives rise to a new conception, that of honor. For the men of this culture, the addition of honor is all. Under the influence of this idea, all becomes sport: hunting, the theft of cattle, love! And thus we arrive at the last station where the feeling of life takes form."

"All those who study relationships and who have investigated these hamitic peoples of the north have found that, to this idea of honor, to this bloody drunkenness of men, there corresponds an equally singular characteristic in women. They are so strongly attached to their blood relations, to their fathers and to their brothers, that for them, the husband takes on importance only in the hours of desire and in instants of passionate abandon.[51] The family is a matriarchal clan. Happiness does

---

51. Vide: *Les Mamelles de Tirésias*: Thérèse.

matriarcal. La femme ne connaît pas le bonheur dans le charme de la maternité satisfaite.[52] Elle est, dès la naissance, la bien-aimée que l'homme recherche. A l'audacieux prétendant qui, la nuit, se glisse dans sa tente et réclame sa possession (que l'époux dorme ou non à côté d'elle, peu importe!) elle ne saurait rien refuser. C'est ainsi qu'à côté du rapt du bétail l'amour devient le but des exploits de l'homme.[53]

"Cette énergie virile engendrée par la lutte pour l'existence à travers les combats les plus rudes, donne naissance à l'idéal de l'homme ambitieux.[54] On célèbre la gloire du vainqueur. Voici que naissent le chant héroïque et l'épopée d'amour.

. . . .

"Un cortège de fantômes mené par une créature féminine. Celle-ci conduit sa suite vers le camp du roi derrière lequel resplendit au milieu des arbres agités par le vent, une masse de blocs de rochers disposés à la manière d'une rose largement épanouie. Ces images sont empreintes d'une sensibilité si chaude et si lourde de sens que nous pouvons les comprendre alors même que l'intelligence n'en saisit pas tous les détails. Les figures de douleur muette et de vie révolue sont tellement expressives que nous n'en avons pas besoin de commentaires. Si beaucoup d'éléments nous restent étrangers c'est uniquement parce qu'un sentiment de la vie, infiniment éloigné de nous, fut ici à l'œuvre. Mais en face de ces images elles-mêmes, tout le monde doit se rendre compte qu'aucune d'elles n'ait rien à voir avec l'inspiration tendant à la spiritualisation de la matière.

"Tout au contraire ces peintures sont l'œuvre d'un sentiment imaginatif de la vie. Ce qu'elles représentent ne se trouve pas dans l'ambiance vivante de leurs créatures, mais est la traduction des phénomènes de la vie intérieure engendrée par le sentiment de la vie. Cet art est né d'une spéculation extrêmement avancée qui de son côté, ne peut sortir que de l'abandon à la vie et du sentiment mystique de l'existence."[55]

52. Apollinaire's anthropologic sense makes him record the ineffectualness of the man of his time in these exploits.

53. Cf. Apollinaire's "L'Otmika:" dealing with "le rapt sacré" of the gypsies.

54. *L'Art africain* par Leo Frobenius, *Cahiers d'art* 8–9, 1930. P. 410ff.

55. André Breton, *Les Pas perdus*.

not come to a woman with the pleasure of fulfilled maternity.[52] She is, from birth, the beloved sought by a man. She could refuse nothing to the daring suitor who, at night, slips into her tent and reclaims his possession (and no matter if the husband by her side sleeps or no!) It is thus that love, next to stealing cattle, becomes the goal of man's exploits.[53]

"This virile energy, engendered in the roughest fights in the battle for existence, gives birth to the ideal of the ambitious man.[54] One celebrates the glory of the conqueror. Thus is born the heroic hymn and the love epic.

. . . .

"A retinue of ghosts led by a female creature. This woman leads her suite toward the king's camp behind which a mass of stone blocks gleams among trees that sway in the wind, arranged like a rose in full bloom. These images are imprinted with a sensitivity so burning and so weighted with meaning that we can understand them even when the mind does not grasp their every detail. The figures of mute sadness and of life gone by are so expressive that we do not need commentaries. If many elements remain strange to us, it is only because one feeling of life, infinitely far from us, was here at work. But in the face of these images themselves, everyone ought to realize that none of them have anything to do with the inspiration leading to matter made spiritual.

"On the contrary, these paintings are the work of life's imaginative feeling. What they represent is not found in the living atmosphere of their creatures, but is the translation of phenomena of interior life engendered by the feeling of life. This art is born of an extremely advanced speculation that can only arise from an abandonment to life and to a mystical feeling of existence."[55]

52. Apollinaire's anthropological sense makes him record the ineffectualness of the man of his time in these exploits.

53. Cf. Apollinaire, "L'Otmika": traitant du "rapt sacré des tziganes."

54. *L'Art Africain* by Leo Frobenius, *Cahiers d'art* 8–9 (1930): 410ff.

55. André Breton, *Les Pas perdus.*

L'Hérésiarque & Cie displays "un bouillant instinct de la querelle théologique"![56] For this reason: that the intelligence of his art recognized a sense of mutation as a constant, rather than the constant of a faith, or an ideal, or a historical record presented as art. His emotions, those emotions recognizable as the art of Apollinaire, never surpassing his destiny, always included the past, a past transformed, but it had preceded him. His culture—the destiny and the will of his time which was also the nature of his intelligence—disclosed it. Made incumbent his constant heresies with respect to this past. Of that intelligence which goes under the name of Apollinaire, as of the heresiarch of his story, the theological truth, as absolute only a past to Apollinaire, must be that the heresiarch ressemble á tous les hommes, car tous sont à la fois pécheurs et saints, quand ils ne sont pas criminels et martyrs." Obviously in Flaubert's *Trois Contes*, stories in which historical record is presented as art or in which art has the effect of historical record, Félicité, Saint Julien and Iaokanaan are martyrs: in the three stories[57] of Apollinaire which recall Flaubert's tales as stories, Cyprienne, Que Vlo-ve and Salomé are at once sinners and saints (a characterization which does not fit the Salomé of Flaubert). The gravity of acceleration of Flaubert's narrative is in each sense history veiling a myth. The surprise or mystic complicity of Apollinaire's is in each case data inciting ethnic comparisons. Flaubert's characters are simple results, the necessary products of historic myths and times presented as artistic unities; even the rhetoric is an unbranched flow. That is why the direction of the myth being evident, if implicit, despite the perfection of his art, his work may be taken up to sponsor a cause.[58] Apollinaire's characters, tho the intelligence they illustrate is never unconscious of causes, move mystically in multiple directions (the lives of people at once sinners and saints are not simple). Like the Wandering Jew of his *Le Passant de Prague*, they stir up all the past behind them

---

56. *L'Hérésiarque et Cie*: *L'Hérésiarque*, Stock, 1910.

57. "La Plante"—conte inédit, *L'Esprit nouveau*, October 1924, "Que Vlo-ve?" And "La Danseuse": *L'Hérésiarque* et Cie.

58. Communism, for instance.

L'Hérésiarque et Cie montre "a fiery instinct of the theological quarrel."[56] Et voice pourquoi: l'intelligence de son art reconnaissait comme valeur constante un sens du changement: plutôt qu'une croyance, un idéal ou un document historique que l'on présente sous la forme de l'art. Ces émotions, ces formes reconnaissables comme étant l'art d'Apollinaire et qui ne dépassaient jamais sa destinée comprenaient toujours le passé, un passé transformé mais qui était tout de même derrière lui. Sa culture—la destinée de la volonté de son époque qui était aussi la nature de son intelligence—la révélait. Ses constantes hérésies à l'égard de ce passé, s'imposaient à lui, à tous. La vérité théologique (absolutisme qui est bien du passé pour Apollinaire) de cette intelligence qui se présente sous le nom de Guillaume Apollinaire, ou sous celui de l'Hérésiarque de son histoire, doit être pour l'un comme pour l'autre que l'Hérésiarque "resembles all men, for all of them are at the same time sinners and saints, if not criminals and martyrs." Evidemment les *Trois Contes* de Flaubert sont des histoires où le document historique est présenté comme art, autrement dit l'art y fait l'effet d'un document historique: Félicité, Saint Julien et Iaokanaan sont martyrs: dans les trois histoires[57] d'Apollinaire qui rappellent les contes de Flaubert par leur sujet: Cyprienne, Que Vlo-ve et Salomé sont à la fois pécheurs et saints (méthode d'incarnation qui ne convient pas à la Salomé de Flaubert). Le récit de Flaubert, dans ses ralentissements et ses accélérations n'est que de l'histoire voilant un mythe. Le choc et la duplicité mystiques du récit d'Apollinaire sont des données appelant des comparaisons ethniques. Les personnages de Flaubert sont des produits simples, l'aboutissement inévitable de mythes et d'époques historiques présentés comme unités artistiques; la rhétorique elle-même est un courant non ramifié. C'est pourquoi, la direction du mythe étant évidente bien qu'implicite, malgré la perfection de son art, Flaubert peut être appelé à faire comparaître son œuvre pour soutenir une cause.[58] Les personnages d'Apollinaire bien qu'ils incarnent une intelligence qui ne perd jamais de vue les causes, se meuvent mystiquement dans des directions multiples (les vies des gens qui sont à la fois pécheurs et saints ne sont pas simples). Comme le Juif Errant de son *Passant de Prague*, ils remuent tout le passé derrière eux et

---

56. *L'Hérésiarque et C*^{ie}: *L'Hérésiarque*, Stock, 1910.

57. "La Plante"; Conte inédit, *L'Esprit nouveau*, October 1924. "Que Vlo-ve?" and "La Danseuse" in *l'Hérésiarque et C*^{ie}.

58. Communism, for example.

and evoke an illimitable future ahead of them. "There are more mysteries in heaven and earth, Horatio . . ." And the transformations of the somas of these characters glint in their present with the fluorescence of various pasts never definitely recognizable as their own. Because causes change, they have hardly any causes, outside of an impulse to radiate them. The Wandering Jew who walks forever in expiation of his original guilt and towards his ultimate redemption, walks even in the embraces of his amours.

Miroir brisé sel renversé ou pain qui tombe
Puissent ces dieux sans figures m'épargner toujours
Au demeurant je ne crois pas mais je regarde et j'écoute et notez
Que je lis assez bien dans la main
Car je ne crois pas mais je regarde et quand c'est possible j'écoute

Tout le monde est prophète mon cher André Billy
Mais il y a si longtemps qu'on fait croire aux gens
Qu'ils n'ont aucun avenir qu'ils sont ignorants à jamais et idiots de
    naissance
Qu'on en a pris son parti et que nul n'a même l'idée
De se demander s'il connaît l'avenir ou non
Il n'y a pas d'esprit religieux dans tout cela
Ni dans les superstitions ni dans les prophéties
Ni dans tout ce que l'on nomme occultisme
Il y a avant tout une façon d'observer la nature
Et d'interpréter la nature
Qui est très légitime[59]

Apollinaire's artistic instinct for the natural simultaneity (rather than the unity) of intelligence is a constant in his work. It is this constant which distinguishes it from such writing as Alfred Jarry's *Ubu Roi*, showing a superficial resemblance to Apollinaire, but, closely, a difference.

59. "Sur les Prophéties"—*Calligrammes*.

évoquent un futur illimitable devant eux. "Il y a plus de choses dans le ciel et sur la terre, Horatio . . . etc." Et les transformations des *somas* de ces personnages brillent dans leur présent de la fluorescence de différents passés qui ne peuvent jamais être reconnus comme les leurs. Les causes changent, donc c'est à peine s'ils ont des causes, en dehors d'une certaine énergie qui les force à s'irradier. Le Juif Errant qui marche toujours pour expier sa faute et vers son ultime rédemption, marche encore quand il fait l'amour.

Broken mirror spilled salt or falling bread
Might these shapeless gods forever spare me
I do not believe but I look and I listen so take note
That I read palms quite well
For I do not believe but I look and when I can I listen

Everyone is a prophet my dear André Billy
But so long ago that people are convinced
That they have no future that they are forever ignorant and idiots
   by birth
That sides have been taken and no one thinks
To wonder if he can or cannot see the future
There is no religious faith in all of this
Not in superstitions not in prophecies
Nor in all that we call occultism
First there is a way of observing nature
And of interpreting nature
That is very legitimate.[59]

L'instinct artistique que possède Apollinaire de la simultanéité naturelle (plutôt que de l'unité) de l'intelligence est une constante de son œuvre. C'est cette constante qui la distingue de l'écriture de l'*Ubu Roi*, de Jarry, qui pourtant en surface ressemble à de l'Apollinaire, et qui en est profondément différent.

59. "Sur les Prophéties," *Calligrammes*.

"Alfred Jarry a été homme de lettres comme on l'est rarement. Ses moindres actions, ses gamineries, tout cela, c'était de la littérature. C'est qu'il était fondé en lettres et en cela seulement. Mais de quelle admirable façon! Quelqu'un a dit un jour devant moi que Jarry avait été le dernier auteur burlesque. C'est une erreur! A ce compte, la plupart des auteurs du XVe siècle, et une grande partie de ceux du XVIe, ne seraient que des burlesques. Ce mot ne peut désigner les produits les plus rares de la culture humaniste. On ne possède pas de terme qui puisse s'appliquer à cette allégresse particulière où le lyrisme devient satirique, où la satire, s'exerçant sur de la réalité, dépasse tellement son objet qu'elle le détruit et monte si haut que la poésie ne l'atteint qu'avec peine, tandis que la trivialité ressortit ici au goût même, et, par un phénomène inconcevable, devient nécessaire. Ces débauches de l'intelligence où les sentiments n'ont pas de part, la Renaissance seul permit qu'on s'y livrat, et Jarry, par un miracle, a été le dernier de ces débauchés sublimes."[60]

Apollinaire's criticism is true enough of Jarry's *Ubu Roi*—it is like the plays of the Renaissance, since, as much as the *gaillardise* of its chandelle verte may singe or spear Shakespeare, the method of its madness is no other than a Falstaff turned Macbeth, morally (or immorally) only carrying out the Shakespearian technique on a ridiculed stage. The ridiculed stage and the burlesque are present in *Les Mamelles de Tirésias*, but Apollinaire's instinct of the natural simultaneity of intelligence removes his work at a great distance from even Shakespeare's accelerated dramatic unities. The simultaneity of intelligence in *Les Mamelles de Tirésias* rockets at a tangent from the theme of Aristophanes' *Lysistrata*, the refusal of women to bear children (in *Les Mamelles* for no such logical reason as that war will destroy them, but for the cause of feminism); and destroying its own rather serious pleas for the repopulation of France by the intensity of the burlesque, even as the breasts of Thérèse are destroyed in their ascent as balloons, leaves the mind with a feeling of having been everywhere and a future of nowhere.

60. 1909, reprinted in *Il y a*, 1925, and *Contemporains pittoresques*, 1928.

"Alfred Jarry was a man of letters as one rarely is. The least of his actions, his childish play, all was literature. For his foundations were in literature and nowhere else. How admirable though! One day someone said in front of me that Jarry had been the last burlesque author. It's a mistake! In this case, most of the authors of the fifteenth century, and a large part of those of the sixteenth, were nothing but burlesques. This word can not refer to the rarest products of a humanist culture. We have no term that applies to this particular elation where lyricism becomes satirical, where satire, practiced on reality, passes so far beyond its object that it destroys it and rises so high that poetry can only reach it with difficulty, while the triviality resurfaces here as a taste, and, by an inconceivable phenomenon, becomes necessary. Only the Renaissance offered the freedom to give oneself up to these debauches of intelligence where emotion played no part, and Jarry, by some miracle, was the last of these sublime debauchers."[60]

La critique est assez juste. *Ubu Roi* ressemble assez aux drames de la Renaissance, car la gaillardise de sa chandelle verte peut bien singer ou lyncher Shakespeare, la logique de sa folie n'est autre qu'un déguisement de Falstaff en Macbeth, et ne transporte que moralement (ou immoralement) la technique shakespearienne sur une scène plongée dans le ridicule. La scène plongée dans le ridicule, et le burlesque sont présents dans *les Mamelles de Tirésias*, mais l'instinct qu'a Apollinaire de la simultanéité naturelle de l'intelligence enlève son œuvre et énergiquement même aux unités dramatiques accélérées de Shakespeare. La simultanéité d'intelligence dans *les Mamelles de Tirésias*, jaillit par la tangente du thème de la *Lysistrata* d'Aristophane: les femmes refusent de mettre des enfants au monde (dans *les Mamelles* elles ne cherchent pas à leur conduite de justification logique telle que la peur de les voir tuer à la guerre; elles ont des principes féministes); mais cette belle propagande qu'Apollinaire prend au sérieux pour la repopulation de la France est anéantie par l'intensité du burlesque, de même que les seins de Thérèse sont anéantis dans leur ascension aérostatique, et cet anéantissement laisse l'esprit dans l'impression d'avoir été partout et que son avenir n'est nulle part.

60. 1909, reprinted in *Il y a*, 1925 and *Contemporains pittoresques*, 1928.

Guillaume continued the implicit contradictions of simultaneity. *Le Bestiaire* ou *Cortège d'Orphée*[61] on the face of it is medieval allegory. But Guillaume's verses after the symbolists are an essential contradiction of themselves, the sadness of themselves, of his day, all days which have been and are to be, diming even the allegorical beasts:

Le Cheval
Mes durs rêves formels sauront te chevaucher,
Mon destin au char d'or sera ton beau cocher
Qui pour rêves tiendra tendus à frénésie,
Mes vers, les paragons de toute poésie.

La Chèvre du Thibet
Les poils de cette chèvre et même
Ceux d'or pour qui prit tant de peine
Jason, ne valent rien au prix
Des cheveux dont je suis épris.

Le Serpent
Tu t'acharnes sur la beauté
Et quelles femmes ont été
Victimes de ta cruauté!
Eve, Eurydice, Cléopâtre;
J'en connais encore trois ou quatre.

Le chat
Je souhaite dans ma maison:
Une femme ayant sa raison,
Un chat passant parmi les livres,
Des amis en toute saison
Sans lesquels je ne peux pas vivre.

Le Lion
O lion, malheureuse image
Des rois chus lamentablement,
Tu ne nais maintenant qu'en cage
A Hambourg, chez les Allemands.

61. 1911, Déplanche, avec bois gravés par Raoul Dufy.

Guillaume poursuivit les implicites contradictions de la simultanéité. *Le Bestiaire* ou *Cortège d'Orphée*[61] est en l'occurrence de l'allégorie médiévale. Mais ces vers après l'époque symboliste sont foncièrement des contradictions d'eux-mêmes, la tristesse d'être eux-mêmes, la tristesse du jour, de tous les jours qui furent et seront, embrume jusqu'à ces bêtes allégoriques:

The Horse

My hard formal dreams will know how to ride
My fate, handsome coachman, a gold carriage will drive
And the reins in his frenzy that he will pull tight
Are my verses, at poetry's height.

The Tibetan Goat

There is nothing of value to me
In this goat's hair nor in the golden fleece
That Jason worked so hard for
Next to the hair that is my captor.

The Snake

You are set against beauty
And what women have been
Victims of your cruelty!
Eve, Eurydice, and Cleopatra;
There are three or four others that occur to me.

The Cat

In my home I would like:
A reasonable wife,
A cat walking among books, that walks in and out,
And friends for every season
Without whom I cannot live.

The Lion

Oh lion unhappy image
Of kings so sadly fallen
Now you are only born in cages
In Hamburg, home of the Germans.

61. Déplanche, 1911, with wood engravings by Raoul Dufy.

Le Lièvre

Ne sois pas lascif et peureux
Comme le lièvre et l'amoureux
Mais, que toujours ton cerveau soit
La hase pleine qui conçoit.

Le Lapin

Je connais un autre connin
Que tout vivant je voudrais prendre.
Sa garenne est parmis le thym
Des vallons du pays de Tendre.

Le Dromadaire

Avec ses quatre dromadaires
Don Pedro d'Alfaroubeira
Courut le monde et l'admira.
Il fit ce que je voudrais faire
Si j'avais quatre dromadaires.

L'Eléphant

Comme un éléphant son ivoire
J'ai en bouche un bien précieux.
Pourpre mort! —J'achète ma gloire
Au prix des mots mélodieux.

La Mouche

Nos mouches savent des chansons
Que leur apprirent en Norvège
Les mouches ganiques qui sont
Les divinités de la neige.

Le Dauphin

Dauphins, vous jouez dans la mer
Mais le flot est toujours amer.
Parfois, ma joie éclate-t-elle?
La vie est encore cruelle.

The Hare
Don't be wanton don't be scared
Like the hare or the lover
But let your brain forever
Be like a full and fertile female.

The Rabbit
I know another coney
That I would like to take alive.
His warren is in the thyme
In the vales of a country called Tender.

The Dromedary
Don Pedro of Alfarubaries
Took all of his four dromedaries
Ran 'round the world and admired it.
Doing just what I'd like to do
If I had four dromedaries.

The Elephant
Like the elephant holding his ivory
In my mouth I hold a treasure quite precious.
Dead purple!—I buy my glory
With words melodious.

The Fly
The songs our flies know
They learned in Norway
From ganic flies turned
Into divinities of snow.

The Dolphin
Dolphins you play in the sea
But tides are bitter sport indeed.
Does joy sometimes burst from me?
Still, life is full of cruelty.

La Poulpe

Jetant son encre vers les cieux,
Suçant le sang de ce qu'il aime
Et le trouvant délicieux,
Ce monstre inhumain, c'est moi-même.

La Méduse

Méduses, malheureuses têtes
Aux chevelures violettes
Vous vous plaisez dans les tempêtes
Et je m'y plais comme vous faites.

L'Ecrevisse

Incertitude, ô mes délices
Vous et moi nous nous en allons
Comme s'en vont les écrevisses
A reculons, à reculons.

La Carpe

Dans vos viviers, dans vos étangs
Carpes, que vous vivez longtemps!
Est-ce que la mort vous oublie
Poissons de la mélancholie.

Les Sirènes

Saché-je d'où provient, Sirènes, votre ennui
Quand vous vous lamentez, au large, dans la nuit?
Mer, je suis, comme toi, plein de voix machinées
Et mes vaisseaux chantants se nomment les années.

The miniature verses are the epic of Apollinaire's early intelligence. Neither the primitive simplicity affected by the beasts, nor the lament or joy of the simple verses, is a cloak. There are several cloaks and each unfolds in the inside of the other. Whatever expostulation the lyricism offers might be in the voice of Guillaume's Wandering Jew, intimately but objectively heard as he walks forever, an exile to dead and, strangely, still living times. The sadness of the verses incised in allegory—art's wornness, art's renewal—is their essential self-contradictory life.

The Octopus

Spewing his ink to the skies,
Sucking the blood of his love
And finding it delicious,
This inhuman monster, tis I.

The Medusa

Medusas, miserable heads
Violet locks
You rejoice in the tempest
And I join you in your quest.

The Crawfish

Uncertainty, oh my delights
We're leaving you and I
Like crayfish departing
Inching slowly slowly backward.

The Carp

In your fishbowls, in your ponds
Carp you live so long!
Has death forgotten you exist
Oh you melancholy fish?

The Sirens

Sirens, you weep throughout the night
Do I know how your troubles arise?
Like the ocean I am filled with artificial voices
My singing ships call themselves the years.

Ces miniatures sont l'épopée des premiers exploits de l'intelligence d'Apollinaire. Ni la simplicité primitive qu'affectent les bêtes, ni la complainte ou la joie de ces simples quatrains ne peut être un manteau. Il y a plusieurs manteaux et chacun se déploie sous un autre. Et si le lyrisme implique quelque commentaire, celui-ci pourrait bien être dans la voie du juif errant, entendue dans l'intimité, mais objective, quand il marche sans espoir d'arrêt, exilé des temps morts et, par étrange, de ceux qui vivent encore. La tristesse des vers gravée dans l'allégorie (art qui s'étiole et qui reprend vie) sont leur vie essentielle qui est faite de ses propres contradictions.

The epic of this intelligence has no place, except perhaps the abstract and yet too painfully tangible intimacy of a village where all artists are intimate—the proverbial thought always a feeling; a sentiment given flare by personal hurt become art: shared suffering with another become apprehensive of suffering as recorded in a lyric. Giving and taking this object which is a song, two people at table. Not the Chansons de Geste, but a bestiary in which the animal life has become an intimate of creation; or, the Chansons when poignantly but never offensively heroic attaining intimacy as over the folk fires over which they were first sung.

The intelligence attracting the data of vicissitudes, become itself, settles, whatever its origin, in a country favorable to the formative desire of the ambient—among a people, their lives, vicarious for all history. Guillaume's beasts are Hellenic; Latin; they are French, subsuming the classic; they lived in the Paris of his time. So did the ragpicker of his story.[62] Pertinax Restif who claimed descent from Restif de la Bretonne, and whose pride "l'empêcha de comprendre: Mais vois: au début de la généalogie, un empereur; à la fin, un chiffonnier content de son sort. Décemment et vertueusement ton fils sera vidangeur. Heureusement pour lui, ce métier n'existe plus guère, et ce sont des machines qui vident les fosses . . ."

"La vie est variable aussi bien que l'Euripe."[63] The voyager who experienced this line, wrote the poem, dedicated to Fernand Fleuret, as the journey of his intelligence. Encompassing fact, intelligence finds extension in the routine of labors, which repay with "pain pétri, de bon pain"

---

62. "Histoire d'une famille vertueuse," *L'Hérésiarque*.
63. "Le Voyageur," *Alcools*.

L'épopée de cette intelligence ne possède aucun lieu, si ce n'est peut-être l'intimité abstraite et pourtant terriblement tangible d'un village où les artistes vivent intimes. La pensée d'un proverbe est un sentiment encore: un sentiment enflammé par la passion personnelle est devenu art: partagée avec un autre homme qui y devient sensible, la souffrance a fait naître le poème lyrique. Communication de cet objet: le chant entre deux hommes à la même table, ce ne sont pas les Chansons de Geste, c'est un bestiaire où la vie animale est entrée dans l'intimité de la création: il y a aussi les Chansons de Geste: par elles poignantes, mais non offensives l'héroïque atteint à l'intimité comme lorsqu'elles furent pour la première fois chantées autour d'un feu.

L'intelligence en attirant et groupant les données des vicissitudes devient elle-même et se fixe, quelles que soient ses origines dans un pays favorable au désir inventif du voyageur: parmi un peuple et ses vies dépositaires de l'histoire tout entière. Les bêtes de Guillaume sont grecques, latines, elles sont françaises, elles ont respiré le classique, et elles ont vécu dans le Paris de son époque. Tel le chiffonnier de son histoire,[62] Pertinax Restif qui se prétendait descendant de Restif de la Bretonne et dont "the understanding was blocked by pride: but look! At the beginning of the genealogy, an emperor; at the end, a ragman happy with his lot. His son will be a decent and virtuous cleaner of outhouses. Luckily for him the profession is nearly obsolete and now we have machines to drain the sewers . . ."

"Life is as variable as Euripe."[63] Le voyageur qui a vu ce vers a écrit le poème qu'il dédie à Fernand Fleuret et qui est l'itinéraire de son intelligence. Encerclant les faits, l'intelligence trouve de l'étendue dans la routine de travaux qui lui sont payés en "kneaded bread, good bread"—

62. "Histoire d'une famille vertueuse," *L'Hérésiarque.*
63. "Le Voyageur," *Alcools.*

the magazines Guillaume wrote for,[64] the works of the Renaissance he
edited for La Bibliothèque des Curieux, the collection, *Les Maîtres de
L'Amour* from 1909 till the end of his life, are given by his bibliographers. The labors are natural since intelligence is avid for fact. "Il était
avide de vérité, de réalité et telle est la base de son érudition. Les faits
lui paraissent irréducibles et convaincants. Seule l'interprétation qu'on
en peut donner le trouva souvent rebelle.[65] To Fleuret, Guillaume wrote
in 1910: "Je suis peiné de vous voir vous enfoncer dans cette érudition,
aimable à la vérité, mais où j'ai du pénétrer par nécessité mais où je ne
voudrais pas que vous vous perdiez." Fleuret, Louis Perceau and Guillaume were at that time collecting their critical Icono-bio-bibliographie
of the *L'Enfer de la Bibliothèque nationale*.[66] The work was modelled

---

64. Cf. the review of André Salmon's *Féeries, Vers et Prose*, July–August 1908:
a discussion of Salmon's symbolism to the renewal of French classicism in the 20th
century. See also the articles, reprinted as the text of *Contemporains pittoresques*,
on Raoul Ponchon, Ernest la Jeunesse, Rémy de Gourmont, Jean Moréas, and Les
Anecdotes de Willy sur Catulle Mendès, in *Les Marges* 1909–1910: "Raoul Ponchon est une fleur merveilleuse, ceux qui la cultive connaissent la certitude d'être
aimés. Il s'éloigne des autres hommes non pas avec tristesse comme l'hypocondre
Bouilly, mais avec colère comme Alceste. Nous voulions, mes amis et moi, il y a
quelques années, dans une petite revue, demander pour Ponchon la croix de la Légion
d'Honneur. Nous nous trompions; le ruban vert du mérite agricole convient mieux à
sa misanthropie." Ponchon's disdain of Henri de Régnier: "il composa au temps où
l'Académie était un monstre qu'on tuait tous les jours, et dont la dépouille fournissait
un vêtement inusable."

Of Rémy de Gourmont: (on the quais of Paris, Apollinaire guessing the un-
kown): "La première étoile apparut distincte, mais brillant à peine; l'inconnu fit un
geste, puis s'en alla marchant très vite. Songé-je? Je crois bien ou il avait envoyé un
baiser à l'étoile. Aussitôt, je nommai l'inconnu. Il devint pour moi: Rémy de Gourmont. —C'était lui-même qu'intéressent toutes choses de l'Univers, les bêtes et les
astres, les livres et les rues, l'humanité et l'amour qui émeut toute la nature. J'eus
depuis l'occasion de la visiter et de la reconnaître."

Jean Moréas: "Il s'en allait pensif, imprimant à ses bras légèrement pliés le mouvement du nocher qui écarte les flots pour faire avancer la barque. C'est ainsi que,
sur le sol magique de la Colchide les Argonautes ont cherché la toison. —La conversation de Moréas était un enseignement plein d'enfoncement et sans nul pédantisme.
—(Moréas interrupting a young savant who had said, not without sadness: "Je ne
me souviens pas d'avoir jamais pleuré—"ne dites pas cela."

Anecdotes de Willy sur Catulle Mendès: (a lady) "Mendès, toute la nuit, il me
lit ses vers—et le matin il me rate."

65. Jean Royère, *Les Marges*, December 15, 1918.

66. Mercure de France, 1912.

il s'agit là, évidemment, entre autres des magazines pour lesquels Guillaume a écrit,[64] des œuvres de la Renaissance qu'il a éditées pour la Bibliothèque des Curieux, de la *Collection des Maîtres de l'Amour* que les bibliographes indiquent et placent entre 1909 et la fin de sa vie. Ces travaux sont naturels puisque l'intelligence est avide de faits. "He was avid for truth, for reality and such is the foundation of his scholarship. Facts appeared irreducible and convincing to him. It was only in interpreting these facts that he was often rebellious.[65] C'est à Fleuret que Guillaume écrivit en 1910: "It pains me to see you sinking into this erudition, faithful to truth, into which I delved out of necessity but I wouldn't want you to lose yourself." Fleuret, Louis Perceau et Apollinaire étaient à ce moment occupés à recueillir leur iconobibliographie critique de *l'Enfer de la Bibliothèque nationale.*[66] Ce travail avait pour modèle *l'Enfer de la*

64. See the review of *Féeries* by André Salmon, *Vers et Prose* (July–August 1908). Therein is explained Salmon's superiority to Banville and the importance Salmon's symbolism might have for reforming French classicism in the twentieth century. See also the articles reprinted in *Contemporains pittoresques* on Raoul Ponchon, Ernest La Jeunesse, Rémy de Gourmont, Jean Moréas, and Willy's Anecdotes on Catulle Mendès in *Les Marges*, 1909–1910: "Raoul Ponchon is a marvelous flower, those who cultivate it can be certain that they will be loved. It is not with the sadness of the hypochondriac Bouilly that he sets himself apart from other men but with the anger of Alceste. Several years ago my friends and I wanted to request the Legion of Honor's cross for Ponchon in a little revue. We were mistaken; the green ribbon of agricultural merit was better suited to his misanthropy." Ponchon's disdain for Henri de Régnier "he wrote at a time when the Academy was a monster to be killed each day and whose fur made an unwearable garment."

On Rémy de Gourmont: (on the quais of Paris, Apollinaire guessing at the unknown): "The first star to appear was distinct but barely shone; the unknown gestured then went on his way at a quick pace. Am I dreaming? I do believe that he'd blown a kiss to the star. I immediately named the unknown: He became for me: Rémy de Gourmont. It is in he himself that all things of the Universe are interested, that animals and the stars, the books and the streets, humanity and love move all of nature. I have since had occasion to visit and to recognize her."

Jean Moréas: "He went on his way, pensive, with his folded arms making the slight gesture of a sea captain who parts the waves to move his boat forward. It is thus that the Argonauts searched for the fleece on the magical soil of Colchis. Moréas's conversation was an education full of cheer and without dull pedantry. (Moréas interrupting a young scholar who had said, not without sadness, "I do not remember ever having wept."—"Don't say that."

Willy's anecdotes about Catulle Mendès: (a lady) "Mendès, all night, he reads me his poetry—and in the morning he misses me."

65. Jean Royère, *Les Marges*, December 15, 1918.

66. Mercure de France, 1912.

on the *Enfer de la Bibliothèque du Vatican*. The preface made clear the intentions of its collaborators: "Des ouvrages comme ceux qui sont conservés à *l'Enfer de la Bibliothèque nationale* ne sont point inutiles aux travailleurs."—Quoting L'Abbé Grégoire: —"ils servent à l'histoire de l'humanité, des mœurs, des coutumes et des arts. —En effet, les satiriques licencieux de XVe, du XVIe, du XVIIIe, siècles sont des poètes que l'on ne peut exclure de l'histoire littéraire sans que leur absence creuse aussitôt, dans la littérature française, un gouffre insondable. —Les pamphlets, les romans de la Révolution aident à la faire comprendre et restent des documents intéressants." The authors in the bibliography include Arétin, Baudelaire, du Bellay, Béranger, Boccaccio, John Cleland, Crébillon fils, Camille Desmoulins, Diderot, Laurent Tailhade, Verlaine, Voltaire etc.[67]

Apollinaire's hérésiarque,[68] Orfei, "qui était originaire d'Alexandrie, en parlait volontiers le dialecte. Son discours était émaillé de paroles grasses, presque obscènes, mais étonnement expressives. C'est le fait des mystiques d'employer de telles paroles, le mysticisme touche de près l'érotisme. Malgré l'intérêt que pourraient avoir certaines expressions pour les philologues, je n'insisterai pas sur ce côté de l'esprit d'Orfei. Ma science très superficielle des dialectes italiens ne m'a d'ailleurs pas permis de tout comprendre, et je n'ai saisi le sens de nombre de mots que grâce à la mimique qui accompagnait les discours de l'hérésiarque."

Apollinaire defined the timely interest and limits of this mysticism bordering on the erotic in his introduction to *L'Œuvre poétique de Charles Baudelaire:*[69]

Exprimer avec liberté ce qui est du domaine des mœurs, on ne connaît pas de courage plus grand chez un écrivain. Choderlos de Laclos s'y applique avec une précision pour la première fois vraiment mathématique.

67. The significance of this book becomes very evident on the realization that all of Apollinaire's "poèmes libres" are still inaccessible or lost under several pseudonyms or in anonymity or in the mere reference of his bibliographers. (dated: April 1932). Apollinaire: "La Rome des Borgias n'est pas à moi (Elle est de René Dupuis [Dalize])"—Letter to Fleuret, 1913.

68. *L'Hérésiarque.*

69. Paris: Bibliothèque Des Curieux, 1917.

bibliothèque du Vatican. La préface exposait les intentions de ses collaborateurs: "Works such as these that are kept in the Hell section of the National Library are far from useless to working people" et, citant l'Abbé Grégoire: "they serve the history of humanity, morals, customs, and the arts." "In effect, the licentious satirists of the fifteeenth, sixteenth, seventeenth centuries are poets whose exclusion from literary history would immediately cut an uncrossable gulf through French literature. . . . The pamphlets and the novels of the Revolution are helpful in understanding it and remain interesting documents." La bibliographie comprend les noms d'Arétin, Baudelaire, du Bellay, Béranger, Boccace, John Cleland, Crébillon fils, Camille Desmoulins, Diderot, Laurent Tailhade, Verlaine, Voltaire, etc. etc. . . . [67]

Apollinaire's l'hérésiarque, Orfei[68] "who came from Alexandria, often spoke in that land's dialect. His conversation was peppered with turns of phrase which, while they were vulgar to the point of obscenity, were also astonishingly expressive. It is in the nature of mystics to use such language, mysticism bordering on eroticism as it does. In spite of the interest that certain expressions might hold for philologists, this is not the side of Orfei's spirit that I wish to emphasize. In any case, my very superficial knowledge of Italian dialects kept me from understanding everything, and it was only thanks to the gestures accompanying the Heresiarque's speech, that I grasped the meanings of some words."

Apollinaire a expliqué ce mysticisme confinant à l'érotisme, son importance et ses limites dans son *Introduction à l'Œuvre poétique de Charles Baudelaire*:[69]

For free expression in the moral domain, greater courage is not known than a writer's. Choderlos de Laclos was the first to apply himself to this with a truly mathematical precision.

---

67. The meaning of this book becomes clear when one realizes that all of Apollinaire's "free poems" are still inaccessible, spread about under different pseudonyms or lost in anonymity or in the vague references of these bibliographies. Apollinaire (April 1932): "The Rome of Borgias is not mine" (it is René Dupuis' (Dalize); Letter to Fleuret, 1913.

68. *L'Hérésiarque.*

69. Bibliothèque des Curieux (Paris, 1917).

"1782, c'est la date mémorable de la publication des *Liaisons Dangereuses* où, officier d'artillerie, il tenta d'appliquer aux mœurs les lois de la triangulation, qui sert aussi bien, comme on sait, aux artilleurs qu'aux astronomes. Etonnant contraste! la vie infinie qui gravite au firmament obéit aux mêmes lois que l'artillerie destinée par les hommes à semer la mort. —Des mesures angulaires calculées par Laclos naquit l'esprit littéraire moderne; c'est là qu'en découvrit les premiers éléments Baudelaire, un explorateur raisonnable et raffiné de la vie ancienne, mais dont les vues sur la vie moderne impliquent toutes une certaine folie. C'est avec délices qu'il avait aspiré les bulles corrompues qui montent de l'étrange et riche boue littéraire de la Révolution où, près de Diderot, Laclos, fils intellectuel de Richardson et de Rousseau, eut comme continuateurs les plus remarquables: Sade, Restif, Nerciat et tous les conteurs philosphiques de la fin du XVIIIe siècle. —La preuve de l'influence des littératures cyniques de la Révolution sur *Les Fleurs du mal* se retrouve partout dans sa correspondence et dans ses notes. —Baudelaire est le fils de Laclos et d'Edgar Poe, mais leur fils aveugle et fou qui, toutefois, avant d'escalader les cimes, avait regardé avec une admirable précision les arts et la vie.

"Il est vrai aussi qu'en lui s'est incarné pour la première fois l'esprit moderne. C'est à partir de Baudelaire que quelque chose est né qui n'a fait que végéter, tandis que naturalistes, parnassiens, symbolistes passsent auprès sans rien voir; tandis que les naturistes, ayant tourné la tête, n'avaient pas l'audace d'examiner la nouveauté sublime et monstrueuse. A ceux qu'étonnerait sa naissance informe de la boue révolutionnaire et de la vérole américaine il faudrait répondre par ce qu'enseigne la Bible touchant l'origine de l'homme issu du limon de la terre.

"Il est vrai que la Nouveauté prit avant tout la face de Baudelaire, qui a été le premier à souffler l'esprit moderne en Europe, mais son cerveau prophétique n'a pas su prophétiser, et Baudelaire n'a pas pénétré cet esprit nouveau dont il était lui-même pénétré, et dont il découvrit les germes en quelques autres venus avant lui.

"Et il vaudrait bien la peine qu'on l'abandonnât, comme ont été abandonnés des lyriques de grand talent tels qu'un Jean-Baptiste Rousseau dès que ressassé par les uns et les autres et mis à la portée du vulgaire, leur lyrisme eut vieilli.

"Cependant, même tombé dans le domaine public, Baudelaire n'en est pas encore là et peut toujours nous apprendre qu'une attitude élégante n'est pas du tout incompatible avec une grande franchise d'expression.

"1782 is the memorable date of the publication of *Dangerous Liaisons* where an artillery officer tried to apply the laws of triangulation to morals, which, as we know, are as useful to artillerymen as they are to astronomers. Astonishing contrast! The infinite life that gravitates in the firmament obeys the same laws as the artillery assigned by man to sow death. . . . The angular measurements calculated by Laclos gave birth to the modern literary spirit; this is where Baudelaire discovered his first elements, a reasonable and refined explorer of ancient life, but whose views on modern life imply a degree of folly. It is with delight that he inhaled the corrupt bubbles arising from the strange and rich literary mud of the Revolution where, close to Diderot, Laclos (the intellectual son of Richardson and of Rousseau), all had the most remarkable followers: Sade, Restif, Nerciat, and all the philosophical storytellers of the end of the eighteenth century. . . . The proof of the influence of the cynical literature of the Revolution on *Les Fleurs du mal* is found throughout his correspondance and in his notes. . . . Baudelaire is the son of Laclos and of Edgar Poe, but their blind and mad son, who, however, before scaling the summits, had looked with an admirable precision at the arts and at life.

"It is also true that the modern spirit was, for the first time, incarnated in him. It was after Baudelaire that something was born, only to stagnate while the naturalists, Parnassians, and symbolists passed nearby and saw nothing; while the nudists, having turned to look, did not have the audacity to examine this sublime and monstrous newness. Those who would be amazed at his crippled birth from the revolutionary mud and the American pox, must be answered with the Bible's teachings on the origin of man, issue of the dust of the ground.

"It is true that the Newness took the face of Baudelaire before all others, he who had been the first to breathe the modern spirit in Europe, but his prophetic brain did not know how to prophesy, and Baudelaire did not penetrate this new spirit by which he was himself penetrated, and thanks to which he discovered the seeds of several others who came before him.

"And it is well worth abandoning, just as great lyrics were abandoned, and their lyricism had aged like those of Jean-Baptiste Rousseau, the moment he was taken up by someone or other and placed at the gate of vulgarity.

"However, even fallen into the public domain, Baudelaire is still not there and can still teach us that an elegant attitude is not at all incompatible with a great frankness of expression.

"*Les Fleurs du mal* sont à cet égard un document de premier ordre.

"La liberté qui règne dans ce recueil ne l'a pas empêché de dominer sans conteste la poésie universelle à la fin du XIXe siècle.

"Son influence cesse à présent, ce n'est pas un mal.

"De cette œuvre nous avons rejeté le côté moral qui nous faisait du tort en nous forçant d'envisager la vie et les choses avec un certain dillettantisme pessimiste dont nous ne sommes plus les dupes.

"Baudelaire regardait la vie avec une passion dégoûtée qui visait à transformer arbres, fleurs, femmes, l'univers tout entier et l'art même, en quelque chose de pernicieux.

"C'était sa marotte et non la saine réalité.

"Toutefois il ne faut point cesser d'admirer le courage qu'eut Baudelaire de ne point voiler les contours de la vie.

"L'usage social de la liberté littéraire deviendra de plus en plus rare et précieux. Les grandes démocraties de l'avenir seront peu libérales pour les écrivains."

In 1910, Apollinaire published his history *Le Théâtre italien*,[70] dealing not only with "la mimique qui accompagnait les discours" but with "l'usage social de la liberté littéraire":

(Jacopone de Todi) —"ce religieux est un poète terrible qui ne craint pas de s'attaquer violemment au pape lui-même et fait pressentir Dante."

(*Les Sacre Representazioni*) "se donnaient aux fêtes des confréries des couvents. Elles étaient souvent jouées par des enfants. Il s'y mêlait de la bouffonerie. La mise en scène était naïve, mais aussi somptueuse que possible. Il s'agissait avant tout d'émerveiller le peuple et de l'amuser." (An aim very near that of the author of *Les Mamelles de Tirésias* and the Dramaturgie of *Le Poète assassiné*.)

"La stricte observation des règles, la majesté du style ne suffisaient point à animer un genre où manquait avant tout l'observation de la réalité. Les tragédies italiennes étaient froides et monotones. Elles n'intéressaient que les humanistes.

---

70. Michaud, Paris, *Le Théâtre italien* includes Choix de Textes, bibliography, gravures, notes etc.

"*Les Fleurs du mal* is, in this respect, a document of the first order.

"The freedom that reigns in this collection did not prevent it from dominating, without contest, the universal poetry of the end of the nineteenth century.

"His influence is fading now; this is not an evil.

"We have rejected the moral side of this work that harms by forcing us to envision life and things with a certain pessimistic dilettantism of which we are no longer the dupes.

"Baudelaire looked at life with a disgusted passion that hoped to transform trees, flowers, women, the entire universe and even art, into something pernicious.

"This was his folly and not sane reality.

"There is, however, no reason to cease admiring Baudelaire's courage in not veiling life's contours. . . .

"The social usage of literary freedom will become rarer and rarer and more precious. The great democracies of the future will not be so liberal with writers."

En 1910 Apollinaire publia son histoire du *Théâtre italien*[70] traitant non seulement "of the comical expressions that accompanied the discourses" mais "of the social usage of literary freedom."

Il parle de Jacopone de Todi: "this religious man is a tremendous poet who is not afraid of violently tackling the pope himself and who offers a premonition of Dante."

Il parle des *Sacre Representazioni* "which were given on the feast days in monastic brotherhoods. They were often performed by children. They had an antic aspect. The set was naive but as sumptuous as possible. It was done above all for the amazement and amusement of the people." (Ce but n'est pas très éloigné de celui que poursuit l'auteur des *Mamelles de Tirésias* ou de la Dramaturgie du *Poète assassiné*).

"The strict observation of rules, the majesty of style is not at all sufficient, does not at all suffice to animate a genre where the observation of reality was missing. Italian tragedies were cold and monotonous. They only interested humanists.

70. *Le Théâtre italien* (Paris, Michaud), contains selected texts, bibliography, engravings, notes, etc.

(Comédie): "La Comédie de la rue se maintenait sous le nom de commedia dell'arte, ou comédie improvisée, elle pénétrait même dans les palais où elle mettait sa fantaisie parmi les scènes mythologiques que venaient rompre et égayer les querelles de masques gracieux ou grotesques, des mêlées de fous et de bossus se battant à coup de vessie de porc. La commedia dell'arte, dont le dévelopement ne s'est pas arrêté jusqu'à Goldoni, eut une influence marquée sur le théâtre moderne.

"Bientôt le drame pastoral fut absorbé par le mélodrame ou opéra en musique.

"On a fixé une origine antique à la plupart des personnages de la comédie italienne. C'est ainsi qu'il faudrait aller chercher Polichinelle dans les Atellanes sous le nom de Maccus, avec l'arlequin qui ne serait que la transformation du mime planipède, de même que le Capitan dériverait du *miles gloriosus* des Latins. On a aussi attribué à ces personnnages une origine mythique: ils figuraient les planètes. Il vaut mieux voir les masques de la comédie italienne dans leurs caractères provinciaux. Le Docteur est bolonais, Pantalon est vénitien, Scaramouche est napolitan.—Au demeurant, le docteur est un pédant, le capitan un poltron qui fait le brave."

A dramatic insight which became a lens to converge and diverge light in his essay "Sur la Peinture:"[71]

"Considérer la pureté, c'est baptiser l'instinct, c'est humaniser l'art et diviniser la personnalité.

"La racine, la tige et la fleur de lys, montrent la progression de la pureté jusqu'à sa floraison symbolique.

"Tous les corps sont égaux devant la lumière et leurs modifications résultent de ce pouvoir lumineux qui construit à son gré.

"Nous ne connaissons pas toutes les couleurs et chaque homme en invente de nouvelles.

"Mais, le peintre doit avant tout se donner le spectacle de sa propre divinité et les tableaux qu'il offre à l'admiration des hommes leur conféreront la gloire d'exercer aussi et momentanément leur propre divinité.

"Il faut pour cela embrasser d'un coup d'œil: le passé, le présent et l'avenir.

71. *Les Peintres cubistes*, cf. Guillaume Janneau, *L'Art cubiste*, Paris 1929, for the importance of Apollinaire as the expounder of cubism.

"The Comedy of the the street continued under the name of *commedia dell'arte* or improvised comedy; it even penetrated the palaces where it placed its fantasy among the mythological scenes that came to break and to enliven the quarrels of the gracious or grotesque masks, of the packs of madmen and hunchbacks beating one another with pork bladders. The *commedia dell'arte*, whose development didn't stop until Goldoni, had a marked influence on modern theater.

"Soon the pastoral drama was absorbed by the melodrama or opera in music.

"Most of the characters of the Italian comedy were assigned an origin in Antiquity. It is thus that Punchinello can be found under the name of Maccus in the Atellanes, with harlequin no more than the transformation of the *planipède* mime, just as the Captain would come from the miles gloriosus. These characters were also assigned a mythic origin: they represented the planets. It is better to see a provincial origin for the Italian comedy's masks. The Doctor is from Bologna, Pantalon is Venetian, Scaramouche is Neopolitan. For all that, the doctor is a pedant, the Captain a coward feigning courage."

Intelligence dramatique qui devint dans son Essai sur la peinture[71] appareil d'optique à faire converger et diverger la lumière.

"To consider purity is to baptize instinct, it is to humanize art and divinize personality.

"The root, the stalk and the *fleur de lys* show the progression of purity all the way to its symbolic flowering.

"All bodies are equal before the light and their modifications result from this luminous power that builds as it pleases.

"We don't know all the colors and every man invents new ones.

"But the painter must, above all, offer the spectacle of his own divinity and the paintings that he offers for the admiration of men will confer upon them the glory of exercizing their own divinity for a moment.

"To do this one must embrace for an instant the past, the present and the future.

---

71. *Les Peintres cubistes*; cf. Guillaume Janneau: *L'Art cubiste*, Paris, 1929 for the role Apollinaire played as Cubism's spokesman.

"La toile doit présenter cette unité essentielle qui seule provoque l'extase.

"Alors, rien de fugitif n'entraînera au hasard. Nous ne reviendrons pas brusquement en arrière. Spectateurs libres nous n'abandonnerons point notre vie à cause de notre curiosité. Les faux-sauniers des apparences ne passeront point en fraude nos statues de sel devant l'octroi de la raison.

"Nous n'errerons point dans l'avenir inconnu, qui séparé de l'éternité n'est qu'un mot destiné à tenter l'homme.

"Nous ne nous épuiserons pas à saisir le présent trop fugace et qui ne peut être pour l'artiste que le masque de la mort: la mode.

"On ne découvrira jamais la réalité une fois pour toutes. La vérité sera toujours nouvelle.

"Autrement, elle n'est qu'un système plus misérable que la nature.

"Lês nouveaux peintres, pas plus que leurs anciens ne se sont proposé d'être des géomètres. Mais on peut dire que la géométrie est aux arts plastiques ce que la grammaire est à l'art de l'écrivain.

"Or, aujourd'hui, les savants ne n'en tiennent plus aux trois dimensions de la géométrie euclidienne. Les peintres ont été amenés tout naturellement et, pour ainsi dire, par intuition,[72] à se préoccuper de nouvelles mésures possibles de l'étendue que dans le langage des ateliers modernes on désignait tout ensemble et brièvement par le terme de *quatrième dimension*.

"Telle qu'elle s'offre à l'esprit, du point de vue plastique, la quatrième dimension serait engendrée par les trois mesures connues: elle figure l'immensité de l'espace s'éternisant dans toutes les directions à un moment déterminé. Elle est l'espace même, la dimension de l'infini; c'est elle qui doue de plasticité les objets. Elle leur donne les proportions qu'ils méritent dans l'œuvre, tandis que dans l'art grec par exemple, un rythme en quelque sorte mécanique détruit sans cesse les proportions.

"L'art grec avait de la beauté une conception purement humaine. Il prenait l'homme comme mesure de la perfection. L'art des peintres nouveaux prend l'univers infini come idéal et c'est à cet idéal que l'on doit une nouvelle mesure de la perfection qui permet à l'artiste-peintre de donner à l'objet des proportions conformes au degré de plasticité où il souhaite l'amener.

---

72. Apollinaire's "pour ainsi dire" perhaps saves him from a criticism of this position, such as Gino Severini's *Du Cubisme au Classicisme*.

"The canvas should present this essential unity that alone provokes ecstasy.

"So nothing fleeting will lead to chance. We will not go brusquely backward. Free spectators, we will not abandon our life because of our curiosity. The false salt merchants of appearances will not falsely pass our statues of salt before the toll of reason.

"We will not wander in the unknown future which, separated from eternity, is but a word destined to tempt man.

"We shall never discover reality once and for all. Truth will always be new.

"We will not exhaust ourselves in seizing the too fleeting present which, for the artist, can only be a mask of death—fashion.

"Otherwise it is a system more miserable than nature.

"The new painters no more purport to be geometers than the older ones. But one can say that geometry is to the plastic arts as grammar is to the art of the writer. . . .

"Or, today, scholars no longer limit themselves to Euclidean geometry's three dimensions. Painters have been led entirely naturally and by intuition, so to speak,[72] to a preoccupation with possible new measures of the scale that in the language of today's studios are referred to in sum and briefly as the *fourth dimension.*

"Just as it presents itself to the mind, from the plastic point of view, it is the three known measures that would engender the fourth dimension. It represents the immensity of space reaching forever in all directions at a given moment. It is space itself, the dimension of the infinite; it is that dimension which endows objects wih plasticity. It gives them the proportions they deserve in the work, whereas in Greek art, for example, a somewhat mechanical rhythm always destroys proportions.

"Greek art had a purely human conception of beauty. It took man as the measure of perfection. The art of new painters takes the infinite universe as the ideal and it is to this ideal that we owe a new measure of the perfection which allows the artist-painter to give the object proportions conforming to that degree of plasticity that he hopes to achieve.

72. Apollinaire's "so to speak" spares him the criticism that is made of Gino Severini's similar position in his *Du Cubisme au Classicisme.*

"Ajoutons que cette imagination de la *quatrième dimension*, n'a été que la manifestation des aspirations, des inquiétudes d'un grand nombre de jeunes artistes regardant les sculptures égyptiennes, nègres et océaniennes, méditant les ouvrages de science, attendant un art sublime, et qu'on n'attache plus aujourd'hui à cette expression utopique, qu'il fallait noter et expliquer, qu'un intérêt en quelque sorte historique.

"Le beau dégagé de la délectation que l'homme cause à l'homme, et depuis le commencement des temps historiques aucun artiste européen n'avait osé cela. Il faut aux nouveaux artistes une beauté idéale qui ne soit plus seulement l'expression orgueilleuse de l'espèce, mais l'expression de l'univers, dans la mesure où il s'est humanisé dans la lumière."

This page is not the portrait of Guillaume Apollinaire, the painter, tho it would be easy to show the resemblance of the literature of his paintings[73] to the literature of his calligrammes. However, when the heroine of his *Les Mamelles de Tirésias* allowed her breasts—balloons—to fly one red, one blue, when she shouted bull-like into the microphone, and then admired herself in the mirror of le kiosque à journaux, Guillaume humanized the universe in the limelight.[74] He called that plastic a drama, which signified action "pour établir ce qui le sépare de ces comédies de mœurs, comédies dramatiques, comédies légères qui depuis plus d'un demi-siècle fournissent à la scène des œuvres dont beaucoup sont excellentes mais de second ordre et que l'on appelle tout simplement des pièces." His preface continued: "pour caractériser mon drame je me suis servi d'un néologisme qu'on me pardonnera car cela m'arrive rarement et j'ai forgé l'adjectif surréaliste qui ne signifie pas du tout symbolique, mais définit assez bien une tendance de l'art qui si elle n'est pas plus nouvelle que tout ce qui se trouve sous le soleil n'a du moins jamais servi à formuler aucun crédo, aucune affirmation artistique et littéraire."

"Pour tenter, sinon une rénovation du théâtre, du moins un effort personnel, j'ai pensé qu'il fallait revenir à la nature même, mais sans l'imiter à la manière des photographes.

"Quand l'homme a voulu imiter la marche, il a créé la roue qui ne ressemble pas à une jambe. Il a fait ainsi du surréalisme sans le savoir.

73. Cf. the reproductions in *L'Esprit nouveau*, October 1924.

74. The first performance of *Les Mamelles de Tirésias* was given by La Revue Sic, June 24, 1917.

"Let us add that this imagination—the *fourth dimension*—was only the manifestation of the aspirations, of the worries of a great number of young artists looking at Egyptian sculptures, negro and Oceanic, pondering the works of science, waiting for a sublime art, and that today it is only a certain historical interest that is attached to this utopian expression which had to be noted and explained.

"The beautiful, released from the delight that man gives to man, and since the beginning of history, no European artist had dared do that. The new artists need an ideal beauty that is no longer only the proud expression of the species, but the expression of the universe, insofar as it humanised itself in the light."

Ces pages ne font pas un portrait de Guillaume Apollinaire, peintre, quand bien même il serait facile de montrer la ressemblance de la littérature de ses tableaux[73] avec la littérature de ses calligrammes. Cependant, quand l'héroïne des *Mamelles de Tirésias* laissait envoler ses seins—un ballon rouge et un ballon bleu, quand elle criait comme un taureau dans le microphone, et puis s'admirait dans le miroir du kiosque à journaux, Guillaume humanisait l'univers au feu de la rampe.[74] Cette plastique, c'était ce qu'il appelait un drame dans le vrai sens du mot, action, "to establish that which separates these comedies of manners, dramatic comedies, light comedies that, for more than half a century, brought works to the stage, many of which were excellent but of a second order and that are simply called plays." Sa préface continuait ainsi: "To characterize my drama I have made use of a neologism, for which I will be excused because I do it rarely, and I created the adjective surrealist which has no symbolic meaning at all but is a fairly good definition of a tendency in art that, if it is not newer than anything under the sun, at least has never served to give form to any credo, any artistic or literary affirmation.

"To attempt, if not a renovation of the theater, at least a personal effort, I thought I would have to return to nature itself but without imitating it as photographers do.

"When man wanted to imitate walking, he created the wheel which does not resemble a leg. He thus took part in surrealism without knowing it.

73. Cf. the reproductions in *L'Esprit nouveau*, October 1924.

74. The first production of *Les Mamelles de Tirésias* was given by the literary review *Sic*, June 24, 1917.

"On a dit que je m'étais servi du moyen dont on use dans les revues; je ne vois pas bien à quel moment. Ce reproche toutefois n'a rien qui puisse me géner, car l'art populaire est un fonds excellent et je m'honorerais d'y avoir puisé si toutes mes scènes ne s'enchaînaient naturellement selon la fable que j'ai imaginée et où la situation principale—un homme qui fait des enfants, est neuve au théâtre et dans les lettres en général, mais ne doit plus choquer que certaines inventions impossibles des romanciers dont la vogue est fondée sur le merveilleux dit scientifique.

"Pour le surplus, il n'y a aucun symbole dans ma pièce qui est fort claire, mais on est libre d'y voir tous les symboles que l'on voudra et d'y démeler mille sens comme dans les oracles sybillins.—il y a des œuvres remarquables dont le symbolisme justement prête à de nombreuses interprétations qui parfois se contrarient."

(From the Prologue)[75]
On tente ici d'infuser un esprit nouveau au théâtre
Une joie une volupté une vertu
Pour remplacer ce pessimisme vieux de plus d'un siècle
Ce qui est bien ancien pour une chose si ennuyeuse
La pièce a été faite pour une scène ancienne
Car, on ne nous aurait pas construit de théâtre nouveau
Une au centre l'autre formant comme un anneau
Autour des spectateurs et qui permettra
Le grand déploiement de notre art moderne
Mariant souvent sans lien apparent comme dans la vie
Les sons les gestes les couleurs les cris les bruits
La musique la danse l'acrobatie la poésie la peinture
Les chœurs les actions et les décors multiples
Vous trouverez ici des actions
Qui s'ajoutent au drame principale et l'ornent
Les changements de ton du pathétique au burlesque
Et l'usage raisonnable des invraisemblances
Ainsi que des acteurs collectifs ou non
Qui ne sont pas forcément extraits de l'humanité
Fait de l'univers entier
Car le théâtre ne doit pas être un art en trompe-l'oeil

75. Written in 1916.

"It has been said that I made use of the variety show's hackneyed techniques; I don't quite see where. This reproach could not bother me, however, because popular art is an excellent well and I would be honored to have drawn from it if all of my scenes didn't naturally follow from the fable I imagined and whose primary situation—a man who gives birth to children, is new to the theater and to literature in general, but ought not to be more shocking than certain impossible inventions of novelists whose fame is based on those marvels that are called scientific.

"What's more, there is not a symbol in my play that is perfectly clear, but anyone is free to see all the symbols that he wants in it and to pull a thousand meanings from it as from the sibylline oracle. There are remarkable works whose symbolism rightly lends itself to numerous interpretations that occasionally contradict one another."

Prologue[75]

Here we attempt to infuse the theater with a new spirit
A joy a voluptuousness a virtue
To replace this old pessimism of more than a century
That's old enough for something so dull
The play was made for an antique stage
For no one would have built us a new theater
A round one with two stages, one in the center the other like a ring
Around the spectators and that will allow
The great deployment of our modern art
Often blending without a visible connection as in life
The sounds the gestures the colors the cries the noises
The music the dance the acrobatics the poetry the painting
The choruses the plots and the multiple sets
Here you will find plots
That add to and ornament a principal drama
Changes in tone from pathetic to burlesque
And the reasonable use of unlikelihoods
Thus the actors collective or not
Who are not necessarily extracts of humanity
But of the entire universe
For theater must not be a trompe-l'œil art

75. Written in 1916.

Il est juste que le dramaturge se serve
De tous les mirages qu'il a à sa disposition
Comme faisait Morgane sur le Mont-Gibel
Il est juste qu'il fasse parler
Les foules les objets inanimés
S'il lui plaît
Et qu'il ne tienne pas plus compte du temps
Que de l'espace
Son univers est sa pièce
A l'intérieur de laquelle il est le dieu créateur
C'est-à-dire la nature même
Et non pas seulement la représentation d'un petit petit morceau
De ce qui nous entoure ou de ce qui s'est jadis passé

The prologue of *Les Mamelles de Tirésias* is the speech of Apollinaire—the poet, once stroller over the two banks of the Seine, the recorder of the boulevardiens of Paris, the Amphion[76] for whom the stones of his adopted city had, in times past, and for all modern intent, moved as in the old myth to the attraction of an art. He has gone to War and come back to the people whom he prefers among all others.

At that time, the cast of his work had for its hypostasis the confirmed light of a consciousness which, in its egress, he solaced with the name of "L'Esprit nouveau." It was opposed to or came out of the irresolution of another hypostasis, the matter of the times, the contingency of war, which engulfed as it were *"l'Esprit nouveau"* under the cast of another name, *Couleur du temps.* —Implicitly, Apollinaire's posthumous play in verse—*Couleur du temps*[77]—was meant for "un théâtre rond à deux scènes" for the verse which falls on the ear with directness, like Villon's, made the local universe the subject of the play. The action, if it is an action, and not as it seems a constant resolution of an action never to be, is of a half dozen people pursuing peace away from a warring world, which they have escaped for a marmoreal antarctic where "il faut que tout meure."

The mise en scène is moved by the airs:

76. Cf. "L'Amphion faux-messie," *L'Hérésiarque.*
77. Published in *La Nouvelle Revue française*, November 1, 1920.

It is right that the playwright should use
All of the mirages at his disposal
As Morgane did on Mount Gibel
It is right that he should give speech
To crowds to inanimate objects
If he likes
And that he should not take into account
Time more than space
His universe is his play
At the interior of which he is the god creator
That is to say nature itself
And not only the representation of a little little bit
Of what surrounds us or of what happened long ago

Le prologue des *Mamelles de Tirésias* est le discours d'un Apollinaire poète, jadis flâneur des deux rives de la Seine, historien des boulevardiers, Amphion[76] pour qui les pavés de sa ville d'adoption au temps passé, et avec une force et un sens tout modernes, s'étaient mis en mouvement attirés par un art. Il est allé au front et est revenu parmi le peuple qu'il préfère à tout autre.

A cette époque la physionomie de son œuvre prenait pour hypostase la clarté nette d'une conscience que sans plus de formalités il appelait *L'Esprit nouveau*. Elle sortait pour s'y opposer de cette autre hypostase irrésolue: la matière de l'époque, la contingence de la guerre qui engouffrait l'Esprit nouveau dans un titre différent: *Couleur du temps*.[77] Cette pièce en vers qui fait partie de l'œuvre posthume d'Apollinaire était destinée à un théâtre rond à deux scènes; car le vers qui tombe droit dans l'oreille tel celui de Villon faisait de l'univers local le sujet de la pièce. L'action, si c'en est une et non la constante résorption d'une action qui ne naîtra jamais, se passe entre une demi-douzaine de gens à la poursuite de la paix hors d'un monde belligérant dont ils se sont échappés pour tomber dans un antarctique marmoréen où "all must die."

La mise en scène se meut par les airs:

---

76. Cf. "L'Amphion faux-messie," *L'Hérésiarque*.
77. Published in *La Nouvelle Revue française*, November 1, 1920.

> Et des nuages dorés
> Folâtrent autour de nous
> Ainsi que des dauphins autour d'une carène

to the ultimate hallucination: the body of a woman encased in the transparency of an iceberg of glass. The strife of the four men of the play over
the image of their vision—a vision like all the struggles of man limited
by the fatal shortsightedness of vision which debates about, and kills
for, the right of safeguarding what it sees—ends in death for all. The
two women who have come with the men, escaping the frame of European weaknesses, will also die, not having anything left to regret, not
the spiritual rights of religion, nor the philosophic rights of country, nor
even the right of having abandoned the dead and the living:

> un petit balcon
> Donnant sur une rue peu passante
> Et le bruit très lointain des tramways
> Banquise de souvenirs glacés

In the frozen void before their death, each of the four men sees the
image of his capacity for vision:

> **Nyctor**
> Eve modèle de la beauté

> **Ansaladin**
> La science qui ne change pas

> **Van Diemen**
> Immobile et très belle à jamais
> C'est la paix même que nous cherchons

> **Le Solitaire**
> Puisque vous le voulez ce sera
> Pour elle que nous nous battrons

The voices of the various gods assembled at the death of the fantastic
history of humanity which has created them are heard:

> And the golden clouds
> Frolic around us
> Like dolphins around a ship's hull

jusqu'à l'ultime hallucination: le corps d'une femme encastré dans la transparence d'un iceberg en verre. Les luttes des quatre hommes autour des images de leur vision (vision limitée comme toutes les luttes de l'homme par une fatale étroitesse de regards qui la pousse à se débattre et à tuer pour le droit de sauvegarder ce qu'elle voit) finissent par la mort de tous. Les deux femmes venues avec les hommes, échappées au cadre des faiblesses européennes, mourront aussi n'ayant plus de regrets à éprouver, ni pour les droits spirituels de la religion, ni les droits philosophiques de la patrie, ni même pour le droit d'avoir abandonné les morts et les vivants:

> a little balcony
> overlooking a seldom traveled street
> And the distant noise of streetcars
> Floes of frozen memory

Dans le vide froid, avant leur mort, chacun des quatre hommes voit l'image qui lui convient:

Nyctor
Eve, model of beauty

Ansaladin
Unchanging science

Van Diemen
Immobile and forever very beautiful
It is peace itself that we seek

Solitaire
Since you want it, it will be
For her that we do battle

Les voix des différents dieux assemblés à la mort de l'histoire fantastique de l'humanité qui les a créés se font entendre:

> Soleil ô vie ô vie
> Apaise les colères
> Console les regrets
> Prends en pitié les hommes
> Prends en pitié les Dieux
> Les Dieux qui vont mourir
> Si l'humanité meurt!

The birth of this death has been pursued ruthlessly, but without its inherent complicity has evolved into the appearance of a new subsistence, the latitude of *l'Esprit nouveau*.

For the world in which Apollinaire died took on the image of many absurdities. To exist and to keep the intelligence active, Guillaume even became censor[78] on *Paris Midi* and astonished his friends by revealing to them dates heading dispatches from New York and London, the text of news proceeding entirely from his imagination: "Il n'y a pas, expliquait-il, de meilleur façon d'influer sur les événements." Not a Frenchman, he could have avoided the War. But an intelligence which could not surpass its own destiny attracted it. "La première édition à 25 exemplaires de *Case d'Armons* a été polygraphiés sur papier quadrillé, à l'encre violette, au moyen de gelatine, à la batterie de tir (45e batterie, 38e Régiment d'artillerie de campagne) devant l'ennemi, et le tirage a été achevé le 17 juin 1915." An achievement of the times, like the wearing of a uniform, both perhaps the action of an insistence for the sake of verisimilitude. He continued his *Vie anecdotique* for the Mercure de France and not disrupting the consecutiveness of his past, the past of his work, he submitted to the *Couleur du temps*; described the superstitions of the English and the poilus of the trenches. Fragments, often showing amazing completeness in themselves, which he hurriedly gathered for the appearance of his novel *La Femme assise*. He reviewed the "ouvrages sur la guerre actuelle:[79]

"Par exemple les Alpins skieurs pareils à des pierrots blancs dansant sur la neige, les Dolomites, montagnes chères à l'aquarelliste Jeanès, déroulent ici leur chaos harmonieux."

78. André Billy, *Apollinaire vivant*.
79. Mercure de France: 16—October— 1916, 16—July—1917.

Sun oh life oh life
Pacify anger
Soothe regrets
Take pity on men
Take pity on Gods
Gods who will die
If humanity dies!

La naissance de cette mort s'est poursuivie sans pitié, mais sans inhérente complicité a entraîné l'apparition d'une nouvelle existence: la latitude de *l'Esprit nouveau*.

Car le monde où est mort Apollinaire a pris l'aspect de nombreuses absurdités. Pour vivre et conserver à l'intelligence son activité, Guillaume devint même un des censeurs[78] de *Paris Midi* et étonna ses amis en leur révélant les dates et les entêtes de dépêches venues de Londres et New York et dont le texte sortait tout entier de son imagination: "There is not, he explained, a better way of influencing events." N'étant pas français, il aurait pu éviter la guerre. Mais une intelligence qui ne pouvait pas dépasser sa destinée l'entraînait. "The first printing of 25 copies of *Case d'Armons* was polygraphed on squared paper, in purple ink, with gelatine, in the shooting battery (Forty-fifth Battery, Thirty-eight Regiment of the country artillery) before the enemy, and the printing took place on June 17, 1915." An achievement of the times, like the wearing of a uniform; two acts that might be the result of a stubborness for the love of likelihood. Il continua sa *Vie Anecdotique* pour le Mercure de France et sans briser le développement de son passé, le passé de son œuvre, il se soumit à la *Couleur du temps*; il décrivit les superstitions des Anglais et des soldats des tranchées. Fragments, à l'occasion étonnemment complets en eux-mêmes, qu'il rassembla en hâte pour sa *Femme assise*. "Il faisait la chronique des livres sur la guerre:[79]

"For example alpine skiers like white pierrots dancing in the snow, Dolomites, mountains dear to the watercolorist Jeanès, unfurl their harmonious chaos here."

78. André Billy, *Apollinaire vivant*.
79. Mercure de France, October 16, 1916, July 16, 1917.

"Ce volume est bien conçu et d'une merveilleuse netteté de clichés—
On ne saurait trop louer de telles publications qui aident les Français à
comprendre l'effort de leurs alliés—observations précises rendues avec
cette véracité imagée. Le vocabulaire est excellent. Il n'exagère point
le pittoresque langage de nos poilus—sang froid que les médecins acquièrent au contact de la souffrance."

He wrote home though to his friends:

"Mais je ne sais par quelle aberration nous ne nous occupons pas du
tout de la guerre."[80]

"Ici, amie, c'est la guerre. Vous le savez: obus-Roi. Ça a le comique
et le tragique de la pièce de Jarry obus partout."[81]

"Il faut surtout être gai, sans ça tout est foutu. Mais tout de même,
vieux, les années de métier, n'y a que ça. Ce n'est pas notre affaire de
guerroyer ou la pensée humaine foutra le camp. On a fait la guerre pendant tout le dix-septième siècle, mais Corneille, Racine, Malherbe ne se
battaient pas, ni Pascal, ni Bossuet. Nous faisons notre devoir aussi bien
que les autres, mais vraiment c'est ailleurs qu'il devrait être. A chacun son
métier maintenant, si j'en reviens ce sera une sacrée cure d'énergie."[82]

And among the absurdities of the time: the cure, the product of
the interactions of multiple awareness, bore a trademark—for public
consumption no doubt—*l'Esprit nouveau*. The article which Apollinaire
wrote by way of hasty definition and which appeared posthumously[83]
dealt with "heritage"—classic good sense, assured critical spirit, restraint
of sentiment, with romantic curiosity—the exploration of truth in ethnic, as well as in imaginary, sense. The article mentioned instigations:
vers libre; researches into form; assonance; alliteration; typographical or
visual lyricism; the literary synthesis of music, painting and poetry. "Qui
oserait dire que les exercises de rhétorique, les variations sur le thème
de: 'Je meurs de soif auprès de la fontaine,' n'ont pas eu une influence
déterminante sur le génie de Villon?" The writer looked forward to a
refinement of the cinema and the phonograph, which would supplant
the present literature and give liberty to poets: "le livre vu et entendu de

80. Letter to Picabia, 12/29/24, in *L'Esprit nouveau*, October 1924.

81. Letter, April 26, 1915, reprinted in *Les Marges,* December 15, 1918.

82. Published in *Les Arts à Paris,* Nîmes, January 2, 1915. Reprinted in *Almanachs de Treich,* April 1924.

83. Mercure de France, December 1, 1918.

"This volume is well-conceived and of a marvellous clarity of clichés. Such publications that help the French in understanding their allies' efforts cannot be over praised . . . precise observations rendered with this imaged truth. The vocabulary is excellent. It doesn't in the least exaggerate the picturesque language of our foot soldiers . . . self-control that doctors acquire in their contact with suffering."

Il écrivait pourtant à ses amis:

"But I don't know by what aberration we do not at all concern ourselves with the war."[80]

"Here, sweet friend, it is war. You know it: King shell. This has the comic and the tragic of Jarry's play [*Ubu Roi*], shells everywhere.[81]

"One must, above all, be happy. Without that, all is lost. But all the same, old man, the career years, that's all there is. It is not our business to wage war or human thought will clear out. There was war throughout the seventeenth century but Corneille, Racine, Malherbe didn't fight, neither did Pascal nor Bossuet. We do our work as well as the others but really we should be elsewhere. To each his career now, if I come back from it, it will be one hell of an energy cure."[82]

Donc retour parmi les absurdités de l'époque: le remède à apporter, produit des interactions d'une conscience multiple, portait une marque de fabrique—probablement pour parler au public—L'*Esprit nouveau*, l'article qu'Apollinaire écrivit pour le définir au plus vite et qui fait partie de ses écrits posthumes[83] traitait de l'héritage classique: le bon sens, la solidité de l'esprit critique, le contrôle des sentiments, et de la curiosité romantique: l'exploration de la vérité dans le sens ethnique aussi bien que dans celui de l'imagination. Parmi les instigations mentionnées: le vers libre, recherches de formes, l'assonance, l'allitération; le lyrisme typographique ou visuel, la synthèse littéraire de la musique, la peinture et la poésie. "Who would dare to say that rhetorical exercises, variations on the theme of 'I'm dying of thirst next to a fountain,' did not have a determining influence on Villon's genius?" L'auteur attendait encore un perfectionnement du cinéma et du phonographe qui devait supplanter la littérature actuelle et donner aux poètes la liberté:

80. Letter to Picabia, December 29, 1914, in *L'Esprit nouveau*, October 1924.

81. Letter, April 26, 1915, reprinted in *Les Marges*, December 15, 1918.

82. Published in *Les Arts à Paris*, Nîmes, January 3, 1915, reprinted in *Les Almanachs de Treich*, April 1924.

83. Mercure de France, December 1, 1918.

l'avenir." Restraints were set, national limits indicated: "les surenchères futuristes, italienne et russe, filles excessives de *l'Esprit nouveau*—la France répugne au désordre." A poet's matter was not to be less than that of the daily paper: there would be accessibility to events by way of telephone, wireless, aeroplane, prophecy, machines. With increased liberty, there would be an increased enforcement of ancient discipline, but there would be no less an enforcement of new disciplines as exigent as the ancient. Wagner and Rousseau were rejected. Art would more and more be the expression of a country, since it has always been the expression of a milieu, a nation, a race. A cosmopolite lyric expression could have only the vague accent of international rhetorical parliamentarism: Guillaume noticed the difference between contemporary Italian and American films. French, *L'Esprit nouveau* meant liberty and order. There would be no sense in a reduction of poetry to imitative harmonies of noises, for tho these have their place with the lyric, tragic or pathetic sense attached, the real noises are often superior to the poetic rendition of them. But today even the ridiculous would be hunted out. *L'Esprit nouveau* leaving the horrible would not debase the noble. *L'Esprit nouveau* would not be decorative or impressionistic, but a study of nature interior and exterior. It would exist as surprise and not be a discursus. To the poet on his way to discovery, the good sense of the past with him, "le moindre fait est le postulat, le point de départ d'une immensité inconnue où flambent les feux de joie des significations multiples." The new spirit was the enemy of aesthetics, of snobs, of formulas, of schools. "Les poètes ne son pas seulement les hommes du beau. Ils sont encore et surtout les hommes du vrai. Les poètes enfin seront chargés de donner par les téléologies lyriques et les alchimies archilyriques un sens toujours plus pur à l'idée divine, qui est en nous si vivante et si vraie, qui est ce perpétuel renouvellement de nous-*mêmes*, cette création éternelle, cette poésie sans cesse renaissante dont nous vivons." The new spirit must not allow the machine, mathematics and science to excel it, but meet these on their ways.

The facts in Apollinaire's last criticism were presented as an advertisement, but they complete the portrait. A letter[84] written in 1917 revealed more of incision in the display: "Très bien votre manifeste du Nord-Sud . . .

---

84. March 1917, to Paul Dermée, *L'Esprit nouveau*, October 1924.

"the seen and heard book of the future." Des contraintes étaient établies, des limites nationales indiquées: "the higher bidding futurists, Italian and Russian, excessive daughters of *L'Esprit nouveau*—France loaths disorder." La matière du poète ne devait être rien de moins que celle du quotidien: les événements devenaient accessibles par le téléphone, la T.S.F., l'avion, la prophétie, les machines. Avec une liberté plus grande viendrait une plus grande application de l'ancienne discipline, mais il n'y en aurait pas moins pour ça une application de la nouvelle, aussi pressante que l'ancienne. Wagner et Rousseau se trouvaient rejetés. Ce serait l'expression d'un pays, car ces lois ont toujours été l'expression d'un milieu, d'une nation, d'une race. Une expression lyrique cosmopolite ne pourrait guère avoir que l'accent vague de la rhétorique du parlementarisme international. Guillaume remarquait la différence entre les films contemporains italiens et américains. En France, *l'Esprit nouveau* signifiait la liberté et l'ordre. Il n'y aurait aucun sens à réduire la poésie à des harmonies imitatives de bruit, car bien que ceux-ci aient leur place ici avec le sens lyrique, tragique ou pathétique qui s'attache à eux, les bruits réels sont souvent supérieurs à leur représentation poétique. Mais de nos jours le ridicule lui-même serait poursuivi. *L'Esprit nouveau* en délaissant l'horrible ne chercherait pas à rabaisser le noble. *L'Esprit nouveau* ne serait ni décoratif ni impressionniste mais une étude intérieure et extérieure de la nature. Il existerait comme surprise et ne serait pas un discursif développement. Pour le poète qui va à la découverte, et que le bon sens du passé accompagne, "the least fact is the postulate, the point of departure for an unknown immensity where flame the fires of joy of multiple meanings." *L'Esprit nouveau* était l'ennemi de l'esthétique, des snobs, des formules, des écoles. "Poets are not only men concerned with beauty. They are still and above all men concerned with truth. Poets will finally be responsible for giving, with lyrical theologies and archilyrical alchemies an ever purer sense of the divine idea, which is so alive and so true in us, which is this perpetual renewal of ourselves, this eternal creation, this poetry unendingly reborn by which we live." *L'Esprit nouveau* ne doit pas se laisser dépasser par la machine, les mathématiques et la science, mais au contraire les rejoindre en chemin.

Les faits présentés par la dernière critique d'Apollinaire prenaient les allures de la réclame; ils peuvent servir à compléter le portrait. Une lettre[84] datée de 1917 révélait des intentions plus pures: "Very good your North-South manifesto . . .

84. March 1917, to Paul Dermée, *L'Esprit nouveau*, October 1924.

"Vous avez eu raison d'insister sur la nécessité d'une prochaine période d'organisation du lyrisme.

"Et aussi d'une contrainte intérieure, qui est indispensable à toute poésie, c'est-à-dire à toute création; il est juste aussi de ramener 'l'étrange magie des mots' à son rôle de moyen poétique.

"Tout bien examiné, je crois, en effet qu'il vaut mieux adopter surréalisme que surnaturalisme que j'avais d'abord employé. Surréalisme n'existe pas encore dans les dictionnaires et il sera plus commode à manier que surnaturalisme déjà utilisé par les Philosophes."

The destiny unsurpassed in the portrait is the destiny of European weaknesses, of an intelligence living the Europe of its time and Europe's various pasts (living Paris, living France, living Italy), and constantly aware of individual and ethnic differences. Of one whose work was often filtered with the light of medieval intelligence, it might be said for the convenience of insight that the destiny of his writing was not unlike the destiny of love as Cavalcanti defined it:

In memory's locus taketh he his state
Formed there in manner as a mist of light
Upon a dusk that is come from Mars and stays
Love is created, hath a sensate name,
His modus takes from soul, from heart his will;
From form seen doth he start, that, understood,
Taketh in latent intellect—
As in a subject ready—
                    place and abode,
Yet in that place it ever is unstill,
Spreading its rays, it tendeth never down
By quality, but is its own effect unendingly
Not to delight, but in an ardour of thought
That the base likeness of it kindleth not.

It is not virtue, but perfection's source
Lying within perfection postulate
Not by the reason, but 'tis felt, I say,
Beyond salvation, holding its judging force,
Maintains intention reason's peer and mate;
Poor in discernment, being thus weakness' friend,
Often his power meeteth with death in the end

"You were right to insist that a period of organization of lyricism should necessarily follow.

"And also of an internal constraint, which is indispensable to all poetry, that is to say, to all creation; it is also right to restore the 'strange magic of words' to its role of poetic means.

"Having examined it all, I believe, in fact, that it is better to adopt surrealism than supernaturalism which I had first employed. Surrealism doesn't yet exist in dictionaries and it will be easier to handle than supernaturalism which is already used by our Philosophers."

La destinée que le portrait ne dépasse pas "is the frame of European weakness," d'une intelligence qui revit la vie de l'Europe de son époque et revit la vie des différents passés de cette Europe (Paris, la France, l'Italie), et qui se rappelle constamment les différences individuelles et les différences ethniques. De celui dont l'œuvre a souvent été tamisée à la lumière de l'intelligence médiévale, on pourrait dire pour plus de pénétration que la destinée de son écriture n'était pas différente de la destinée de l'amour tel que le définit Cavalcanti:

> In memory's locus taketh he his state
> Formed there in manner as a mist of light
> Upon a dusk that is come from Mars and stays
> Love is created, hath a sensate name,
> His modus takes from soul, from heart his will;
> From form seen doth he start, that, understood,
> Taketh in latent intellect—
> As in a subject ready—
>   place and abode,
> Yet in that place it ever is unstill,
> Spreading its rays, it tendeth never down
> By quality, but is its own effect unendingly
> Not to delight, but in an ardour of thought
> That the base likeness of it kindleth not.
>
> It is not virtue, but perfection's source
> Lying within perfection postulate
> Not by the reason, but 'tis felt, I say,
> Beyond salvation, holding its judging force,
> Maintains intention reason's peer and mate;
> Poor in discernment, being thus weakness' friend,
> Often his power meeteth with death in the end

But he withstayed
                    or from true course
                                        betrayed
E'en though he meet not with hate
                                or villeiny
Save that perfection fails, be but a little;
Nor can man say he hath his life by chance
Or that he hath not established seigniory
Or loseth power, e'en lost to memory.

He comes to be and is when will's so great
It twists itself from out all natural measure;
Leisure's adornment puts he then never on,
Never thereafter, but moves changing state,
Moves changing colour, or to laugh or weep
Or wries the face with fear and little stays,
Yea, resteth little
                    yet is found the most
Where folk of worth be host.
And his strange property sets sighs to move
And wills man look into unformèd space
Rousing there thirst
                    that breaketh into flame.
None can imagine love
                    that breaketh into flame.
None can imagine love
                    that knows not love;
Love doth not move, but draweth all to him;
Nor doth he turn
                    for a whim
                                to find delight
Nor to seek out, surely,
                    great knowledge or slight.

                    *   *   *

In quella parte
                    dove sta memoria
Prende suo stato
                    si formato
                                chome

But he withstayed
              or from true course
                             betrayed
E'en though he meet not with hate
                           or villeiny
Save that perfection fails, be but a little;
Nor can man say he hath his life by chance
Or that he hath not established seigniory
Or loseth power, e'en lost to memory.

He comes to be and is when will's so great
It twists itself from out all natural measure;
Leisure's adornment puts he then never on,
Never thereafter, but moves changing state,
Moves changing colour, or to laugh or weep
Or wries the face with fear and little stays,
Yea, resteth little
                  yet is found the most
Where folk of worth be host.
And his strange property sets sighs to move
And wills man look into unformèd space
Rousing there thirst
                  that breaketh into flame.
None can imagine love
                  that breaketh into flame.
None can imagine love
                  that knows not love;
Love doth not move, but draweth all to him;
Nor doth he turn
              for a whim
                         to find delight
Nor to seek out, surely,
                  great knowledge or slight.

                    *   *   *

In quella parte
              dove sta memoria
Prende suo stato
              si formato
                         chome

Diafan dal lume
         d'una schuritade
La qual da Marte
         viene e fà dimora
Elgli é creato
         e a sensato
            nome
D'alma chostume
         di chor volontade
Vien da veduta forma ches s'intende
Che'l prende
         nel possibile intelletto
Chome in subgetto
         locho e dimoranza
E in quella parte mai non a possanza
Perchè da qualitatde non disciende
Risplende
         in sé perpetuale effecto
Non a diletto
         mà consideranza
Perche non pote laire smiglglianza:—
Non é virtute
         ma da questa vene
Perfezione
         ches si pone
            tale
Non razionale
         ma che si sente dicho
Fuor di salute
         giudichar mantene
E l antenzione
         per ragione
            vale
Dicerne male
         in chui é vizio amicho
Di sua virtu seghue ispesso morte
Se forte
         la virtù fosse impedita
La quale aita
         la contrara via

Diafan dal lume
        d'una schuritade
La qual da Marte
        viene e fà dimora
Elgli é creato
        e a sensato
           nome
D'alma chostume
        di chor volontade
Vien da veduta forma ches s'intende
Che'l prende
        nel possibile intelletto
Chome in subgetto
        locho e dimoranza
E in quella parte mai non a possanza
Perchè da qualitatde non disciende
Risplende
        in sé perpetuale effecto
Non a diletto
        mà consideranza
Perche non pote laire smiglglianza:—
Non é virtute
        ma da questa vene
Perfezione
        ches si pone
           tale
Non razionale
        ma che si sente dicho
Fuor di salute
        giudichar mantene
E l antenzione
        per ragione
           vale
Dicerne male
        in chui é vizio amicho
Di sua virtu seghue ispesso morte
Se forte
        la virtù fosse impedita
La quale aita
        la contrara via

Nonche opposito natural sia
Mà quanto che da ben perfett e torte
Per sorte
        non po dir om ch abbi vita
Che stabilita
        non a singnioria
A simil puo valer quant uom l obblia:
Lesser é quando
        lo volere a tanto
Ch oltre misura
        di natura
            torna
Poi non si addorna
        di riposo maj
Move changiando
        cholr riso in pianto
E lla fighura
        con paura
            storna
Pocho soggiorna
        anchor di lui vedraj
Che n gente di valore il piu si trova
La nova
Qualità move a sospirj
E vol ch om mirj
        in un formato locho
Inmaginar nol puo hom che nol prova
E non si mova
        perch'a llui si tirj
E non si aggirj
        per trovarvi giocho
E certamente gran saver nè pocho:[85]

Translating, as it were, the locus of this definition, Apollinaire, before the event of the War, wrote down his *Futurist Manifesto*:[86]

85. "*Donne mi Prega.*"
86. Communiqué par M. Marinetti, *L'Esprit nouveau*, October 1924.

Nonche opposito natural sia
Mà quanto che da ben perfett e torte
Per sorte
                non po dir om ch abbi vita
Che stabilita
                non a singnioria
A simil puo valer quant uom l obblia:
Lesser é quando
                lo volere a tanto
Ch oltre misura
                di natura
                        torna
Poi non si addorna
                di riposo maj
Move changiando
                cholr riso in pianto
E lla fighura
                con paura
                        storna
Pocho soggiorna
                anchor di lui vedraj
Che n gente di valore il piu si trova
La nova
Qualità move a sospirj
E vol ch om mirj
                in un formato locho
Inmaginar nol puo hom che nol prova
E non si mova
                perch'a llui si tirj
E non si aggirj
                per trovarvi giocho
E certamente gran saver nè pocho:[85]

Comme pour traduire la zone définie ici, Apollinaire (c'était avant l'entrée en scène de la guerre), rédigea son manifeste futuriste:[86]

85. *"Donne mi Prega."*
86. Communiqué par M. Marinetti, *L'Esprit nouveau*, October 1924.

L'Antitradition Futuriste
Manifeste-synthèse

ABAS LEPominir Aliminé Sskorsusu
        otalo EIScramir Menigme
ce moteur à toutes tendances impressionisme fauvi-
sme cubisme expressionnisme pathétisme dramatisme orphisme
paroxysme
DYNAMISME PLASTIQUE

MOTS EN LIBERTE

INVENTION DE MOTS

DESTRUCTION
Suppression de la douleur poétique
                des exotismes snobs

	S	de la copie en art	I
	U	des syntaxes déjà condam-	N
	P	nées par l'usage dans	F
	P	toutes les langues	I
	R	de l'adjectif	N
	E	de la ponctuation	I
	S	de l'harmonie typographique	T
	S	des temps et personnes des verbes	I
	I	de l'orchestre	F
	O	de la forme théâtral	
Pas	N	du sublime artiste	
de	D	du vers et de la strophe	
regrets	E	des maisons	
	L'	de la critique et de la	
	H	satire	
	I	de l'intrigue dans les	
	S	récits	
	T	de l'ennui	
	O		
	I		
	R		
	E		

The Futurist Anti-Tradition
Synthesis Manifesto

ABAS LEPominir Aliminé Sskorsusu
    otalo EIScramir Menigme
this motor has all tendencies of impressionism fauvi-
sm cubism expressionnism patheticism dramatism orphism
paroxysm dynamism

PLASTIC DYNAMISM

WORDS IN LIBERTY

INVENTION OF WORDS

DESTRUCTION

Suppression of poetic pain

		of snobbish exoticisms	
	S	of copied art	I
	U	of syntaxes already condem	N
	P	ned by their usage in	F
	P	every language	I
	R	of the adjective	N
	E	of punctuation	I
	S	of typographic harmony	T
	S	of verb tenses and persons	I
	I	of the orchestra	V
	O	of theatrical form	E
No	N	of the sublime artist	
regrets	O	of line and stanza	
	F	of houses	
	H	of criticism and	
	I	satire	
	S	of intrigue in	
	T	narratives	
	O	of boredom	
	R		
	Y		

CONSTRUCTION

1 - *Techniques sans cesse renouvelées ou rhythmes*

                Littérature pure *Mots en*
                liberté Invention de

L   *mots*   L
A   Plastique pure (5 sens)   A
       Création invention prophétie

P   V
U   *Description onomato-*   A
R   *péique*   R
E   Musique totale et *Art*   I
T   *de bruits*   E
E   Mimique universelle   T
             et Art des lumières   E
             Machinisme Tour-
             Eiffel Brooklyn et
Continuité   gratte-ciels
simultanéité   Polyglottisme
en opposition   Civilisation pure
    au   Nomadisme épique
particularisme   exploratorisme urban
   et à la   *Art des Voyages* et des
division   promenades
            Antigrâce
            Frémissements directs
                à grands spectacles
            libres cirques
            music-halls etc

2 - *Intuition vitesse ubiquité*

            Livre ou vie captivée ou phonocinémat-
            ographie ou *Imagination sans fils*
            Trémolisme continu ou onamatopées
            plus inventées qu'imitées
blows   Danse travail ou Choréographie pure
   and   Langage véloce caractéristique
wounds   impressionnant chanté sifflé
            mimé dansé marché couru
            Droit des gens et guerre continuelle
            Féminisme intégral où différenci-
                ation innombrable des sexes

CONSTRUCTION

1 - *Endlessly renewed techniques or rhythms*

Pure literature Words in freedom
Invention of words
Pure plastic (5 senses)
Creation invention prophecy

P   V
U   *Onomato-*   A
R   *poetic description*   R
I   Total music and *Art*   I
T   *of noise*   E
Y   Universal gestures   T
       and Art of lights   Y

Machinism Eiffel
Tower Brooklyn and

Continuity   sky scrapers
simultaneity   Polyglottism
in opposition Pure civilisation
to   Epic nomadism
particularism urban exploratorism
and to   *Art of Travels* and of
division   promenades
Anti-grace
Direct tremblings
at great spectacles
Free circuses
music-halls etc

2 - *Intuition speed ubiquity*

Book or captive life or phonocinemat-
ography or *Imagination without strings*
Continued quaverings or onamatopeas
more invented than imitated
blows   Dance work or pure Choreography
and   Language velocity characteristic
wounds   impressive sung whistled
mimed danced walked run
People's rights and continual war
Integral feminism or innumerable differentiation
of the sexes

Humanité et appel à l'outr'homme
Matière ou *transcendantalisme physique.*
Analogies et Calembours tremplin
lyrique et seul science des langues
calicot Calicut Calcutta tafla
Sophia le Sophi suffisant Uffizi officier
officiel o ficelles Aficionado Dona-Sol Donatello
Donateur donne à tort torpilleur

ou ou ou flute crapaud naissance des peuples apremines

MER. . . . DE. . . .
     aux

Critiques
Pédagogues
Professeurs
Musées
Quattrocentistes
Dixseptièmesièclistes
Ruines
Patines
Historiens
Venise Versaille Pompei
Bruges Oxford Nuremberg
Tolède Bénarès etc
Défenseurs de paysages
Philogogues

Essayistes
Néo et post
Bayreuth et Florence
Montmartre et Muniche
Lexique
Bongoûtismes
Orientalismes
Dandysmes
Spiritualistes
ou réalistes
(sans sentiment
de la réalité
et de l'esprit
Académismes

Les frères siamois D'Annunzio et Rostand
Dante Shakespeare Tolstoi Goethe

Dilettantismes merdoyantes
Eschyle et théâtre d'Orange
Inde Egypte Fiesole et la théosophie
Scientisme
Montaigne Wagner Beethoven Edgar Poe

Humanity and call to the outside man
Matter or *physical transcendentalism*
Analogies and Puns lyrical
springboard and the only science of language
calicot Calicut Calcutta tafla
Sophia the sufficient Sophi Uffizi officer
official o fishel Aficionado Dona-Sol Donatello
Donator do not tour torpor

or or or flute toad birth of apremine peoples

O SHI-T-ON
   the

Critics	Essayists
Pedagogues	*Neo and post*
Professors	Bayreuth and Florence
Museums	Montmartre and Munich
Quattrocentists	Vocabulary
Seventeenthcenturists	Goodtastism
Ruins	Orientalisms
Patinas	Dandyisms
Historians	Spiritualists
Venice Versailles Pompei	or realists
Bruges Oxford Nuremberg	(without feeling
Toledo Benares etc.	for reality
Defenders of countrysides	and the spirit of
Philogogues	Academyisms

The Siamese brothers D'Annunzio and Rostand
Dante Shakespeare Tolstoy Goethe

Shitty dilettantisms
Eschylus and the theatre in Orange
India Egypt Fiesole and theosophy
Scientism
Montaigne Wagner Beethoven Edgar Poe

Walt Whitman et Baudelaire
Rose[87]
aux
Marinetti Picasso Boccioni Apollinaire
Paul Fort Mercereau Max Jacob Carrà
Delaunay Henri Matisse Braque
Depaquit Séverine Severini Derain
Russolo Archipenko Pratella
Balla F. Divoire N. Beaudin
T. Varlet Buzzi Palazzeschi Maquaire
Papini Soffici Folgore Govini
Montfort R. Fry Cavacchioli
D'Alba Altomare Tridon
Metzinger Gleizes Jastrebzoff
Royère Canudo Salmon Castiaux
Laurencin Aurel Agero Léger Valentine
de Saint-Point Delmarle Kandinsky
Stravinsky Herbin A Billy G.
Sauvebois Picabia Marcel Duchamp
B. Cendrars Jouve H. M. Barzun
G. Polti MacOrlan F. Fleuret
Jaudon Mandin R. Dalize
M. Brésil F. Carco Rubiner
Betuda Manzella-Frontini

87. "Je me souviens qu'un matin nous nous promenions avec Toussaint Luca dans le sale quartier piemontais du Carnier, et plus précisément dans la petite portion de ce quartier nommé le Tonkin. Sur la route une troupe de gamins et de gamines entourait Apollonie, une femme de ménage qui, âgée, était encore belle, brune, et bien faite. Les gamins et gamines, qui la connaissaient bien, la voyant passer tous les jours, avaient pris l'habitude de se moquer d'elle et, parce qu'elle était brune et peu soignée, ils l'appelaient *Biffabrenn*, ce qui signifie à peu près breneuse en piemontais. . . . Ils chantaient: 'Madama Biffabrenn, Madama Biffabrenn.' Tout à coup, la femme de ménage, irritée par les cris injurieux des gamins, se retourna avec un geste qui fit reculer la troupe et leur cria le mot de Cambronne. Aussitôt un chœur répondit: "Merda-rosa, merd'ati ros'a mi." C'est de cette scène inoubliable que j'ai tiré plus tard quelques éléments de mon manifeste milanais, *l'Antitradition Futuriste*, qui vient d'être imité avec bonheur par les nouveaux artistes et poètes anglais, dans le premier numéro de leur revue trimestrielle: *Blast*. Written in August 1914, p. 179, *Anecdotiques*.

Walt Whitman and Baudelaire
    Rose[87]
    to
Marinetti Picasso Boccioni Apollinaire
Paul Fort Mercereau Max Jacob Carrà
Delaunay Henri Matisse Braque
Depaquit Séverine Severini Derain
Russolo Archipenko Pratella
Balla F. Divoire N. Beaudin
T. Varlet Buzzi Palazzeschi Maquaire
Papini Soffici Folgore Govini
Montfort R. Fry Cavacchioli
D'alba Altomare Tridon
Metzinger Gleizes Jastrebzoff
Royère Canudo Salmon Castiaux
Laurencin Aurel Agero Léger Valentine
de Saint-Point Delmarle Kandinsky
Stravinsky Herbin A Billy G.
Sauvebois Picabia Marcel Duchamp
B. Cendrars Jouve H. M. Barzun
G. Polti MacOrlan F. Fleuret
Jaudon Mandin R. Dalize
M. Bresil F. Carco Rubiner
Betuda Manzella-Frontini

87. "I remember that one morning we were walking with Toussaint Luca in the dirty Piedmontese quarter of the *Carnier* and more specifically in the small part of this quarter called Tonkin. In the street a group of boys and girls surrounded Apollonie, a cleaning woman who, though old was still beautiful, a well-built brunette. The boys and girls, who knew her well, seeing her go by every day, had taken to teasing her and because she was brown-haired and ill-kempt, calling her *Biffabrenn*, which means basically *breneuse* in Piedmontese. . . . They sang: "Madama Biffabrenn, Madama Biffabrenn." All of a sudden, the cleaning woman, irritated by the children's hurtful cries, turned with a gesture that made the troupe draw back, and cried the word "Cambronne" at them. Right away a chorus answered: "Shitta-Rosa, shit for you and rose for me." It is from this unforgettable scene that I later took several elements of my Milanese manifesto, the *Futurist Antitradition*, which was just recently and happily imitated by the new English artists and poets in the first issue of their trimestral review: *Blast*. Written in August 1914, *Anecdotiques*, 179.

A. Mazza T. Derême Giannat-
tusio Tavolato De Gonzagues-
Frick C. Larronde etc.

Paris le 29 juin 1913 jour
de Grand Prix à 65 mètres
au-dessus du Boul. S.-Germain
Direction Du Mouvement Futuriste
Corso Venezia 61—Milan

Guillaume Apollinaire
(202 Blvd. Saint-Germain, Paris)

A. Mazza T. Derême Giannat-
tusio Tavolato De Gonzagues-
Frick C. Larronde etc.

Paris June 29, 1913 day
of the 65-meter Grand Prix
above the Boulevard Saint-Germain
Direction of the Futurist Movement
Corso Venezia 61—Milan

> Guillaume Apollinaire
> (202 Blvd. Saint-Germain, Paris)

Le Poète ressuscité

"Le ciel presque nocturne a des lueurs d'aiguilles. Langues de feu où sont-elles mes pentecôtes. Pour mes pensées de tous les pays de tous les temps.[1]

"Oi! oi, ce qui signifie 'hélas!' en hébreu.[2]

"L'hébreu? c'est à peine si la plupart d'entre nous le savent lire au moment de la Barmitzva. Nos savants hébraïsants font sourire les rabbins étrangers; et la traduction française qui existe du Talmud est, au dire des juifs allemands ou polonais, un monument de l'ignorance des rabbins de France. Donc, j'ignore la religion juive, elle est abolie comme le paganisme, ou plutôt, non de même que le paganisme, elle survit dans le catholicisme.[3]

"Ottomar Scholem et Abraham Lœweren sont en colère Parce que pendant le sabbat on ne doit pas fumer Tandis que les chrétiens passent avec des cigares allumés Et parce qu'Ottomar et Abraham aiment tous deux Lia aux yeux de brebis et dont le ventre avance un peu Pourtant tout à l'heure dans la synagogue l'un après l'autre Ils baiseront la thora en soulevant leur beau chapeau Parmi les feuillards de la fête des cabanes Ottomar en chantant sourira à Abraham Ils déchanteront sans mesure et les voix graves des hommes feront gémir un Léviathon au fond du Rhin comme une voix d'automne Et la synagogue pleine de chapeaux on agitera les loulabims *Hanoten ne Kamoth bagoim tholahoth baleoumim.*[4]

"Et leurs vers étaient admirables.

"Les repas n'en finissaient pas, et la même serviette servait tour à tour aux quatre poètes, mais on ne le leur disait pas.

"Cette serviette, petit à petit, devint sale.

1. "Palais," *Alcools*.
2. "Le Passant de Prague," *L'Hérésiarque et Cⁱᵉ*.
3. "Le Juif latin," *L'Hérésiarque et Cⁱᵉ*.
4. "La Synagogue," *Alcools*.

The Poet Resurrected

"The sky nearly dark is lit with points of light. Tongues of fire where are my Whit Sundays. For my thoughts of all countries and all times.[1]

"Oy! Oy! which means 'Alas!' in Hebrew.[2]

"Hebrew? Most of us can barely read it by the time we reach our bar mitzvah. Foreign rabbis laugh at our Hebraists; and, according to German or Polish Jews, the French translation of the Talmud is a monument to the ignorance of French rabbis. So, I am ignorant when it comes to Judaism. It has been done away with as completely as paganism. Or no, rather it survives but within Catholicism, just like paganism.[3]

"Ottomar Scholem and Abraham Lœweren are angry because Christians go by with lit cigars on the Sabbath, when smoking is not allowed And because Ottomar and Abraham both love Leah of the sheep's eyes whose stomach sticks out a little But soon, inside the synagogue, one after the other they will raise their lovely hats and kiss the Torah On the feast of sheds Ottomar will smile at Abraham through the branches as he sings They will become endlessly disillusioned and, upon hearing the men's deep voices, a Leviathan at the bottom of the Rhine will sigh with the voice of autumn And in the synagogue filled with hats they will shake the loulabims *Hanoten ne Kamoth bagoim tholahoth baleoumim.*[4]

"And their verses were admirable.

"The meals were never-ending and one by one each of the four poets used the same napkin but no one told them this.

"Little by little, the napkin became dirty.

1. "Palais," *Alcools.*

2. "Le Passant de Prague," *L'Hérésiarque et Cie.*

3. "Le Juif latin," *L'Hérésiarque et Cie.*

4. "La Synagogue," *Alcools.*

"Voici du jaune d'œuf près d'une traînée sombre d'épinards. Voilà des ronds de bouches vineuses et cinq marques grises laissées par les doigts d'une main au repos. Une arête de poisson a percé la trame du lin comme une lance. Un grain de riz séché, collé dans un angle. Et de la cendre de tabac assombrit certaines parties plus que les autres.

"Et des saisons passèrent.

"Les poètes se servaient tour à tour de la serviette et leurs poèmes étaient admirables.

"Léonard Délaisé crachait sa vie plus comiquement encore, et David Picard se mit aussi à cracher.

"La serviette vénéneuse infesta tour à tour, après David, Georges Oastréole et Jaime Saint-Félix, mais ils ne le savaient pas.

"Semblable à une loque ignoble d'hôpital, la serviette se tacha du sang qui venait aux lèvres des quatre poètes, et les dîners n'en finissaient pas.

"Au commencement de l'automne, Léonard Délaissé cracha le reste de sa vie.

"Dans différents hôpitaux, sécoués par la toux comme des femmes par la volupté, les trois autres poètes moururent à peu de jours d'intervalle. Et tous les quatre laissaient des poèmes si beaux qu'ils semblaient enchantés.

"Les convives morts, la serviette devint inutile.

"L'amie de Justin Prérogue voulut la mettre au sale.

"Et elle la déplia en pensant: 'Elle est vraiment trop sale et elle commence à sentir mauvais.'

"Mais la serviette dépliée, l'amie de Justin Prérogue eut un étonnement et appela son ami qui s'émerveilla:

"C'est un vrai miracle! Cette serviette si sale, que tu étales avec complaisance, présente, grâce à la saleté coagulée et de diverses couleurs, les traits de notre ami défunt, David Picard.

"Tous deux, en silence, regardèrent quelques instants l'image miraculeuse et puis, doucement, firent tourner la serviette.

"Mais ils pâlirent aussitôt en voyant apparaître l'épouvantable aspect à mourir de rire de Léonard Délaissé s'efforçant de cracher.

"Et les quatre côtés de la serviette offraient le même prodige.

"Justin Prérogue et son amie tournèrent longtemps comme des astres autour de leur soleil, et cette Sainte Véronique, de son quadruple regard, leur enjoignait de fuir sur la limite de l'art aux confins de la vie.[5]

"Justin Prérogue et son amie virent Georges Oastréole indécis et Jaime Saint-Félix sur le point de raconter une histoire.

5. "La Serviette des poètes," *L'Hérésiarque.*

"Here a bit of egg yolk near a dark streak of spinach. Here the rings of wine-stained mouths and five gray marks left by the fingers of a resting hand. A fishbone has pierced the weave of the linen like a lance. A grain of dried rice stuck at an angle. And tobacco ash darkens certain parts more than others.

"And seasons passed.

"One by one the poets used the napkin and their poems were admirable.

"Léonard Délaissé spit his life even more comically and David Picard began to spit too.

"The poisonous napkin infected them one by one, after David, Georges Oastréole and Jaime Saint-Félix, but they did not know this.

"Like a vile hospital rag, the napkin was stained with the blood of the four poets' lips, and the dinners were never ending.

"At the beginning of autumn, Léonard Délaissé spat out what remained of his life.

"Shaken with coughing like voluptuous women, the three remaining poets died in different hospitals, all within a few days of each other. And all four left poems so beautiful that they seemed enchanted.

"With the guests dead, the napkin was useless.

"Justin Prérogue's girlfriend wanted to put it with the dirty linen.

"And she unfolded it, thinking, 'Really, it's so dirty it's starting to smell.'

"But Justin Prérogue's girlfriend had a shock when she unfolded the napkin and she called her boyfriend, who was filled with wonder:

"It's a real miracle! In the congealed, multicolored dirt of this filthy napkin you've so complacently unfolded, there's a portrait of our late friend, David Picard.

"Both looked silently at the miraculous image for several moments and then, gently, turned the napkin over.

"But they grew pale as soon as they did so, seeing the appalling image of Léonard Délaissé doing his best to spit as he choked with laughter.

"And they found the same wonder on all four sides of the napkin.

"Justin Prérogue and his girlfriend turned around it for a long time like stars around their sun, and this Saint Veronica of the quadruple gaze enjoined them to flee to the furthermost bounds of life on the frontier of art.[5]

"Justin Prérogue and his girlfriend saw Georges Oastréole undecided and Jaime Saint-Félix on the verge of telling a story.

5. "La Serviette des poètes," *L'Hérésiarque.*

"Laisse cette serviette, dit brusquement Justin Prérogue.

"Le linge tomba et s'étala sur le plancher.

"Que Vlo-ve? c'est à dire: *Que voulez-vous?*

"La guitare de Que Vlo-ve? était un peu du vent qui gémit toujours dans les Ardennes de Belgique . . .

"Que Vlo-ve? était la divinité de cette forêt où erra Geneviève de Brabant, depuis les bords de la Meuse jusqu'au Rhin, par l'Eiffel volcanique aux mers mortes que sont les mares de Daun, l'Eiffel où jaillit la source de Saint Apollinaire, et où le lac de Maria Laach est un crachat de la Vierge . . .

"Les yeux de Que Vlo-ve, clignotants et chassieux, à chaire des paupières rouges de jambon cru, larmoyaient sans cesse et les larmes lui brûlaient les lèvres comme l'eau des fontaines acides qui abondent dans les Ardennes.

"Il était le compère des sangliers, le cousin des lièvres, des écureuils, et la vie secouait son âme comme le vent d'est secoue les grappes orangées aux sorbiers des oiseaux . . .

"Que Vlo-ve? wallon, wallonant de Wallonie.

"Que Vlo-ve? Préférait son sobriquet à son nom: Poppon Remach Lehez. Mais si on le saluait de son surnom: *Li bai valet* (le beau garçon), il faisait résonner l'âme de sa guitare et tapait sur le ventre de son interlocuteur en disant:

"Il sonne creux comme ma guitare, il jase la soif, il n'a plus de *péket* à pisser.

"On se prenait par le bras et sans se tutoyer, car on ne se tutoye jamais en wallon, on allait, nom de Dieu! boire du *péket* qui est de la plus vulgaire eau-de-vie de grains, à laquelle, en parlant français, on donne par euphémisme le nom de genièvre.

"Et c'eût été bien extraordinaire que dans un coin de l'auberge on ne découvrit pas Guyame le poète, qui avait le don d'ubiquité, car on le voyait chez tous les débitants de bière et de *péket*, entre Stavelot et Malmedy. Et combien de fois était-il arrivé que des gars s'étaient battus, parce que l'un disait:

"J'ai bu hier avec Guyame à la *Station*, il était telle heure.

"Menteur, disait un autre, à la même heure, Guyame était avec nous à l'estaminet du *Bonnet à poil*, et il y avait là le *percepteur des postes et receveur des contributions*.

"Et, de fil en aiguille, les gars finissaient par se flanquer des beignes en l'honneur du poète.

"Don't touch that napkin, Justin Prérogue said brusquely.

"The clothe fell and spread out on the floor.

"Whadda ya wan'? that is to say, *What do you want?*"

"Whadda ya wan'?'s guitar was a bit of the sighing wind of the Belgian Ardennes . . .

"Whadda ya wan'? was the divinity of this forest where Geneviève de Brabant wandered from the edge of the Meuse to the Rhine, past the volcanic Eiffel to the dead seas' pools of Daun, the Eiffel, where Saint Apollinaire's fountain gushes, and where the lake of Maria Laach is the Virgin's spittle . . .

"Whadda ya wan'?'s eyes, blinking and hunted, the flesh of the lids as red as raw ham, teared continuously and the tears burned his lips like water from the acid fountains that abound in the Ardennes.

"Wild boars were his comrades, his cousins, hares and squirrels, and life shook his soul like the east wind shook the orangey grapes in the birds' sorbiers . . .

"Que Vlo-ve wallon, wallonning from Wallonie.

"Whadda ya wan'? preferred his sobriquet to his name: Poppon Remach Lehez. But if he was called by his surname: *Li bai valet* (the handsome lad), he would make his guitar's soul hum and tap on his interlocutor's stomach and say:

"It sounds hollow like my guitar, it prattles with thirst, there is no more *péket* to piss.

"Arm in arm, though never calling each other *tu*, because no one ever calls anyone *tu* in Wallon, they would go, 'zounds! to drink *péket*, that crudest of grain liquors, euphemistically called geneva gin in French.

"And it was quite extraordinary if Guyame the poet was not to be found in some corner of the inn. His was the gift of ubiquity, for he was seen at all of the beer and *péket* merchants between Stavelot and Malmedy. And how many times had the guys come to blows because one of them said:

"I drank with Guyame at the *Station* yesterday, at such and such a time.

"Liar, another would say, Guyame was with us at the *Naked Hat* tavern then, along with the *postal tax collector and the receiver of contributions.*

"And, one thing leading to another, the guys would end up clinking their glasses in honor of the poet.

"Guyame était phtisique et logeait à l'hospice, à Stavelot. Comme on lui donnait partout à boire gratis, Guyame allait boire partout. Et, dès qu'il avait bu, il en contait des contes bleus, des histoires de brigands, de l'autre monde ou à dormir debout! Il en déclamait des vers contre la famille protestante de la place de l'Eglise, contre le bossu du Francorchamps, et contre la fille rousse des Trois-Ponts, qui allait toujours en automne ramasser les champignons! Pouah! les champignons donnent la crève aux vaches, et elle en bouffait, la rousotte, sans mourir! Ah! la sorcière! . . . Mais il chante aussi la gloire des airelles, des myrtilles et le bien que font aux tripes humaines du lait et des myrtilles, c'est à dire le *tchatcha* archidivin, ambrosiaque. Il faisait souvent des vers pour les servantes qui pèlent les *krompires*, les bonnes pommes de terre, les *magna bona* . . . [6]

> Vous y dansiez petite fille
> Y danserez vous mère-grand
> C'est la maclotte qui sautille
>   Toutes les cloches sonneront
> Quand donc reviendrez-vous, Marie
> Sais-je où s'en iront tes cheveux
> Crépus comme mer qui moutonne
> Sais-je où s'en iront tes cheveux
> Et tes mains feuilles de l'automne
> Que jonchent aussi nos aveux.[7]

> Passent les jours et passent les semaines
>   Ni temps passé
>   Ni les amours reviennent
> Sous le pont Mirabeau coule la Seine.

> Vienne la nuit sonne l'heure
> Les jours s'en vont je demeure.[8]

"J'entendis très bien mes deux poèmes, mais j'ignore si les auditeurs les ont compris aussi bien que moi.

6. "Que Vlo-ve?" *L'Hérésiarque.*
7. "Marie," *Alcools.*
8. "Le Pont Mirabeau," *Alcools.*

"Guyame was consumptive and stayed at the hospice in Stavelot. Since he drank for free everywhere he went, Guyame drank everywhere. And, as soon as he had drunk, he would tell sexy stories, stories of brigands, of the other world or of sleeping standing up! He declaimed verses against the Protestant family on the church square, against the hunchback of Francorchamps, and against the redheaded girl of Three-Bridges, who always collected mushrooms in the fall! Ugh! Mushrooms kill cows, and that carrot top would eat them and live! Ah! The witch! . . . But he also sang the glory of bilberries, of blueberries and the benefits of milk and blueberries to human guts, that is to say the super-divine, ambrosius *cha cha*. He often wrote verses for the servants who peeled *krompires*, good potatoes, the *magna bona*. . . . [6]

> There you danced as a little girl
> A grandmother there you shall dance
> Today it's the maclotte that twirls
>   Every clock shall sound its chants
> Marie when will you return
> Do I know where your hair will blow
> Woolly like the whitening seas
> Do I know where your hair will blow
> And your hands foliage of autumn
> That our promises scatter so[7].
>
> Days pass and weeks go by
>   Past loves
>   Past times won't come again
> Under Mirabeau Bridge flows the Seine.
>
> Night comes I hear the hour toll
> Days go by I remain.[8]

"My two poems were quite clear to me but I do not know if my listeners understood them as well as I did.

6. "Que Vlo-ve?" *L'Hérésiarque*.
7. "Marie," *Alcools*.
8. "Le Pont Mirabeau," *Alcools*.

"Après l'enregistrement, on fit redire mes poèmes à l'appareil et je ne reconnus nullement ma voix.[9]

"Essaye de l'attraper, toi qui as été Parisien.[10]

> Ecoutez, moi je suis le gosier de Paris
> Et je boirai encore s'il me plaît, l'univers
>
> Ecoute mes chants d'universelle ivrognerie
>
> Et la nuit de septembre s'achevait lentement
> Les feux rouges des ponts s'éteignaient dans la Seine
> Les étoiles mouraient le jour naissait à peine.[11]

"Il faut maintenant prendre son courage à deux mains, car voici l'instant difficile. Il s'agit de dire la gloire et la beauté du gueux déguenillé Que Vlo-ve? et du poète Guillaume Wirin, dont les guenilles couvraient aussi un bon gueux gueusant. Allons d'ahan! . . . Apollon! mon Patron, tu t'essouffles, va-t-en! Fais venir cet autre, Hermès le voleur, digne plus que toi de chanter la mort du Wallon Que Vlo-ve? sur laquelle se lamentent tous les elfes de l'Amblève. Qu'il vienne, voleur subtil, aux pieds ailés.

"Hermès, dieu de la lyre et voleur de troupeaux, qu'il jette sur Que Vlo-ve? et sur la Chanceresse toutes les mouches ganiques que l'on croit, au nord, tourmentes certaines vies comme une fatalité. Qu'il amène avec soi mon second Patron, en mitre et pluvial, l'évêque saint Apollinaire. Ce dernier voilera le calvaire de bois peint qui patit au carrefour.

"Guyame se leva et alla pisser à la porte. En revenant il dit:

"Je voudrais être dans les fagnes derrière la baraque Michel, je serais assis dans les bruyères et les airelles, et plus heureux que saint Remacle en sa chasse, *nom de Dio!* Il y en a-t-il des boules d'or au ciel clair de ce soir *nom de Dio di nom di Dio*, le ciel est plein de couilles lumineuses qu'on appelle astres, planètes, étoiles, lunes.

"*V'n'en savez nin comme ça, vous qu'avez* trois couilles. Il en faut plus que ça pour atteindre le quorum et ressembler au ciel, allons, un peu de guitare, là, *nom di Dio!* . . . Que Vlo-ve?

9. *Anecdotiques*, page 174.

10. "Que-Vlo-ve?" *L'Hérésiarque.*

11. "Vendémiaire," *Alcools.*

"After the recording, they replayed them on the machine and I did not recognize my voice at all.[9]

"Try to catch it, you who were once a Parisian.[10]

> Listen, I am the throat of Paris
> And if I please I'll drink, the universe
>
> Listen to my songs of universal drunkenness
>
> And the September night slowly drew to a close
> The bridges' red lights disappeared in the Seine
> The stars were dying the day had barely risen[11]

"Now we must take our courage in both hands, for this is the difficult moment. We must speak of the glory and the beauty of the ragged beggar Whadda ya wan'? and of the poet Guillaume Wirin, whose rags also covered a right-begging beggar. Let's go forth! Apollo! My Patron, you're out of breath, go on! Send that other one, Hermes, the thief, more worthy than you are to haunt the death of the Wallon Whadda ya wan'? for whom all of the elves of the Amblève lament. Let him come, subtle thief on winged feet.

"Hermes, god of the lyre and thief of the flock, that he might cast a spell on Whadda ya wan'? and on Lady Luck, as powerful as one of those plagues of flies that, in the north, are said to torment certain lives like fate. That he might bring my second Patron, with his miter and his pluvial, Bishop Saint Apollinaire. He will be the one to veil the painted wooden calvary to raise the suffering Christ at the crossroads.

"Guyame rose and went to piss out doors. Coming back he said:

"I would like to be in the marshes behind Michel's place, I would sit among the heather and bilberries, and be happier than Saint Remacle on a hunt, *'zounds*! There are golden balls in the clear sky tonight! *'zounds 'zounds 'zounds*! the sky is full of luminous balls that we call stars, planets, meteors, moons.

"*You don't know nothing, you with* three balls. You need more than that to reach a quorum and get yourself to heaven, alright, a little guitar there, *'zounds*! . . . whadda ya wan'?

9. *Anecdotiques*, page 174.

10. "Que Vlo-ve?" *L'Hérésiarque*.

11. "Vendémiaire," *Alcools*.

Nost' ogne avi li quat pis blancs
Et les creges à l'advinant.

Et l'trou di cou tot neur
Tot neur comme du tcherbon

"Tisez-vous! dit le *babo*, je veux aller schlof avec la Chancesse.

"*Nom di Dio!* cria Que Vlo-ve? vous le *babo*, vous n'avez même pas de censes pour payer votre *péket,* vous irez schlôf à *Mâmdi* ou à *Stavleu.* Allons, vite! Vous allez boire un *vêre sol* hawai. Faites claquer vosse lainwe, et puis allez-vous en!

"Le babo but le verre de *péket,* fit claquer sa langue, puis:

"Venez un peu, Que Vlo-ve? Je veux v'grusiner *one saquoué.*

"Que Vlo-ve? fit sa question:

"Que Vlo-ve?

"Puis il prit son couteau et jeta sa guitare sur les lombes.

"Ensuite il s'approche du babo.

"Guyame divaguait:

"De jolies petites vieilles dansent la maclotte dans un jardin de tournesols; les beaux soleils! Que Vlo-ve? m'*coye binamège*, ne vous battez pas. Le babo vous étranglera come la rampioule étrangle les arbres . . .

"Le babo râlait doucement:

"*Nom di Dio! Nom di Dio! Nom di Dio!*

"Ses yeux se renversèrent. Que Vlo-ve? se redressa en tenant la main du babo. De son couteau il se mit à couper le bras à la jointure. Le babo cria:

"Aïe! Aïe! *vo direz à ma Mareye* que je lui envoie *un betch* d'amour.

"Que Vlo-ve continuait à couper . . .

"*N'jassez nin* comme ça, dit la Chanceresse, j'v's'ainme bai valet.

"Elle s'approcha de Que Vlo-ve? Le cadavre les séparait. Ils s'embrassèrent. Mais le bras du mort étant remonté dans la pochette droit et pareil à une tige fleurie de cinq pétales, se trouva entre eux.

"Dans la triste lumière ils embrassèrent la main morte.

"La Chanceresse sur la porte cria longtemps:

"Que Vlo-ve? *li bai valet!* Que Vlo-ve? Que Vlo-ve?"

Our cow has four white udders
And she has two white ears.

But her asshole is so black
As black as a lump of coal

"Shut up! said the *babo*, I want to go schlof with Lady Luck.

"'*Zounds*! cried Whadda ya wan'? you *babo*, you don't even have any money to pay for your *péket* and yet you'll go schlof at Mamdi or at Stavleu. All right, quickly! You'll drink a glass of hawaii, click your tongue and out with you!

"The babo drank the glass of *péket*, clicked his tongue, then:

"Come here a minute, Whadda ya wan'? I want to shake you up a bit.

"Whadda ya wan'? asked his question:

"Whadda ya wan'?

"Then he took his knife and swung his guitar up onto his hip.

"Then he approached the babo.

"Guyame babbled:

"The pretty little old ladies dance the *maclotte* in a sunflower garden, the lovely suns! Whadda ya wan'? *m'coye binamège* don't fight. The babo will strangle you like a vine strangles a tree. . . .

"The babo groaned softly.

"'*Zounds*! '*Zounds*! '*Zounds*!

"His eyes rolled back in his head. Whadda ya wan'? raised himself up clutching the babo's hand. With his knife he began to cut his arm at the joint. The babo cried:

"Ow! Ow! Tell my Mareye that I send her a loving kiss.

"Whadda ya wan'? kept cutting . . .

"Don't talk like that, said Lady Luck, I love yuh, handsome lad.

"She approached Whadda ya wan'? The corpse lay between them. They kissed. But the dead man's arm, having come straight out of his breast pocket like a stem flowered with five petals, stood between them.

"In the sad light they kissed the dead hand.

"At the door, Lady Luck cried for a long time:

"Whadda ya wan'? Handsome lad! Whadda ya wan? Whadda ya wan'?"

"Mais Que Vlo-ve? marchait maintenant sur la route. Il prit sa guitare et gratta son chant de mort. En marchant et jouant, il regardait les étoiles habituelles, dont les lueurs versicolores palpitaient. Il songea:

"Je les connais toutes de vue, mais *nom di Dio!* Je vais subitement les connaître chacune en particulier, *nom di Dio!*[12]

Sirènes j'ai rampé vers vos
Grottes tiriez aux mers la langue
En dansant devant leurs chevaux
Puis battiez de vos ailes d'anges
Et j'écoutais ces chœurs rivaux

Une arme o ma tête inquiète
J'agite un feuillard défleuri
Pour écarter l'haleine tiède
Qu'exhalent contre mes grands cris
Vos terribles bouches muettes

Il y a là-bas la merveille
Au prix d'elle que valez-vous
Le sang jaillit de mes otelles
A mon aspect et je l'avoue
Le meurtre de mon double orgueil

Si les bateliers ont ramé
Loin des lèvres à fleurs de l'onde
Mille et mille animaux charmés
Flairant la route à la rencontre
De mes blessures bien-aimées

Leurs yeux étoiles bestiales
Eclairent ma compassion
Qu'importe ma sagesse égale
Celle des constellations
Car c'est moi seul nuit qui t'étoile

12. "Que Vlo-ve?" *L'Hérésiarque.*

"But Whadda ya wan'? was now walking down the road. He took his guitar and strummed his song of death. Walking and playing, he looked at those same stars as they pulsed with multicolored gleamings. He dreamed:

"I know them all by sight, but *'zounds*! soon I'll see each one up close, *'zounds*![12]

Sirens I slithered up to your caves
You stuck out your tongues at the seas
And dancing in front of their horses
You beat your angelic wings
And I listened to the battling choruses

A gun oh my troubled head
I wave a branch stripped of flowers
To disperse the lukewarm breath
That your terrible mute mouths
Exhale against my great cries

There are marvels ahead
What good are you next to them
Blood gushes from my deep wounds
Seeing me and I confess
The murder of my double pride

If the ferrymen have rowed
Far from lips with waves' flowers
Thousands and thousands of spell-bound beasts
Sniff out a path to the meeting
Of my beloved wounds

Their eyes bestial stars
Shed light on my compassion
What matter that my wisdom matches
The wisdom of constellations
For I am night sprinkling you with stars

12. "Que Vlo-ve?" *L'Hérésiarque.*

Sirènes enfin je descends
Dans une grotte avide J'aime
Vos yeux Les degrés sont glissants
Au loin que vous devenez naines
N'attirez plus aucun passant

Dans l'attentive et bien-apprise
J'ai vu feuilloler nos forêts
Mer le soleil se gargarise
Où les matelots désiraient
Que vergues et mats reverdissent

Je descends et le firmament
S'est changé très vite en méduse
Puisque je flambe atrocement
Que mes bras seuls sont les excuses
Et les torches de mon tourment

Oiseaux tiriez aux mers la langue
Le soleil d'hier m'a rejoint
Les otelles nous ensanglantent
Dans le nid des Sirènes loin
Du troupeau d'étoiles oblongues[13]

"Or, l'Amblève était proche et coulait froide, entre les aunes qui l'emmantellent. Les elfes faisaient craquer leurs petits souliers de verres sur les perles qui couvrent le lit de la rivière. Le vent perpétuait maintenant les sons tristes de la guitare. Les voix des Elfes traversaient l'eau, et Que Vlo-ve? du bord les entendait jaser:

"Mnieu, mnieu, mnieu.

"Puis il descendit dans la rivière, et, comme elle était froide, il eut peur de mourir. Heureusement les voix des Elfes se rapprochaient:

"Mnié, mnié, mnié.

"Puis, *nom di Dio!* dans la rivière il oublia brusquement tout ce qu'il savait, et connut que l'Amblève communique souterrainement avec le Lethé, puisque ses eaux font perdre connaissance. *Nom di Dio!* Mais les elfes jasaient si joliment maintenant, de plus en plus près:

"Mnié, mnié, mnié . . .

13. "Lul de Faltenin," *Alcools*.

Sirens at last I descend
Into an avid cave I love
Your eyes The descent is slippery
You are dwarfed in the distance
No longer tempting passersby

While careful and well-learned
I saw our forests stripped of leaves
Sea, the gargling sun
Where sailors would wish
For sails and masts to green again

I descend and the firmament
Quickly changed into a medusa
As I am horribly burning
My arms the only excuses
And the torches of my torment

Birds stick out your tongues at the seas
Yesterday's sun has come back to me
The wounds have soaked us with blood
In the nest of Sirens
Far from the herd of oblong stars[13]

"Yet, the Amblève was close and flowed cold between the alders that enveloped it. The elves clicked their little glass slippers on the pearls that covered the riverbed. The wind now followed up the sad sounds of the guitar. The Elves' voices crossed the water, and on the bank, and Whadda ya wan'? heard them chattering:

"Mee, mee, mee.

"Then he climbed into the river, and, as it was cold, he was afraid of dying. Happily the Elves' voices were getting closer:

"Meep, meep, meep.

"Then, *'zounds!* in the river he suddenly forgot all that he knew, and understood all at once that underground the Amblève met Lethe, with its watery amnesia. *'Zounds!* But the Elves chattered so prettily now, closer and closer:

"Meep, meep, meep . . .

13. "Lul de Faltenin," *Alcools.*

"Et partout, à la ronde, les Elfes des *pouhons*, ou *fontaines* qui bouillonnent dans la forêt, leur répondaient . . . [14]

"La gaucherie, émerveillée et minutieuse, de l'art primitif qui règne ici a de quoi toucher ceux mêmes qui n'ont pas la foi. Il y a là des tableaux de tous genres, le portrait seul n'y a point de place.[15]

"C'est le beau lys que tous nous cultivons C'est la torche aux cheveux roux que n'éteint pas le vent C'est le fils pâle et vermeil de la douloureuse mère C'est l'arbre toujours touffu de toutes les prières C'est la double potence de l'honneur et de l'éternité C'est l'étoile à six branches C'est le Christ qui monte au ciel mieux que les aviateurs Il detient le record du monde pour la hauteur Pupille Christ de l'œil Vingtième pupille des siècles il sait y faire Et changé en oiseau ce siècle comme Jésus monte dans l'air.[16]

"Notre histoire est noble et tragique.[17]

"Tu regardes les yeux pleins de larmes ces pauvres émigrants Ils croient en Dieu ils prient les femmes allaitent des enfants Ils emplissent de leur odeur le hall de la gare Saint-Lazare Ils ont foi dans leur étoile comme les roi-mages Ils espèrent gagner de l'argent dans l'Argentine Et revenir dans leur pays après avoir fait fortune Une famille transporte un édredon rouge comme vous transportez votre cœur Cet édredon et nos rêves sont aussi irréels Quelques-uns de ces émigrants restent ici et se logent rue des Rosiers ou rue des Ecouffes dans des bouges Je les ai vus souvent le soir ils prennent l'air dans la rue Et se déplacent rarement comme les pièces aux échecs Il y a surtout des Juifs leurs femmes portent perruque Elles restent assises exsangues au fond des boutiques

"A la fin tu es lasse de ce monde ancien, Bergère ô tour Eiffel le troupeau des ponts bêle ce matin Tu en as assez de vivre dans l'antiquité grecque et romaine Ici même les automobiles ont l'air d'être anciennes La religion seule est restée toute neuve la religion Est restée simple comme les hangars de Port-Aviation Seul en Europe tu n'es pas antique ô Christianisme L'Européen le plus moderne c'est vous Pape Pie X Et toi que les fenêtres observent la honte te retient D'entrer dans une église et de t'y confesser ce matin Tu lis les prospectus les catalogues les affiches qui

14. "Que Vlo-ve?" *L'Hérésiarque & Cⁱᵉ*.

15. "Les Pèlerins piémontais," *L'Hérésiarque*.

16. "Zone," *Alcools*.

17. "Cors de chasse," *Alcools*.

"And all around in a circle, the *pouhons* Elves, or *fountains* that bubble in the forest, answered them . . . [14]

"The clumsiness, filled with wonder and meticulous, of the primitive art that reigns here has something that touches precisely those who do not have faith. Here there are paintings of all types, with only the portrait missing.[15]

"It is the lovely lily that all of us cultivate It is the redheaded torch that the wind cannot extinguish It is the pale and ruddy son of the sorrowful mother It is the tree forever thick with prayers It is the double gallows of honor and eternity It is the six-pointed star It is Christ who rises into the sky better than aviators He holds the world record for height Pupil Christ of the eye Twentieth pupil of centuries he knows what to do there And changed into a bird this century rises like Jesus into the air.[16]

"Our history is noble and tragic.[17]

"You look tearfully at these poor immigrants They believe in God they pray their wives nurse babies They fill the Gare Saint-Lazare with their smell Like the wise men they have faith in their star They hope to earn money in Argentina And back to their country when they've made their fortune A family carries a red eiderdown like you carry your heart This eiderdown and our dreams are equally unreal Some of these immigrants live here in misery on the rue des Rosiers or rue des Ecouffes I've often seen them at night they take the air in the street and seldom move like chess pieces Most of them are Jews their wives wear wigs They sit anaemically in the back rooms of shops

"In the end you are tired of this ancient world, Shepherdess oh Eiffel Tower the flock of bridges bleats this morning You have had enough of living in Greek and Roman antiquity Here even automobiles look ancient Only religion has stayed brand new religion Has stayed simple like airport hangars In all of Europe only you are not antiquated oh Christianity You are the most modern of Europeans Pope Pius X And you are watched by the windows shame holds you back From going into a church and confessing this morning You read the ads the catalogues the

14. "Que Vlo-ve?" *L'Hérésiarque et C*[ie].

15. "Les Pèlerins Piémontais," *L'Hérésiarque.*

16. "Zone," *Alcools.*

17. "Cors de chasse," *Alcools.*

chantent tout haut Voilà la poésie ce matin et pour la prose il y a les
journaux Il y a les livraisons à 25 centimes pleines d'aventures policières
Portraits des grands hommes et mille titres divers.[18]

> ces vieilles photographies
> Te souviens-tu du jour où une abeille tomba dans le feu.[19]

"Des enfants De ce monde ou bien de l'autre chantaient de ces rondes
Aux paroles absurdes et lyriques Qui sans doute Sont les restes Des plus
anciens monuments poétiques De l'humanité.

"Et la terre plate à l'infini Comme avant Galilée Se couvrit de mille
mythologies immobiles Un ange en diamant brisa toutes les vitrines Et
les mortes m'accostèrent Avec des mines de l'autre monde.

"Car y a-t-il rien qui vous élève Comme d'avoir aimé un mort ou une
morte On devient si pur qu'on en arrive Dans la glacière de la mémoire
A se confondre avec le souvenir On est fortifié pour la vie et l'on n'a plus
besoin de personne.[20]

"Voleur connais-tu mieux les lois malgré les hommes[21]

> Réjouissons-nous non parce que notre amitié à
> été le fleuve qui nous a fertilisés
> Terrains riverains dont l'abondance est la nourriture
> que tous espèrent
> Ni parce que nos verres nous jettent encore une fois
> le regard d'Orphée mourant
> Ni parce que nous avons tant grandi que beaucoup
> pourraient confondre nos yeux et les étoiles
> Ni parce que les drapeaux claquent aux fenêtres
> des citoyens qui sont contents depuis cent ans
> d'avoir la vie et de menues choses à défendre
> Ni parce que fondés en poésie nous avons des es droits
> sur les paroles qui forment et défont l'Univers
> Ni parce que nous pouvons pleurer sans ridicule et
> que nous savons rire

18. "Zone," *Alcools.*

19. "Le Voyageur," *Alcools.*

20. "La Maison des morts," *Alcools.*

21. "Le Larron," *Alcools.*

posters that sing out loud This is poetry this morning as for prose there
are newspapers They deliver detective stories for 25 centimes Portraits
of great men and one thousand different titles.[18]

> these old photographs
> Do you remember the day a bee fell into the fire.[19]

"Children Of this world or the other Sang in rounds Those absurd
and lyrical verses That are certainly The remains of humanity's most
Ancient poetic monuments.

"And the earth was infinitely flat Like before Galileo Covered itself with a thousand motionless mythologies A diamond angel broke all
the shop windows And the dead women accosted me With their other-
worldly looks.

"For nothing raises you up Like having loved the dead man or
women You become so pure that you come to The ice-box of memory
Getting lost recalling You grow strong for life And you no longer need
anyone.[20]

"Thief do you know the laws better in spite of men[21]

> Let us rejoice not because our friendship
>   is the river that has given us life
> The soils the banks whose abundance has been the food
>   that all men desire
> Nor because our glasses once more throw back
>   the gaze of a dying Orpheus
> Nor because we have grown so tall
>   that our eyes might be mistaken for stars
> Nor because flags smack at the windows
>   of citizens who for a 100 years have been happy
>   with a life and a few trifles to defend
> Nor because standing as we do on poetry we have a share
>   in the language that makes and breaks the Universe
> Nor because we can cry without shame
>   nor because we know how to laugh

18. "Zone," *Alcools*.
19. "Le Voyageur," *Alcools*.
20. "La Maison des morts," *Alcools*.
21. "Le Larron," *Alcools*.

Ni parce que nous fumons et buvons comme autrefois
Réjouissons-nous parce que directeurs du jeu et des poètes
L'amour qui emplit ainsi que la lumière
Tout le solide espace entre les étoiles et les planètes
L'amour veut qu'aujourd'hui mon ami André Salmon
    se marie[22]

"J'ai toujours aimé particulièrement les beaux bras. Il est des gens qui attachent une grande importance à la perfection du pied. J'avoue qu'elle me touche, mais le bras est à mon avis ce que la femme doit avoir de plus parfait. Il agit toujours, on l'a constamment sous les yeux. On pourrait dire qu'il est l'organe des grâces et que par ses mouvements adroits, il est l'arme véritable de l'Amour, alors que, recourbé, ce bras délicat imite un arc dont, étendu, il figure la flèche.[23]

"J'ai eu le courage de regarder en arrière Les cadavres de mes jours Marquent ma route et je les pleure Les uns pourrissent dans les églises italiennes Ou bien dans de petits bois de citronniers Qui fleurissent et fructifient En même temps et en toute saison D'autres jours ont pleuré avant de mourir dans des tavernes Ou d'ardents bouquets rouaient Aux yeux d'une mûlatresse qui inventait la poésie Et les roses de l'électricité s'ouvrent encore Dans le jardin de ma mémoire.[24]

Juin ton soleil ardente lyre
Brûle mes doigts endoloris
Triste et mélodieux délire
J'erre à travers mon beau Paris
Sans avoir le cœur d'y mourir

Les dimanches s'y éternisent
Et les orgues de Barbarie
Y sanglotent dans les cours grises
Les fleurs aux balcons de Paris
Penchent comme la tour de Pise

22. "Poème lu au mariage d'André Salmon," *Alcools*.

23. *Le Poète assassiné*, Paris, Au Sans Pareil, 1927 (first published by l'Edition, 1916).

24. "Les Fiançailles," *Alcools*.

Nor because we smoke and drink as we always have
Let us rejoice because Love director of fire and of poets
Not only fills like light
All the solid space between stars and planets
But Love desires that today my friend André Salmon
      should marry[22]

"I've always had a particular love for beautiful arms. There are those who attach great importance to the perfection of a foot. I admit that this affects me but in my opinion it is the arm which should be most perfect on a woman. Always in motion, we have it constantly before our eyes. One could say that it is the organ of the Graces and that with its deft movements, it is the true weapon of Love, as when bent, this delicate arm forms an arc and, when extended, makes an arrow.[23]

"I had the courage to look back The corpses of my days Mark my way and I weep for them Some rot in Italian churches Or even in little forests of lemon trees That bloom and bear fruit At the same time and in every season Other days have wept before dying in taverns Where brilliant bouquets turned In the eyes of a mulatto woman who invented poetry And the roses of electricity open again In the garden of my memory.[24]

June your sun brilliant lyre
Burns my aching fingers
Sad and melodious frenzy
I wander through my beautiful Paris
And don't have the heart to die there

Here Sundays stretch forever
And organ-grinders
Weep in these gray courtyards
Flowers on Paris balconies
Lean like the Tower of Pisa

22. "Poème lu au mariage d'André Salmon," *Alcools*.

23. *Le Poète assassiné*, Paris, Au Sans Pareil, 1927 (d'abord publié par l'Edition, 1916).

24. "Les Fiançailles," *Alcools*.

Soir de Paris ivres du gin
Flambant de l'électricité
Les tramways feux verts sur l'échine
Musiquent au long des portées
De rails leur folie de machines

Les cafés gonflés de fumée
Crient tout l'amour de leurs tziganes
De tous leurs siphons enrhumés
De leurs garçons vétus d'un pagne
Vers toi toi que j'ai tant aimée

Moi qui sais des lais pour les reines
Les complaintes de mes années
Des hymnes d'esclave aux murènes
La romance du mal-aimé
Et des chansons pour les sirènes[25]

"Pardonnez-moi mon ignorance Pardonnez-moi de ne plus connaître l'ancien jeu des vers Je ne sais plus rien et j'aime uniquement Les fleurs à mes yeux redeviennent des flammes Je médite divinement Et je souris des êtres que je n'ai pas créés Mais si le temps venait où l'ombre enfin solide Se multipliait en réalisant la diversité formelle de mon amour J'admirerais mon ouvrage.

"J'observe le repos du dimanche Et je loue la paresse Comment comment réduire L'infiniment petite science Que m'imposent mes sens.[26]

"Eh bien! mon garçon, on écoutait les rumeurs de notre beau jardin? Il est plein de souvenirs, ce paradis terrestre. Tycho Brahé y fit l'amour autrefois avec une jolie juive qui lui disait tout le temps: —Chazer,— ce qui signifie cochon en jargon.

"C'était l'année de l'Exposition Universelle, et la tour Eiffel, qui venait de naître, saluait d'une belle erection la naissance héroïque de Croniamantal.

"Et Viersélins Tigoboth s'avança, des baisers pleins les lèvres:

"J'v'ainme! I fait pahule! O binaméïe!"

"Macarée s'aperçut bientôt qu'elle avait conçu de Viersélins Tigoboth.

25. "La Chanson du Mal-Aimé," *Alcools*.

26. "Fiançailles," *Alcools*.

Paris nights drunk on gin
Electrically blaze
Streetcars' green lights on the iron spine
Music along the length
Of the rails' mechanical folly

Smoke-filled cafés
Shout out their gypsies' love
From all of their hacking throats
From all waiters in their aprons
Toward you whom I so dearly loved

I who know old songs for queens
The ballads of my years
Slave songs for sea-eels
The romance of the poorly beloved
And songs for sirens[25]

"Excuse my ignorance Excuse me for no longer knowing the ancient game of verse I don't know anything any more and I only love Flowers in my eyes become flames again I contemplate divinely And I smile at beings that I did not create But if the time came where the shadow solid at last Multiplied in realizing the formal diversity of my love I would admire my work.

"I observe Sunday's rest And I praise laziness how how to reduce The infinitely small science That my senses impose upon me.[26]

"Well then, my boy, you were listening to the murmurings of our lovely garden? This terrestial paradise is full of memories. Tycho Brahe long ago made love to a pretty Jewish girl who would always say to him: —Chazer—which is slang for pig.

"It was the year of the World's Fair, and the Eiffel Tower, which had just been born, saluted the heroic birth of Croniamantal with a lovely erection.

"And Viersélins Tigoboth came forth, his lips full of kisses:

"I love yuh! The full moon! Oh, m'love!"

"Macarée soon understood that she had conceived by Viersélins Tigoboth.

25. "La Chanson du Mal-Aimé," *Alcools*.
26. "Fiançailles," *Alcools*.

"Heureux enfant qui peut à treize ans faire de telles questions! dit M. Janssen. Les âmes sont vagabondes, j'ai la conscience des vies précédentes de mon âme. Elle n'a jamais animé que des corps stériles de savants. Il n'y a rien qui doive vous étonner dans mon affirmation. Des peuples entiers respectent les animaux et proclament la métempsychose, croyance honorable, évidente, mais outrée, puisqu'elle ne tient aucun compte des formes perdues et l'éparpillement inévitable. Leur respect eut dû s'étendre aux végétaux et même aux minéraux. Car la poussière des chemins, qu'est-ce autre chose que la cendre des morts? Il est vrai que les Anciens ne prêtaient de vie aux choses inertes. Des rabbins ont cru que la même âme habita les corps d'Adam, de Moïse et de David. En effet, le nom d'Adam se compose en Hébreu d'Aleph, Daleth et Mem, premières lettres des trois noms. La nôtre habita comme la mienne dans d'autres corps humains, dans d'autres animaux où fut éparpillée et continuera ainsi après votre mort puisque tout doit resservir. Car peut-être il n'y a plus rien de nouveau et la création a cessé peut-être. . . . J'ajoute que je n'ai pas voulu de l'amour, mais je le jure, je ne recommencerais pas une vie semblable. J'ai mortifié ma chair et pratiqué de dures pénitences. Je voudrais que votre vie fût heureuse.

"M. Janssen enseigne encore à Croniamantal l'anglais et le rendit familier avec Shakespeare. Il lui donna surtout le goût des anciens auteurs français. Parmi les poètes français, il estimait avant tout Villon, Ronsard et sa Pléiade, Racine et La Fontaine. Sur son conseil, Croniamantal lut des romans de chevalerie dont plusieurs auraient pu faire partie de la bibliothèque de Don Quichotte.

"Son esprit habitué aux formes poétiques concevait l'amour comme une conquête.

"En rapportant ce qui précède, je crois voir élucidé l'importante question du lieu natal de Croniamantal. Laissons les 123 villes dans 7 pays sur 4 continents se disputer l'honneur de lui avoir donné naissance.

"Nous savons maintenant, et les registres de l'état civil sont là pour un coup qu'il est né du pet paternel, à la Napoule aux cieux d'or, le 25 août 1889, mais fut déclaré à la mairie seulement le lendemain matin."

POÉSIE

"Dans les premiers jours de l'année 1911, un jeune homme mal habillé montait la rue Houdon en courant. Son visage extrêmement mobile paraissaît tour à tour plein de joie ou d'inquiétude. Ses yeux dévoraient tout

"Happy child who can, at thirteen years old, ask such questions, said Mr. Janssen. Souls are vagabonds, I am aware of the past lives of my soul. It has only given life to scholars' sterile bodies. The assertion should not surprise you at all. Entire populations respect animals and proclaim metempsychosis, an honorable but outrageous belief since it does not take into account lost forms and the inevitable scattering. Their respect should have extended to vegetable and even to minerals. For what is the dust of roads but ashes of the dead? It is true that the Ancients did not ascribe any life to inert things. Rabbis believed that the same soul inhabited the bodies of Adam, Moses, and David. In fact, the name Adam in Hebrew is composed of Aleph, Daleth, and Mem, the first letters of the three names. Like mine my soul lived in other human bodies in other animals or was scattered and will continue thus after your death since all things must serve more than once. For perhaps nothing is new and perhaps creation has ceased. . . . I must add that I did not want love, but I swear, I would not start this life over again. I have mortified my flesh and practiced hard penance. I would like you to live a happy life.

"Mr. Janssen continued to teach English to Croniamantal and familiarized him with Shakespeare. Above all he gave him a taste for old French authors. Among French poets, he esteemed Villon, Ronsard, and the Pléiade, Racine and La Fontaine above all others. At his advice, Croniamantal read novels about knights, several of which could have been in Don Quixote's library.

"Accustomed as it was to these poetic forms, his mind conceived of love as a conquest.

"In reporting the preceding, I believe I have elucidated the important question of Croniamantal's birthplace. We shall allow the 123 cities in 7 countries on 4 continents to dispute the honor of having borne him.

"We now know, and for once the registers of the civil state are there to show it, that he was born of a paternal fart, in Napoule of the golden skies, August 25, 1889, but was declared at the town hall only the next morning."

POETRY

"In the first days of the year 1911, a badly dressed young man ran up the rue Houdon. His extremely mobile face seemed alternately filled with joy and worry. His eyes devoured all that they saw and when his

ce qu'ils regardaient et quand ses paupières se rapprochaient rapidement comme des machoires, elles engloutissaient l'univers qui se renouvelait sans cesse par l'opération de celui qui courait en imaginant les moindres détails des mondes énormes dont il se repaissaît. Les clameurs et les tonnerres de Paris éclataient au loin et autour du jeune homme qui s'arrêta tout essoufflé, tel un cambrioleur trop longtemps poursuivit et prêt à se rendre. Ces clameurs, ce bruit, indiquaient bien que des ennemis étaient sur le point de le traquer, comme un voleur. Sa bouche et son regard exprimèrent la ruse, et marchant maintenant avec lenteur, il se réfugia dans sa mémoire, et allait de l'avant, tandis que toutes les forces de sa destinée et de sa conscience écartaient le temps pour qu'apparut la vérité de ce qui est, de ce qui fut et de ce qui sera.

"Le jeune homme entra dans une maison sans étage. Sur la porte ouverte, une pancarte portait:

Entrée des Ateliers

"Il suivit un couloir où il faisait si sombre et si froid qu'il eut l'impression de mourir et de toute sa volonté, serrant les dents et les poings, il mit l'éternité en miettes. Puis soudain il eut de nouveau la notion du temps dont les secondes martelées par une horloge qu'il entendit alors tombaient comme des morceaux de verre et la vie le reprit tandis que de nouveau le temps passait. Mais au moment où il se disposait à toquer contre une porte, son cœur battit plus fort, crainte de ne trouver personne. Il toquait à la porte et criait:

"C'est moi, Croniamantal."

"Et derrière la porte les pas lourds d'un homme fatigué, ou qui porte un faix très pesant, vinrent avec lenteur et quand la porte s'ouvrit ce fut dans la brusque lumière la création de deux êtres et leur mariage immédiat.

"Dans l'atelier, semblable à une étable, un innombrable troupeau gisait éparpillé. C'étaient les tableaux endormis et le pâtre qui les gardait souriait à son ami.

"Sur une étagère, des livres jaunes empilés simulaient des mottes de beurre. Et repoussant la porte mal jointe, le vent amenait là des êtres inconnus qui se plaignaient à tout petits cris, au nom de toutes les douleurs. Toutes les louves de la détresse hurlaient alors derrière la porte, prêtes à dévorer le troupeau, le pâtre et son ami, pour préparer à la même place la fondation de la Ville nouvelle. Mais dans l'atelier il y avait des joies de toutes les couleurs. Une grande fenêtre tenait tout le côté du nord et l'on ne voyait que le bleu du ciel pareil à un chant de femme. Croniamantal

eyelids met quickly, like jaws, they swallowed up the universe, ceaselessly renewing itself by imagining the tiniest details of enormous worlds on which they gorged themselves. The clamoring and the thundering of Paris exploded in the distance and around the young man who stopped out of breath like a thief who, after a long chase, is ready to give himself up. These clamors, this noise, certainly indicated that his enemies were on the verge of tracking him down, like a thief. His mouth and his look gave him away, and now, walking slowly, he took refuge in his memory, and went ahead, while all of the forces of his destiny, and of his conscience, pushed time aside, that the truth of what is, of what was, and of what will be, might appear.

"The young man entered a single story house. On the open door a sign read:

STUDIO ENTRANCE

"He walked down a hallway where it was so dark and so cold that he felt as if he was dying and, with all his will, gritting his teeth and tightening his fists, he broke eternity into bits. Then, suddenly, he perceived time again, whose seconds, hammered out by a clock, fell like pieces of glass only to be taken up again by life, while time was still passing. But as he was about to knock at the door and, afraid of finding no one at home, his heart beat faster. He knocked at the door and cried out:

"It's me, Croniamantal."

"And behind the door, the heavy steps of a tired man, or one carrying a heavy load, came slowly and, when the door opened, there was in the sharp light the creation of two beings and their immediate marriage.

"The studio itself was like a cowshed and scattered about inside were innumerable members of a flock. These were sleeping paintings and their shepherd was smiling at his friend.

"Yellow books were piled on a shelf like blocks of butter. And the wind burst through the badly hung door, carrying with it strange spirits who moaned and cried for all the world's sorrows. Behind the door, the she-wolves of distress howled, ready to devour the flock, the shepherd, and his friend, in preparation for the building of the new City in that very place. But inside the studio there were joys of all colors. A large window took up the entire northern side and all you could see was the sky, as blue as a woman's song. Croniamantal removed his overcoat,

ôta son pardessus qui tomba par terre comme le cadavre d'un noyé et s'asseyant sur un divan, il regarda longtemps sans rien dire la nouvelle toile posée sur le chevalet. Vétu de toile bleue et les pieds nus, le peintre regardait aussi le tableau où dans la brume glaciale deux femmes se souvenaient.

"Il y avait encore dans l'atelier une chose fatale, ce grand morceau de miroir brisé, retenue au mur par des clous à crochet. C'était une insondable mer morte, verticale et au fond de laquelle une fause vie animait ce qui n'existe pas. Ainsi, en face de l'Art, il y a son apparence dont les hommes ne se défient point et qui les abaisse lorsque l'Art les avait élevés. Croniamantal se courba en restant assis et appuyant les avant-bras sur les genoux, il détourna les yeux de la peinture pour les porter sur une pancarte jetée à terre et sur laquelle était tracé au pinceau l'avertissement suivant:

> Je suis chez le Bistro
> L'Oiseau du Bénin

"Il lut et relut cette phrase tandis que l'oiseau du Bénin regardait son tableau en remuant la tête, en se reculant, en se rapprochant. Ensuite il se tourna vers Croniamantal et lui dit:

—J'ai vue ta femme hier soir.

—Qui est-ce? demanda Croniamantal.

—Je ne sais pas, je l'ai vue mais je ne la connais pas, c'est une vraie jeune fille comme tu les aimes. Elle a le visage sombre et enfantin de celles qui sont destinées à faire souffrir. Et parmi sa grâce aux mains qui se redressent pour repousser, elle manque de cette noblesse que les poètes ne pourraient pas aimer car elle les empêcherait de pâtir. J'ai vu ta femme, te dis-je. Elle est la laideur et la beauté; elle est comme tout ce que nous aimons aujourd'hui. Et elle doit avoir la saveur de la feuille du laurier.

"Mais Croniamantal qui ne l'écoutait point, l'interrompit pour dire:

"J'ai fait hier mon dernier poème en vers reguliers:

> Luth
> Zut!

et mon dernier poème en vers irreguliers."

"(Prends garde que dans la deuxième strophe le mot fille est pris en mauvaise part)."

which fell to the ground like a drowned man's corpse and, sitting down on a divan, he gazed for a long time without speaking at the new canvas on the easel. The painter, dressed in blue cloth, his feet bare, also looked at the painting where two women remembered in the glacial fog.

"There was still one deadly thing in the studio, a large piece of broken mirror, held to the wall with crochet nails. It was an unfathomable vertical dead sea, at the bottom of which a false life animated the nonexistent. So, Art faces its own appearance, which men trust and which drags them down when Art had raised them up. Croniamantal bent over and, remaining seated with his forearms on his knees, turned his eyes away from the painting and rested them instead on a sign thrown on the ground. The following warning was traced there with a paintbrush:

> I am at the Bistro
> The Bird of Benin

"He read and reread this sentence while the Bird of Benin looked at his painting and shook his head, drawing back, leaning in again. Then he turned to Croniamantal and said to him:

"I saw your wife last night.

"Who is she? asked Croniamantal.

"I don't know, I saw her but I don't know her, she's a real young girl, the way you like them. She has the serious and childlike look of one whose destiny it is to cause suffering. And with grace in her hands that draw back to push forward, she lacks that nobility that poets cannot love, for it keeps them from suffering. I'm telling you, I saw your wife. She is ugliness and beauty; she is all that we like today. And I'll bet she tastes like a laurel leaf.

"But Croniamantal, who wasn't listening at all, interrupted him to say:

"Yesterday I wrote my most recent poem in regular verse:

> Luth
> Zut!

and my last poem in irregular verse."

"(Note that in the second stanza the word girl should be taken the wrong way)."

PROSPECTUS POUR UN NOUVEAU MÉDICAMENT

Puis les étoiles du matin
Redevinrent les étoiles du soir
Et réciproquement
Il s'écria—Au nom de Maroe
Et de son gypaète préféré
Fille d'Amammoer
Prépare la boisson des héros
—Parfaitement noble guerrier
Ma Ma ramaho nia nia

"Je n'écrirai plus qu'une poésie libre de toute entrave, serait-ce celle du langage.
"Ecoute, mon vieux!

MAHEVIDANOMI RENANOCALIPNODITOC EXTARTINAP —v.s.
   A.Z.
Tél:: 33-122 Pan: Pan
   oeaoiiiioktin
   iiiiiiiiiiii

Croniamantal

"Messieurs les Théâtres, je suis venu pour vous lire ma pièce *Jéximal Jélimite.*

Les Théâtres

"De grâce, attendez un peu, Monsieur, que l'on vous ait mis au courant de nos usages. Vous voici parmi nous, parmi nos acteurs, nos auteurs, nos critiques et nos spectateurs. Ecoutez attentivement et ne parlez presque plus.

Le Critique

"Aujourd'hui, pour qu'une pièce réussisse, il est important qu'elle ne soit pas signée par son auteur.

Croniamantal

"Au revoir, messieurs, je suis votre serviteur. Et si vous le permettez, je reviendrai dans quelques jours. J'ai idée que ma pièce n'est pas encore au point.

PROSPECTUS FOR A NEW MEDICATION

Then the morning stars
Become stars of the night again
And vice versa
He exclaimed—In the name of Maroe
And of his favorite gypaète
Daughter of Amammoer
Prepare the hero's drinks
—Perfectly noble warrior
Ma Ma ramaho nia nia

"From now on the poetry I'll write will be free of all fetters, even those of language.

"Listen, my boy!

MAHEVIDANOMI RENANOCALIPNODITOC EXTARTINAP —V.S.
    A.Z.
Tel: 33-122 Bang. Bang.
    oeaoiiiioktin
    iiiiiiiiiii

Croniamantal

"Gentlemen of the Theater, I have come to read you my play *Jéximal Jélimite*.

The Theater

"For goodness sake, wait a moment, Sir, while we fill you in on our customs. Here you are among us, among our actors, our authors, our critics and our spectators. Listen carefully, and speak very little.

The Critic

"Today, for a play to succeed, it is important that it not be signed by its author.

Croniamantal

"Goodbye gentlemen, I am your humble servant. And if you allow me, I'll come back in a couple of days. I think my play is not quite finished.

"Celle qui chante pour m'attirer sera ignorante comme moi-même et dansante avec des lassitudes.

"Pas plus loin, fillette aux bras nus! J'irai moi-même vers vous. Quelqu'un se tait sous l'aubépine et pourrait nous entendre.

"Divinité! quelle es-tu? Où est ta forme éternelle?

"Le voilà plus beau qu'auparavant et que tous. . . . Ecoute, ô poète, je t'appartiens désormais.

"Ô poète, adores-tu la source? Ô mon Dieu, rendez-moi mon amant! Viens! je sais de si belles chansons.

"La source a son murmure.

"Eh bien! couche avec ton amante froide, qu'elle te noie! Mais si tu vis, tu m'appartiens et tu m'obéiras.

"Comme Orphée, tous les poètes étaient près d'une malemort. Partout les éditeurs avaient pillés et les recueils de vers brûlés. Dans chaque ville des massacres avaient eu lieu. L'admiration universelle allait pour le moment à cet Horace Tograth qui d'Adélaide (Australie) avait déchaîné la tempête et semblait avoir à jamais détruit la poésie. La science de cet homme, racontait-on, tenait du miracle. Il dissipait les nuages ou amenait un orage au lieu qu'il voulait. Les femmes, dès qu'elles le voyaient étaient prêtes à faire sa volonté. Au demeurant, il ne dédaignait pas les virginités féminines ou masculines. Dès que Tograth avait su quel enthousiasme il avait éveillé dans tout l'univers, il avait annoncé qu'il irait dans les principales villes du globe après que l'Australie aurait été débarrassée de ses poètes érotiques ou élégiques. En effet, on apprit à quelque temps de là le délire des populations de Tokio, de Pékin, de Yakoutsk, de Calcutta, du Caire, de Buenos-Ayres, de San Francisco, de Chicago, à l'occasion de la visite de l'infâme allemand Tograth. Il laissa partout une impression surnaturelle à cause de ses miracles qu'il disait scientifiques, de ses guérisons extraordinaires qui portèrent au sublime sa réputation de savant et même de thaumaturge.

"Et elle tendit à Tograth un petit papier rose sur lequel se trouvait ce lamentable acrostiche:

Mon aimée adorée avant que je m'en aille
Avant que notre amour, Maria, ne déraille,
Râle et meure, m'amie, une fois, une fois,
Il faut nous promener tous deux seuls dans les bois
Alors je m'en irai plein de bonheur je crois.

"She who sings to entice me will be as ignorant as I and dancing with weariness.

"Go no further, bare-armed girl! I will go to you myself. There is someone keeping quiet under the hawthorn and he might hear us.

"Divinity! Which one are you? Where is your eternal form?

"Here he is more beautiful than before and that all. . . . Listen, oh poet, from now on, I belong to you.

"Oh poet, do you love the spring? Oh my God, return my lover to me! Come! I know such beautiful songs.

"The spring has its murmur.

"Well then, sleep with your cold lover that she might drown you! But if you live, you belong to me and you will obey me.

"Like Orpheus, all poets were close to a virile death. Publishing houses everywhere had been looted and collections of verse burned. There had been massacres in every city. Universal admiration was, for the moment, for this Horace Tograth who had unleashed the storm from Adelaide (Australia) and seemed to have destroyed poetry forever. It was said that this man's science seemed miraculous. He dispersed clouds or sent storms where he wished. Women, as soon as they saw him, were ready to do his bidding. For all that, he did not scorn feminine or masculine virginity. As soon as Tograth knew what enthusiasm he had awakened in the universe, he had announced that, once Australia had been cleansed of its erotic or elegiac poets, he would visit the major cities of the globe. In fact, it was revealed some time later that the populations of Tokyo, Peking, Yakoutsk, Calcutta, Cairo, Buenos Aires, San Francisco, Chicago had gone into a frenzy on the occasion of the infamous German, Tograth's visit. He left a supernatural impression everywhere because of the miracles that he called scientific, extraordinary cures that raised his reputation as a scholar and even as a miracle worker to sublime levels.

"And she handed Tograth a little pink slip of paper on which this pathetic acrostic was written:

> My beloved adored I must go
> And before our love, Maria, is derailed,
> Rants and dies, my sweet, for once, for once,
> It is for us two to walk alone in the wood
> And then I believe I will go full of joy.

"Ce n'est pas seulement de la poésie, dit Tograth, elle est en outre, idiote."

"Croniamantal s'avança auprès de Tograth et apostropha la foule:

"Canailles, asssassins!"

"Des rires éclatèrent. On cria:

"A l'eau, le couillon!"

"Et Tograth, regardant Croniamantal, lui dit:

"Mon ami, que cette affluence ne vous offusque point. Moi, j'aime la populace, bien que je descende dans des hôtels où elle ne fréquente point."

"Le poète laissa parler Tograth, puis il reprit, s'adressant à la foule:

"Canaille, ris de moi, tes joies sont comptées, on te les arrachera une à une. Et sais-tu, populace, quel est ton héros?"

"Tograth souriait et la foule était devenue attentive. Le poète poursuivit:

"Ton héros, populace, c'est l'Ennui apportant le Malheur."

"Un cri d'étonnement sortit de toutes les poitrines. Des femmes firent le signe de la croix. Tograth voulut parler, mais Croniamantal le saisit brusquement par le cou, le jeta sur le sol et l'y maintint en posant un pied sur sa poitrine. En même temps il parla:

"C'est l'Ennui et le Malheur, le monstre ennemi de l'homme, le Léviathan gluant et immonde, le Béhémoth souillé de stupres, de violes et par le sang des merveilleux poètes. Il est le vomissement des antipodes, ses miracles ne trompent pas plus les clairvoyants que les miracles de Simon, le magicien n'en imposaient aux Apôtres. Marseillais, Marseillais, pourquoi vous dont les ancêtres s'en sont venus du pays le plus purement lyrique, vous êtes-vous solidarisés avec les ennemis des poètes, avec les barbares de toutes les nations? Le plus étrange miracle de l'allemand revenu d'Australie, le connaissez-vous? C'est d'en avoir imposé au monde et d'avoir été un instant plus fort que la création même, que la poésie éternelle."

"Mais Tograth, qui avait pu se dégager, se dressa, sali de poussière et ivre de rage, il demanda:

"Qui es-tu?"

"Et la foule cria:

"Qui es-tu, qui es-tu?"

"Le poète se tourna vers l'orient et parla d'une voix exaltée:

"It's not only poetry, said Tograth, it's idiotic, besides."

"Croniamantal advanced toward Tograth and shouted at the crowd:

"You rabble! You Murderers!"

"There were bursts of laughter. Someone cried out:

"Throw the jerk in the water!"

"And Tograth, looking at Croniamantal, said to him:

"My friend, let not this crowd offend you. I love commoners myself, though they are never to be found at the hotels I frequent."

"The poet let Tograth speak, then he began again, addressing the crowd:

"Laugh at me, you rabble, your joys are numbered, one by one they will be torn from you. And you, commoners, do you know who your hero is?"

"Tograth was smiling and the crowd grew quiet. The poet pushed on:

"Your hero, you commoners, is Boredom bringing with it Misfortune."

"A cry of surprise rose from every breast. Women crossed themselves. Tograth wanted to speak but Croniamantal grabbed him bruskly by the neck, threw him to the ground and held him there with one foot on his chest. He spoke at the same time:

"It is Boredom and Misfortune, man's monstrous enemy, the vile and sticky Leviathan, the Behemoth soiled with excesses, rapes, and the blood of marvelous poets. It is the vomit of the antipodes, his miracles no more fool the clairvoyants than the miracles of Simon, the magician, fooled the Apostles. People of Marseilles, why do you, whose ancestors came from the most purely lyrical country, why do you show solidarity with the barbarians of every nation? Do you know the strangest miracle of the German come back from Australia? It is to have imposed himself on the world and to have been for a moment stronger than creation itself, stronger than eternal poetry."

"But Tograth, who had been able to extricate himself, drew himself up and, covered with dust and drunk with rage, demanded:

"Who are you?"

"And the crowd cried out:

"Who are you? Who are you?"

"The poet turned towards the Orient and spoke in an exalted voice:

"Je suis Croniamantal, le plus grand des poètes vivants. J'ai souvent vu Dieu face à face. J'ai supporté l'éclat divin que mes yeux humains temperaient. J'ai vécu l'éternité. Mais le temps étant venu, je suis venu me dresser devant toi."

"Tograth accueillit d'un éclat de rire terrible ces dernières paroles. Les premiers rangs de la foule ayant vu rire Tograth rirent aussi, et le rire en éclats, en roulades, en trilles se communiqua bientôt à la populace tout entière, à Paponat et à Tristouse Ballerinette. Toutes les bouches ouvertes faisaient face à Croniamantal qui perdait contenance. On cria parmi les rires:

"A l'eau, le poète . . . Au feu, Croniamantal! .. Aux chiens, l'amant du laurier!"

"Un homme qui était au premier rang et avait un gros gourdin en appliqua un coup à Croniamantal, dont la grimace douloureuse fit redoubler les rires de la foule. Une pierre habilement lancée vint frapper le nez du poète, dont le sang jaillit. Une marchande de poisson rendit la foule, puis se plaçant devant Croniamantal, lui dit:

"Hou! le corbeau, Je te reconnais. Peuchaire! tu es un policier qui s'est fait poète; tiens, vache, tiens, conteur de bourdes."

"Et elle lui asséna une gifle formidable en lui crachant au visage. L'homme que Tograth avait guéri de la calvitie s'approcha en disant:

"Regarde, mes cheveux, est-ce un faux miracle, ça?"

"Et levant sa canne, il la poussa si adroitement qu'elle creva l'œil droit. Croniamantal tomba à la renverse; des femmes se précipitèrent sur lui et le frappèrent. Tristouse trépignait de joie, tandis que Paponat essayait de la calmer. Mais du bout de son parapluie, elle alla crever l'autre œil de Croniamantal, qui la vit en cet instant et s'écria:

"Je confesse mon amour pour Tristouse Ballerinette, la poésie divine qui console mon âme."

"Alors de la foule des hommes crièrent:

"Tais-toi, charogne! Attention les madames!"

"Les femmes s'écartèrent vite, et un homme qui balançait un grand couteau posé sur sa main ouverte le lança de telle façon qu'il vint se planter dans la bouche ouverte de Croniamantal. D'autres hommes firent de même. Les couteaux se fichèrent dans le ventre, la poitrine, et bientôt il n'y eut plus sur le sol qu'un cadavre hérissé comme une bogue de châtaigne marine.

"I am Croniamantal, the greatest of living poets. I have often seen God face to face. I withstood the divine radiance that was tempered by my human eyes. I have lived eternity. But the time is come and I am here to stand before you."

"Tograth welcomed these last words with a terrible laugh. The first rows of the crowd, having seen Tograth laugh, also laughed and the laughter in bursts, in rolls, in trills, soon spread to all the commoners, to Paponat and Tristouse Ballerinette. Croniamantal was faced with all of these open mouths and began to lose his composure. Amidst the laughter there were cries:

"Throw the poet in the water! . . . Into the fire with Croniamantal! . . . To the dogs, the laurel lover!"

"A man in the first row who had a big club struck Croniamantal, whose pained grimace redoubled the crowd's laughter. A skillfully tossed stone hit the poet on the nose, and blood gushed forth. A fish peddler pushed through the crowd and then, standing before Croniamantal, she said to him:

"Hey, you crow. I recognize you. Cheapskate! You're a policeman calling himself a poet; here, you cow, take this, you liar."

"And spitting in his face she struck him a terrible blow. The man that Tograth had cured of baldness came up saying:

"Look at my hair, is that a false miracle?"

"And lifting his cane, he gave it a deft push so that it poked out Croniamantal's right eye. He fell over; the women rushed forward and hit him. Tristouse stamped her feet with joy, while Paponat tried to calm her. But with the end of her umbrella, she poked out Croniamantal's other eye, the one with which he looked at her, crying out:

"I confess my love for Tristouse Ballerinette, that divine poetry that consoles my soul."

"The men in the crowd then cried out:

"Shut up, swine! Watch out, ladies!"

"The women quickly moved away, and a man who was swinging a big knife in his open hand threw it so that it landed in Croniamantal's open mouth. Other men did the same. The knives were driven into his stomach, his chest, and soon there was nothing left on the ground but a bristling corpse like the spiky shell of a sea-urchin.

"Un fracas inouï, pareil à un coup de tonnerre éclata. Le vieux prophète serra les lèvres en hochant la tête et regarda par terre puis il se courba et tendit l'oreille assez près du sol. Lorsqu'il se redressa, il murmura:

"La Terre même ne veut plus du contact insupportable des poètes."

"Donnerkeil! Uijeh! eh! eh! eh! Eh! dites donc, là-haut, vous feriez bien de retourner à vos affaires au lieu d'embêter les joyeux bougres que leur sort force à marcher par de pareilles nuits.. Eh! les mères, n'êtes-vous plus sous la domination de Salomon? . . . Ohé! ohé Tseilourkop! Meicabl! Farwasher Ponim! Beheime! Vous voulez m'empêcher de boire d'excellents vins de Moselle avec M.M. les étudiants de la Bouresia qui sont trop heureux de trinquer avec moi à cause de ma science bien connue et de mon lyrisme inimitable, sans compter tous mes dons de sorcellerie et de prophétie.

"Esprit Maudit! Sachez que j'aurais bu aussi des vins du Rhin, sans compter les vins de France. Je n'aurais pas négligé de sabler le champagne en votre honneur, mes vieilles amies! . . . A minuit, à l'heure où l'on fait Christkindchen, j'aurais roulé sous la table et aurais dormi du moins pendant la soûlerie. . . . Mais vous déchaînez les vents, vous faites un vacarme infernal pendant cette nuit angélique qui devrait être paisible. Vous ne l'ignorez pas nous sommes dans la période des jours alcyoniens . . . et, en fait, de calme, vous semblez vous créper le chignon, là-haut, belles dames. . . . Pour amuser Salomon sans doute. . . . Herrgottsoerra . . . , qu'entends-je? . . . Lilith! Naama! Aguereth! Mahala! . . . Ah! Salomon, pour ton plaisir, elles vont tuer tous les poètes sur cette terre.

"Ah! Salomon! Salomon! roi jovial dont les amuseuses sont ces quatre spectres nocturnes qui se dirigent de l'Orient vers le Nord, tu veux ma mort, car je suis aussi poète comme tous les prophètes juifs et prophète comme tous les poètes.

"Adieu, la soûlerie de ce soir. . . . Vieux Rhin, il faut que je tourne le dos. Je m'en vais me préparer à mourir en dictant mes plus lyriques et dernières prophéties . . ."

"Tristouse ne le regretta pas longtemps. Elle prit le deuil de Croniamantal et monta à Montmartre, chez l'oiseau du Bénin, qui commença par lui faire la cour, et après qu'il en eut eu ce qu'il voulait, ils se mirent à parler de Croniamantal.

"Il faut que je lui fasse une statue, dit l'oiseau du Bénin. Car je ne suis pas seulement peintre mais aussi sculpteur.

"C'est ça, dit Tristouse, il faut lui élever une statue.

"An unprecedented din burst like thunder. The old prophet squeezed his lips together, shaking his head and looking down, then he bent over and put his ear close to the ground. When he stood up again he murmured:

"The Earth itself wants no more of this unbearable contact with poets."

"Donnerkeil! Uijeh! hey, hey, hey, Hey! You, up there, you'd do better to get back to your own business than to bother these happy devils whose lot forces them to walk on nights such as this. . . . Hey, you mothers, aren't you still under Salomon's dominion? Hey! hey Tseilourkop! Meicabl! Farwascher Ponim! Beheime! You want to keep me from drinking excellent Moselle wines with the gentle students of Bouresia who are only too glad to raise their glasses with me, thanks to my well-known science and my inimitable lyricism, and that's not counting all my gifts of sorcery and prophecy.

"Evil Spirits! Know that I would also have drunk the wines of the Rhine, not counting the wines of France. I would have taken a sip of champagne in your honor, my old lady friends! . . . At midnight, at the hour of Christkindchen, I would have rolled under the table and slept during my drunkenness. . . . But you unleash the winds, you create an infernal racket during this angelic night that should be peaceful. You know we are in our halcyon days . . . and, in fact days of calm, you seem to comb back your buns, up there, lovely ladies . . . To amuse Solomon, no doubt . . . Herrgottsoera . . . , what's that I hear? . . . Lilith! Naama! Aguereth! Mahala! . . . Ah! Solomon for your pleasure, they will kill all the poets on this earth.

"Ah! Solomon! Solomon! jovial king who keeps four nocturnal ghosts to entertain him, facing north from the Orient, you want me to die, for like all Jewish prophets I too am a poet and, like all poets, I'm a prophet.

"Goodbye to this night's binge . . . Old Rhine, I must turn my back. I am off to prepare myself to die while dictating my most lyrical and final prophecies . . ."

"Tristouse did not miss him for long. She wore black for Croniamantal and went up to Montmartre to the bird of Benin, who started by courting her. After he had taken what he wanted, they began to speak of Croniamantal.

"I have to make him a statue, said the bird of Benin, for I am not only a painter, but a sculptor, too.

"That's it, said Tristouse, we must erect a statue for him.

"Où ça? demanda l'oiseau du Bénin; le gouvernement ne nous accordera pas d'emplacement. Les temps sont mauvais pour les poètes.

"On le dit, répliqua Tristouse, mais ce n'est peut-être pas vrai. Que pensez-vous du bois de Meudon, Monsieur l'Oiseau du Bénin?

"J'y avais bien pensé, mais je n'osais le dire. Va pour le bois de Meudon.

"Une statue en quoi? demanda Tristouse. En marbre? En bronze?

"Non, c'est trop vieux, répondit l'oiseau du Bénin, il faut que je lui sculpte une profonde statue en rien, comme la poésie et comme la gloire.

"Bravo! Bravo! dit Tristouse en battant des mains, une statue en rien en vide, c'est magnifique, et quand la sculpturez-vous?

"Demain, si vous voulez; nous allons dîner, nous passerons la nuit ensemble, et dès le matin nous irons au bois de Meudon.[27]

"Quelques temps après cette sombre tragédie, l'ami Méritarte nous convia à un régal de comédie. Il veut d'abord une soupe madrilène à la glace qui provoqua des sourires. Mais tout le monde éclata de rire quand notre hôte nous eut renseignés sur l'origine taurine des *criadillas* qui suivirent. Les plaisanteries respirent de plus belle autour d'une tête de veau dont la bouffonerie nous plut au point que nous ne laissâmes que le persil dont on l'avait parée. Un gigot bien saignant ne fut pas moins goûté, l'ail qui le parfumait et les haricots de Soissons sur lesquels il reposait mollement nous ayant paru des ressorts éminemment comiques. Bref, nous rîmes comme des bossus, et le petit vin blanc que nous versait Méritarte favorisait notre gaîté.

"Mais l'ami Méritarte voulait élever son art jusqu'au lyrisme. Il nous servit, un soir, un potage aux vermicelles, des œufs à la coque, une salade de laitue aux fleurs de capucines et du fromage à la crême. Nous déclarâmes que c'était là de la poésie sentimentale et dépité, l'ami Méritarte affirma qu'il s'éleverait jusqu'au ton de l'ode. Il est vrai qu'un mois plus tard il nous servait un cassoulet par lequel son art atteignait enfin au sublime. Il s'essaya même à l'épopée, avec une bouillabaisse dont la saveur méditéranéenne nous rappela sur le champ les poèmes d'Homère.[28]

"Dans la clairière, l'oiseau du Bénin se mit à l'ouvrage. En quelques heures, il creusa un trou ayant environ un demi-mètre de largeur et deux mètres de profondeur.

27. *Le Poète assassiné.*

28. "L'ami Méritarte," *Le Poète assassiné.*

"Where? asked the bird of Benin; the government will not give us the space. Times are bad for poets.

"That's what they say, replied Tristouse, but it might not be true. What do you think of the forest of Meudon, Mr. Bird of Benin?

"I had thought of that, but I didn't dare say it. We'll go for the forest of Meudon.

"A statue made of what? asked Tristouse. Marble? Bronze?

"No, too old-fashioned, answered the bird of Benin, this great statue must be sculpted out of nothing, like poetry and like glory.

"Bravo! Bravo! said Tristouse clapping her hands, a statue made out of nothing, of emptiness, it's magnificent, and when will you sculpt it?

"Tomorrow if you like; we'll have dinner, we'll spend the night together, and when morning comes we will go to the forest of Meudon.[27]

"Some time after this dark tragedy, friend Méritarte invited us to a delightful theatrical comedy. First he wants a cold vichyssoise that provoked smiles. But everyone burst out laughing when our host informed us of the taurine origin of the *criadillas* that followed. The best jokes were made over a veal's head whose buffoonery was so pleasing to us that we left nothing but the parsley that garnished it. A rare leg of lamb was equally much appreciated, the garlic that flavored it and the Soissons beans on which it softly rested seeming eminently comical to us. In brief, we laughed like hunchbacks, and the delightful white wine that Méritarte poured for us only added to our gaiety.

"But friend Méritarte wanted to raise his art to lyricism. One night he served us a vermicelli soup, soft boiled eggs, salad with lettuce and nasturtium blossoms and a cheese topped with cream. We declared that this was sentimental poetry and, piqued, friend Méritarte asserted that he would rise to the tone of the ode. It is true that a month later he served us a cassoulet in which his art finally attained the sublime. He even tried an epic, with a bouillabaisse whose Mediterranean flavor immediately recalled Homer's poems.[28]

"In the clearing, the bird of Benin got to work. In a few hours he had dug a hole about a half a meter long and two meters deep.

27. *Le Poète assassiné.*

28. "L'ami Méritarte," *Le Poète assassiné.*

"Ensuite on déjeuna sur l'herbe.

"L'après-midi fut consacré par l'oiseau du Bénin à sculpter l'intérieur du monument à la semblance de Croniamantal.

"Le lendemain, le sculpteur revint avec des ouvriers qui habillèrent le puits d'un mur en ciment armé large de huit centimètres, sauf le fond qui eut 38 centimètres, si bien que le vide avait la forme de Croniamantal, que le trou était plein de son fantôme.

Cueillons la marjolaine
La nuit.[29]

Bouche qui est l'ordre même.[30]

Moi l'horizon je fais la roue comme un grand Paon
Ecoutez renaître les oracles qui avaient cessé
          Le grand Pan est ressuscité.[31]

Il y a l'amour qui m'entraîna avec douceur
Il y a des hommes dans le monde qui n'ont jamais été
          à la guerre.[32]

C'est moi qui commence cette chose des siècles à venir
Ce sera plus long à réaliser que la fable d'Icare volant.

Je lègue à l'avenir l'histoire de Guillaume Apollinaire
Qui fut à la guerre et sut être partout
Dans les villes heureuses de l'arrière
Dans tout le reste de l'univers
Dans ceux qui meurent en piétinant dans le barbelé
Dans les femmes dans les canons dans les chevaux
Au zénith, au nadir, aux 4 points cardinaux
Et dans l'unique ardeur de cette veillée d'armes.
Que c'est beau ces fusées qui illuminent la nuit
Elles montent sur leur propre cime et se penchent pour regarder
Ce sont des dames qui dansent avec leur regard pour yeux, bras et cœurs

J'ai reconnu ton sourire et ta vivacité

29. *Le Poète assassiné.*
30. "La Jolie rousse," *Calligrammes,* Mercure de France, 1918.
31. "Chant de l'Horizon en Champagne," *Calligrammes.*
32. *Il y a, Calligrammes.*

"Then we lunched on the grass.

"The bird of Benin devoted the afternoon to sculpting Croniamantal's features on the inside of the monument.

"The next day, the sculptor returned with workers who fitted the pit with a cement wall eight centimeters thick, except at the bottom where it was 38 centimeters. The empty space was shaped like Croniamantal and the hole was filled with his ghost.

Let us gather marjoram
at night.[29]

Mouth that is order itself.[30]

I the horizon do a cartwheel like a great Peacock
Listen as the oracles gone silent are reborn
    Great Pan is risen.[31]

There is love that gently carries me
There are men in the world who have never been
    to war.[32]

It is I that begins this thing of centuries to come
It will take longer to come true than the tale of flying Icarus.

I leave to the future the story of Guillaume Apollinaire
Who went to war and knew how to be in many places
In the happy cities of the homefront
In all the rest of the universe
In those who die pushing through barbed wire
In women in cannons in horses
At the zenith, at the nadir, at the 4 cardinal points
And in the special fervor of this night before battle.
These rockets that light up the night are so beautiful
They rise to their own height and bend to look down
They are ladies who dance with their gaze for eyes, arms, and hearts

I recognized your smile and your vivacity

29. *Le Poète assassiné.*
30. "La Jolie rousse," *Calligrammes,* Mercure de France, 1918.
31. "Chant de l'Horizon en Champagne," *Calligrammes.*
32. *Il y a, Calligrammes.*

C'est aussi l'apothéose quotidienne de toutes mes Bérénices
　　　dont les chevelures sont devenues des comètes
Ces danseuses surdorées appartiennent à tous les temps et à toutes les races
Elles accouchent brusquement d'enfants qui n'ont que le temps
　　　de mourir.

Et ce serait sans doute bien plus beau
Si je pouvais supposer que toutes ces choses dans lesquelles
　　　je suis partout
Pouvaient m'occuper aussi
Mais dans ce sens il n'y a rien de fait
Car je suis partout à cette heure il n'y a cependant
　　　que moi qui suis en moi.[33]

Rails qui ligotez les nations
Nous ne sommes que deux ou trois hommes
Libres de tous liens
Donnons nous la main[34]

Nous tenterons en vain de prendre du repos
On commencera à minuit
Quand on a le temps on a la liberté
Bigorneaux Lotte multiple soleils et l'Oursin du couchant
Une vieille paire de chaussures jaunes devant la fenêtre

O Paris
Du rouge au vert tout le jaune se meurt
Paris Vancouver Hyères Maintenon New York et les Antilles
La fenêtre s'ouvre comme une orange
Le beau fruit de la lumière[35]

Je me suis enfin détaché
De toutes choses naturelles.[36]

Nous nous ressemblions comme dans l'architecture du
　　　siècle dernier

33. "Merveille de la guerre," *Calligrammes*.
34. "Liens," *Calligrammes*.
35. "Les Fenêtres," *Calligrammes*.
36. "Les Collines," *Calligrammes*.

It is also the daily apotheosis of all my Berenices
    whose locks have turned to comets
These overgilded dancers belong to all times and all races
They suddenly give birth to children who barely have the time
    to die.

And it would certainly be more beautiful
If I could think that my being in all of these things
    everywhere
Could also keep me busy
But in fact there is none of that
For if I am everywhere at this hour there is
    only myself in myself.[33]

Rails that bind nations
We are but two or three men
Free of all ties
Let us join hands.[34]

We will try in vain to rest
At midnight we will begin
When you have time you have freedom
Winkles Cod multiple Suns and the sunset's Sea urchin
A pair of old yellow shoes by the window

Oh Paris
From red to green all the yellow dies
Paris Vancouver Hyères Maintenon New York and the Antilles
The window opens like an orange
Beautiful fruit of the light[35]

I have finally released myself
From all natural things.[36]

We resemble each other the way the architecture of
    the last century did

---

33. "Merveille de la guerre," *Calligrammes.*
34. "Liens," *Calligrammes.*
35. "Les Fenêtres," *Calligrammes.*
36. "Les Collines," *Calligrammes.*

Ces hautes cheminées pareilles à des tours
Nous allons plus haut maintenant et ne touchons plus
    le sol[37]
          le trolley
A travers l'Europe vétue de petits feux multicolores.[38]

MUTATION

Des allumettes qui ne prenaient pas
    Et tout
        A tant changé
          en moi

Tout
    Sauf mon Amour
        Eh! oh! Ha![39]

    orgues
            aux fétus de la paille où tu dors
L'hymne de l'Avenir est paradisiaque.[40]

Quels sont les grands oublieurs
Qui donc saura nous faire oublier telle ou telle
    partie du monde
Où est le Christophe Colomb à qui l'on devra l'oubli
    d'un continent.[41]

Décidément je ne respecte aucune gloire

Nuit violente et violette et sombre et pleine d'or par
    moments
Nuits des hommes seulement
Nuit du 24 septembre
Demain l'assaut

37. "Le Musicien de Saint-Merry," *Calligrammes.*

38. "A Travers l'Europe," *Calligrammes.*

39. "Mutation," *Calligrammes.*

40. "La Nuit d'avril 1915," *Calligrammes.*

41. "Toujours," *Calligrammes.*

These chimneys high as towers
We go higher now and no longer touch the ground[37]
         the trolley
Across Europe dressed in small multicolored fires.[38]

MUTATION

Matches that won't light
    And all
       Is so very changed
          in me

All
    But my Love
      Hey! Ho! Ha![39]

      organ music
         in the haystack where you sleep
The hymn of the Future is heavenly.[40]

Who are the great forgettors
Who can make us forget this or that
    part of the world
Where is that Christopher Columbus to whom we will owe the forgetting
    of a continent.[41]

I really respect no glory at all

Night violent and violet and dark and filled with gold at
    moments
Nights of men only
Night of September 24th
Tomorrow we attack

37. "Le Musicien de Saint-Merry," *Calligrammes.*
38. "A Travers l'Europe," *Calligrammes.*
39. "Mutation," *Calligrammes.*
40. "La Nuit d'avril 1915," *Calligrammes.*
41. "Toujours," *Calligrammes.*

Nuit violente ô nuit dont l'épouvantable cri profond
   devenait plus intense de minute en minute
Nuit criait comme une femme qui accouche
Nuit des hommes seulement[42]

"Pas sentimental à l'excès comme le sont ces gens sans mesure que leurs actions dépassent sans qu'ils sachent s'amuser.[43]

"J'entends déjà le son aigre de cette voix à venir Du camarade qui se promènera avec toi en Europe tout en restant en Amérique une femme mince déguisée en homme Intelligence car voilà ce que c'est qu'une femme intelligente Et il ne faudrait pas oublier les légendes.[44]

"Et cet aveugle était l'homme qui, en 1840, avait découvert l'or en Californie.

"Elvire peignait avec une fantaisie délicate et non sans force, des bouquets éclatants où paraissaient des marguerites aux pétales noires et cette vie qu'animaient l'art, l'amour, la danse à Bullier et le cinéma, continua jusqu'au moment de la déclaration de guerre.

"Au reste, l'année 1914 commença par une gaieté folle. Comme au temps de Gavarni, l'époque fut dominée par le Carnaval. La danse était à la mode, on dansait partout, partout avaient lieu des bals masqués. La mode féminine se prêtait si bien au travesti que les femmes déguisaient leurs cheveux sous des couleurs éclatantes et délicates qui rappelaient celles des fontaines lumineuses qui m'étonnèrent, quand j'étais enfant, à l'exposition de 1889. On aurait dit encore des lueurs stellaires et les Parisiennes à la mode avaient droit, cette année, qu'on les appelât des *Bérénices*, puisque leurs chevelures méritaient d'être mises au rang des constellations.

"Dans un petit théâtre, quelques mois avant la guerre, j'ai vu danser la furlana (prononcer fourlana), que les danseurs, avant de la danser, qualifièrent de danse du pape; c'étaient des pas si lascifs que le pape serait bien étonné d'être mentionné à ce propos.

"En 1914, comme aujourd'hui du reste, on ne goûte que les légendes brèves ou plutôt personne ne sait plus en faire de longues.

42. "Désir," *Calligrammes*.
43. "A l'Italie," *Calligrammes*.
44. "Arbre," *Calligrammes*.

Violent night oh night whose horrible deep scream
    grew more intense with every minute
Night that screamed like a woman in labor
Night of men only.[42]

"Not overly sentimental like those immoderate people who go too far without knowing how to have fun.[43]

"I already hear the high tone of this voice coming From the friend who will wander with you in Europe remaining all the while in America a thin woman disguised as a man Intelligence for this is what it is to be an intelligent woman And legends are not to be forgotten.[44]

"And this blind man is the one who, in 1840, discovered gold in California.

"Elvire painted with a fantasy that was delicate but not without power. In her startling bouquets apppeared black-petaled daisies and this life that animated art, love, dancing at Bullier and the cinema, all continued until the moment war was declared.

"For the rest, the year 1914 began with a mad gaiety. As in the times of Gavarni, the period was dominated by the Carnival. Dancing was in fashion, people danced everywhere, masked balls were taking place everywhere. Women's fashion lent itself so well to this transvestite style that women did up their hair in shocking and delicate colors, like those of the luminous fountains that amazed me as a child at the 1889 Fair. They were like stellar lights and fashionable Parisian women had the right, that year, to be called *Bérénices*, since their hair was worthy of being placed among the constellations.

"In a little theater, a few months before the war, I saw the furlana (pronounced fourlana) dance, and the dancers, before doing the dance, called it the Pope's dance; the steps were so lascivious that the pope would have been quite surprised to have been mentioned in connection with it.

"In 1914, like today, only brief legends were appreciated or, more to the point, no one knew how to make longer ones anymore.

42. "Désir," *Calligrammes.*

43. "A l'Italie," *Calligrammes.*

44. "Arbre," *Calligrammes.*

"Epoque de bals et de mascarades! l'époque était légère; on ne danse jamais plus que dans le temps des révolutions et des guerres et quel singulier poète a donc inventé ce lieu commun véritablement prophétique: *danser* comme sur un volcan?

"Le type le plus caractéristique de cette époque de bals et de ballets russes, ce fut incontestablement Elvire que je revois à Bullier, avec ses cheveux lilas, ses fourures blanches et son monocle; on l'appelait la vrille et nul doute que cet accoutrement, chevelure lilas, monocle et fourrure blanche ne se fut généralisé l'an suivant si la guerre n'était venue. Un Gavarni eut peut-être surgi et nous aurions eu au bal de l'Opéra de délicieuses Vrilles comme au temps de Gavarni il y avait de charmants débardeurs.

"M. et Mme. Delaunay étaient des novateurs. Il ne s'embarrassaient pas de l'imitation des modes anciennes et, comme ils voulaient être de leur temps, ils ne cherchaient point à innover dans la forme de la coupe des vêtements, suivant en cela la mode du jour; mais ils cherchaient à influencer en utilisant des matières nouvelles infiniment variées de couleurs.

"Voici, par exemple, un costume de M. Robert Delaunay: veston violet, gilet beige, pantalon nègre. En voici un autre: manteau rouge à col bleu, chaussettes rouges, chaussures jaune et noire, pantalon noir, veston vert, gilet bleu de ciel, minuscule cravate rouge.

"Voici la description d'une robe simultanée de Mme. Sonia Delaunay Terek: tailleur violet, longue ceinture violette et verte et, sous la jaquette, un corsage divisé en zones de couleurs vives tendres ou passées, où se mêlent le vieux rose, la couleur tango, le bleu nattier, l'écarlate etc., apparaîssant sur différentes matières, telles que drap, taffetas, tulle, pilou, moire et poult-de-soie juxtaposés.

"Tant de variété méritait de n'avoir point passé inaperçue. Elle mettait de la fantaisie dans l'élégance.

"Et si, en se rendant à Bullier, on ne les voyait aussitôt, on savait que les réformateurs du costume se tenaient généralement auprès de l'orchestre, d'où ils contemplaient non sans mépris les vêtements monotones des danseurs et des danseuses.

"Elvire les intriguait à cause de son monocle et de ses cheveux aux couleurs changeantes, mais elle refusa toujours de se lier avec eux, préférant passer son temps à danser avec Mavise.

"Nicolas Varinoff les menait aussi parfois dans les bals-musettes; celui de Gravillières, où les musiciens se tenaient sur un petit balcon; la Fauvette, rue de Vanves et le Boulodrome de Montmartre, endroit charmant où la musique était, à mon gré, plus plaisante que celle de M. Strauss.

"Time of balls and masquerades! It was a period of lightness; there is never more dancing than during times of revolution and war and what an odd poet then invented this truly prophetic platitude: *to dance* as on a volcano?

"The most characteristic figure at these balls and Russian ballets, was, without a doubt, Elvire, whom I can still see at Bullier, with her lilac hair, her white furs, and her monocle; she was called the twister and there is no doubt that this accoutrement, along with her lilac hair, monocle, and white fur, would have been all the rage the following season if it had not been for the war. A Gavarni might have perhaps arisen and we would have had delicious Twisters at the Opera ball, as in Gavarni's time there were charming dockers.

"Mr. and Mrs. Delaunay were innovators. They did not bother imitating old styles and, since they wanted to be of their time, they didn't even try to innovate with the cut of their clothes; in that, at least, they followed the fashion of their time; but they showed their influence by using new materials in an infinite variety of colors.

"Here, for example, is one of Mr. Robert Delaunay's suits: purple jacket, beige vest, black pants. Here is another: red coat with a blue collar, red socks, yellow and black shoes, black pants, green jacket, sky-blue vest, tiny red tie.

"Here is the description of one of Mrs. Sonia Delaunay Terek's simultaneous dresses: purple suit, long purple and green belt and, under the jacket, a corsage divided into bright, soft, and faded sections of color where antique rose, tango, straw blue, scarlet, etc., appeared on different materials like cotton, taffeta, tulle, velvet, moire, and intertwined silks.

"Such variety was worthy of notice. She brought fantasy into elegance.

"And if they were not seen straightaway at Bullier's, one knew that the suit's reformers usually stuck close to the orchestra, from which position they scornfully contemplated the dancers' monotone clothing.

"Elvire intrigued them with her monocle and the changing colors of her hair, but she always refused to ally herself with them, preferring to spend her time dancing with Mavise.

"Nicolas Varinoff was another who occasionally led them to other dances; those of Gravillières, where the musicians perched on a little balcony; Fauvette, rue de Vanves and the Boulodrome in Montmartre, a charming spot where the music was, in my opinion, more pleasant than that of Mr. Strauss.

"La guerre éclata donc, brisant comme erre cette vie adorable et légère.

Nicolas Varinoff fut extrêmement frappé par l'événement imprévu et, peu de jours après la Marne, il déclarait à Elvire, qui se pressait contre lui caressante comme une chatte, que le temps de l'amour était interrompu et que les occupations qui l'entraînaient particulièrement durant la nuit ne seraient reprises, en ce qui le concernait, qu'à la fin des hostilités. Mais comme Elvire n'accordait à la guerre qu'un intérêt médiocre, cette décision lui parut incohérente, et, au firmament de leur liaison, le dédain se prit à monter comme une lune rousse.

. . . .

"Douce poésie! le plus beau des arts! Toi qui, suscitant en nous le pouvoir créateur, nous met tout proche de la divinité; les déceptions n'ont pas abattu l'amour que je te portais dès ma tendre enfance! La guerre même a augmenté le pouvoir que la poésie exerce sur moi et c'est grâce à l'une et l'autre que le ciel désormais se confond avec ma tête étoilée. Douce poésie! je regrette que l'incertitude des temps ne me permette pas de me livrer à tes inspirations touchant la matière de ce livre, mais je suis pressé. La guerre continue. Il s'agit avant d'y retourner, d'achever le roman et la prose est ce qui convient le mieux à ma hâte.

"En s'apprêtant pour aller rue Delambre et en cherchant la copie de la lettre où il était question de sa grand-mère, elle se disait:

"Je ne sais pas pourquoi, après tout, il n'y aurait pas un mormonisme féministe, des femmes ayant plusieurs maris. Ce serait rigolo. Et d'abord ça existe, pas pour les maris, mais pour les amants. Il faudra que je fasse un portrait d'Anatole de Saintariste en lieutenant, à côté de sa poule Corail. Elle est difficile à déssiner cette petite."

"Pour terminer cette lettre, je dois vous annoncer qu'un pasteur anglican vient de faire paraître un livre où implicitement il s'efforce de donner un démenti aux vérités ethniques qui forment le fond de notre religion et qui, avant ce siècle, ont été proclamées par les écrivains catholiques, détenteurs de toute la vérité, jusqu'à l'apparition de l'ange Moroni à Joseph. Ce pasteur, dans son voyage d'Asie, s'étant trouvé chez les Nestoriens, prétend avoir reconnu en eux les représentants de dix tribus d'Israël dont on avait perdu les traces historiques jusqu'au jour où le livre de Mormon a prouvé qu'ayant émigré en Amérique, il ne restait aujourd'hui qu'une faible partie d'une des nations issues d'elles et la plus mauvaise, celle des Lamanites, juifs punis de Dieu, mais qui n'en sont pas moins les derniers représentants de son peuple, c'est-à-dire la race Rouge que nous respectons. Cet ouvrage, plein de mauvaise foi, ne fait même pas allusion à nos vérités et sa publication a été pour moi une nouvelle occasion

"Then war exploded, breaking this light and adorable life like glass.

"Nicolas Varinoff was quite struck by the unforeseen event and, a few days after the Marne, he declared to Elvire, who was rubbing up against him like a cat, that the time of love had been interrupted, and that he would forsake those occupations that particularly pleased him at night, until the end of hostilities. But, as Elvire accorded only a mediocre interest to the war, she couldn't understand this and, at the height of their attachment, disdain began to rise like a harvest moon.

. . . .

"Sweet poetry! The most beautiful of arts! You, who set off our creative powers, bring us near to divinity; deceptions have not diminished the love that I have held for you since my tender childhood! Even the war added to poetry's power over me and it is thanks to the one and the other that the sky these days is confused with my starry head. Sweet poetry! How I regret that the uncertainty of the day does not allow me to abandon myself to the guidance of your inspirations in the matter of this book, but I'm in a hurry. The war goes on. Before going back, it's a matter of finishing the novel and prose, what is best suited to my haste.

"In preparing herself to go to the rue Delambre to look for the copy of the letter that spoke of her grandmother, she said to herself:

"I don't know why, after all, there shouldn't be a feminist Mormonism, with women having several husbands. That would be good for a laugh. And anyway it exists, not for husbands, but for lovers. I must paint a portrait of Anatole de Saintariste as a lieutenant, at the side of Corail, his mistress. That little one is hard to draw."

"To end this letter, I should tell you that an Anglican pastor has just put out a book in which he implicitly does his best to deny the ethnic truths that form the basis of our religion and that, before this century, were proclaimed by Catholic writers, possessors of the whole truth, up to the appearance of the angel Moroni to Joseph. This pastor, in his travels in Asia, found himself among the Nestorians, and claims to have recognized in them the representatives of the ten tribes of Israel whose historical traces have been lost until the day when the Book of Mormon proved that, having emigrated to America, there remains today only a small part of one of the nations that came from them and the worst, that of the Lamanites, Jews punished by God, but who are nonetheless the last representatives of His people, that is to say, the Red race that we respect. This work, full of bad faith, doesn't even make allusion to our truths and the publication was for me a new occasion for recognizing

de reconnaître l'infernale ignorance et l'outrecuidante méchanceté de ces sectes que l'iniquité a suscitées sur la terre. Au contraire, les prêtres catholiques ont connu la vérité par révélation avant la révélation complète des plaques à Joseph Smith qui estimait grandement le catholicisme. Ils vivent avec dignité, avec désintéressement et sont pleins de sanctification. Ils étaient les gardiens de la vérité et notre Eglise n'est au catholicisme que sa continuation moderne et adaptée aux nouvelles révélations.

"C'était dans l'Utah, sur la place qui occupe le centre de la grande ville du Lac Salé, vers trois heures de l'après-midi. La caravane avait apparu d'abord comme les petites fumées d'une fusillade. Elle se condensèrent en de mouvants points noirs. Né à l'horizon, d'où il serpentait comme une procession de fourmi, le cortège avait vite grandi; près des fourgons recouverts de toile, des charrettes, des piétons, hommes et femmes, chargés de fardaux, s'étaient montrées les silhouettes des cavaliers armés, et l'on avait entendu les clameurs des gens, le grincement des roues, le hennissement des chevaux.

"Puis, par groupes, se succédant sans ordre, à intervalles, les piétons, les cavaliers, les attelages étaient entrés dans la capitale des Saints-du-dernier-jour.

"Après une traversée de cinq mois, sans la vue d'aucune terre que le sombre roc du cap Horn, une troupe d'émigrants avait débarqué en Californie pour se joindre aux sectaires polygames de l'Amérique. Il avait fallu voyager péniblement à travers le grand désert du sel et tous: hommes et femmes, descendus des chevaux, sortis des fourgons, regardaient, assis sur le sol, la cité bâtie en amphithéâtre contre les monts Wasatch dont les neiges éternelles se coloraient délicatement de rose tendre et de vert pâle. Ces voyageurs poudreux, ces jeunes filles inquiètes et amaîgries attendaient avec impatience le retour de l'apôtre, Lorenzo Snow, qui s'était rendu chez le Prophète, et la fatigue leur imposait le silence.

"De larges rues sortaient de la place et, régulièrement espacée, des maisons de bois se carraient dans des vergers pleins d'abricotiers et de pêchers couverts de fruits.

"Autour de la place, d'élégantes boutiques de modistes, de luthiers, de grannetiers, de marchands de tabac, de spiritueux, de produits comestibles, d'instruments aratoires, annonçaient leurs marchandises sur des enseignes multicolores et la plupart d'entre elles, pour marquer que le commerçant était mormon, portait la figure d'un œil peint en bleu.

"Il y avait aussi des comptoirs de changeurs et dans des pots violets, devant un hôtel, de petits orangers arrondissaient leurs mappemondes de feuillages.

the infernal ignorance and the outrageous wickedness of these cults that iniquity has inspired on earth. On the contrary, Catholic priests knew the truth by revelation before the complete revelation of the plaques by Joseph Smith who greatly esteemed Catholicism. They live dignified and disinterested lives and are full of blessedness. They were the guardians of truth and our Church is nothing to Catholicism but its modern continuation adapted to new revelations.

"It was in Utah, on the square at the center of great Salt Lake City, around three o'clock in the afternoon. First the caravan looked like little bursts of smoke from gunfire. They condensed into dark moving points. Born at the horizon, whence they twisted like a procession of ants, the retinue grew quickly; near the canvas-covered wagons, the carts, the walkers, overburdened men and women, appeared as the silhouettes of the armed cavalry and one heard the clamoring of the people, the creaking of the wheels, the neighing of horses.

"Then, in groups, following one another at irregular intervals, the walkers, those on horseback, the teams, entered the capital of the Latter-day-Saints.

"After a five-month journey, without sight of any land but the dark rock of Cape Horn, a group of emigrants had come ashore in California to join the polygamous sects of America. They had had to travel painfully across the Great Salt Desert and all, men and women, dismounted their horses, came out of the wagons, sat down on the ground, looked around at the town built in an amphitheater against the Wasatch Range whose eternal snows were delicately colored soft pink and pale green. These dusty travelers, these young girls, so worried and thin, waited impatiently for the return of the apostle, Lorenzo Snow, who had gone to meet the Prophet and, in their exhaustion, they were silent.

"Wide roads took off from the square and, regularly spaced wooden houses nestled in apricot and peach orchards filled with fruit.

"Around this square, elegant boutiques of milliners, instrument-makers, seed merchants, sellers of tobacco, spirits, edible products, instruments for plowing, proclaimed their merchandise on multicolored signs and most of them, to mark that a merchant was Mormon, sported the image of a painted blue eye.

"There were also moneychangers' stalls and, in purple pots in front of a hotel, little orange trees rounding out their globes with leaves.

"Bientôt, pour examiner les émigrants, tous les boutiquiers vinrent sur le pas de leur porte. Les uns fumaient la pipe, d'autres chiquaient et lançaient parfois sur le sol un long jet de salive mordorée; quelques-uns enfin, un canif dans la main droite, taillaient à petits coups un morceau de bois qu'ils tenaient dans la main gauche.

"Des enfants peu à peu entouraient les nouveaux venus et minces, l'air vicieux, les petits garçons donnaient la main aux fillettes, leur prenaient la taille, les embrassaient effrontement en bavardant, en riant, en faisant des grimaces à l'adresse des voyageurs.

"Une de ces petites filles fumait la cigarette, l'écartant après chaque bouffée qu'elle expirait les yeux fermés. C'étaient les premiers nés de la ville naissante.

"Cités! vous êtes les monuments les plus sublimes de l'Art humain. Le mouvement indéfini de la marche humaine s'élève vers l'immobilité infinie. La lassitude fait souhaiter au monde le repos plein d'activité de la vie végétative. Des vagabonds s'arrêtent et, se tenant les uns près des autres comme les arbres dans la forêt, ils plantent des racines artificielles, leurs maisons se dressent, la ville projette ses ombres. Et l'unité merveilleuse du nouvel établissement, avec ses tours et ses demeures, ses aqueducs et ses cloaques, ses architectes et ses pontifes, apparaît tout entière dans le nom de la cité.

"Ces enfants jouaient au soleil et on ne leur avait pas enseigné la pudeur. Ils vivaient dans une société où la religion prescrit et honore l'œuvre de chair et les serails paternels exaltaient leur concupiscence.

"Trois Indiens sortirent fièrement d'un débit de boissons. C'étaient des Utes, vétus de vieux pantalons, coiffés de bonnets en fourrure de vison et chaussés de mocassins précieux qu'ornaient des perles en verroterie blanche et verte et un mouchoir rouge était noué à leur cou nu. Ces Peaux-Rouges marchaient avec dignité, sachant qu'on les regardait comme le reste des Lamanites, dernière nation issue des dix tribus d'Israël qui furent perdus après la captivité de Babylone et dont le livre de Mormon referme l'histoire, la grandeur et les malheurs sur le continent américain.

"Ils formaient la noblesse de la nouvelle cité où, en faveur de leur origine on les laissait vivre pouilleux, débauchés et misérables. Et les traditions qu'ils observaient encore, malgré leur décadence morale, avaient servi de modèle aux réformateurs mormons.

"Soon, all of the merchants came outdoors to examine the emigrants. Some smoked pipes, others chewed, and every so often sent a stream of bronze saliva to the ground; finally, some, penknife in their right hands, carved a bit of wood held in their left hands with little strokes.

"Little by little children surrounded the newcomers; the little boys, who were thin with a nasty expression, took the little girls by the hand, held them by the waist, brazenly kissed them while chatting, laughing, making faces for the travelers' benefit.

"One of these little girls was smoking a cigarette, pulling it away after each puff that she exhaled with eyes closed. These were the firstborn of the new city.

"Cities! you are the most sublime monuments of human Art. The endless movement of human progress rises toward infinite immobility. Laziness makes us wish the world might have a rest filled with the activity of a vegetative life. Vagabonds stop and, sticking close to one another like trees in the forest, they plant artificial roots, their houses rise up, the city projects its shadows. And the marvelous unity of the new establishment, with its towers and its residences, its aqueducts and its cesspools, its architects and its pontiffs, all appear as one in the name of the town.

"These children played in the sun. No one had ever taught them a sense of decency. They lived in a society where religion prescribes and honors the world of the flesh and the paternal scraglios exalted their concupiscence.

"Three Indians came proudly out of a drinking establishment. They were Utes, dressed in old pants, wearing mink hats and, on their feet, precious moccasins decorated with pearls and white and green glass beads, and a red handkerchief knotted around their bare necks. These Redskins walked with dignity, knowing that they were believed to be the last of the Lamanites, the last nation of the ten tribes of Israel that were lost after the Babylonian captivity and whose story ended in the book of Mormon, their greatness and misfortunes on the American continent.

"They made up the nobility of the new town where, due to their ancestry, they were allowed to live a squalid, debauched, and miserable life. And the traditions that they still observed, in spite of their moral decadence, had served as a model for Mormon reformers.

"Il y avait le cortège des onze femmes du Soleil de Perfection, Robin Farmesneare. Elles portaient le nom de leur mari précédé de leur nom paternel. Toutes onze étaient enceintes et leur grossesse à toutes paraîssait avancée; leurs ventres énormes se balançaient devant elles et leur donnaient une noble apparence.

"Et les émigrants s'étonnaient que tant de fécondité se manifestait après la stérilité du désert de sel. La religion qu'elles avaient embrassée en Europe peu de mois auparavant, était celle de la fécondité. Puis, se mêlant à la troupe des femmes étrangères, les fécondes matrones vantaient leur bonheur, décrivaient les joies de leur foyer, louaient la force et l'intelligence de leur époux:

"Venez avec moi, jeune fille, nous sommes déjà quatre épouses et nous vivons en commun auprès de notre époux. Venez partager nos tendresses communes. Nos enfants sont encore petits, ils ne sauront jamais laquelle d'entre nous est leur mère et leur piété filiale nous entourera toutes cinq.

"Venez avec moi, ô jeune fille, je suis venue aussi d'Europe, un jour. J'avais perdu mon seul amour. Et c'est ici la ville sans amour. Et quel bonheur est semblable à celui de la chair satisfaite quand l'esprit ne peut plus connaître la jalousie?

"Sur la place de l'Union, Brigham Young avait levé les mains et tous les hommes, Mormons et Gentils, s'étaient découverts. Alors le prophète se mit à parler. Il vanta la noblesse de la religion nouvelle, disant qu'elle était ouverte à toutes les vérités au fur et à mesure qu'elles apparaîssaient. Il se réjouit que les Dieux eussent envoyé des anges parmi la nation sacrée. Il ordonna aux riches de distribuer leur superflu aux pauvres. Il exalta la polygamie, faisant l'éloge de l'œuvre de chair.

"C'est la joie immense de l'homme de pouvoir procréer comme la divinité. Et l'on voudrait limiter le pouvoir créateur de l'homme au ventre d'une seule femme! N'est-ce pas insulter la génération? Ce pouvoir créateur de l'homme cesse-t-il pendant la grossesse de son épouse? Et pourquoi, pendant qu'elle dure, interdire à l'époux de procréer? Croissez et multipliez, enfants de Dieu! La volupté nous divinise, nous montons au paradis quand nous la ressentons. Naissez, naissez, fils et filles des Saints, croissez et multipliez au nom de Merer, par Odiroth, Merevors, Marinikambinissim.

"There was the retinue of eleven women of the Sun of Perfection, Robin Farmesneare. They carried the name of their husband preceded by their paternal name. All eleven were pregnant and all of their terms appeared to be advanced; their enormous bellies held before them gave them a noble appearance.

"And the emigrants were surprised that such fertility was found here after the sterility of the salt desert. The religion that they had embraced in Europe only a few months before was that of fertility. Then, mixing into the group of foreign women, the fertile matrons boasted of their happiness, describing the joys of their hearth, praising the strength and intelligence of their husbands:

"Come with me, young girl, we are already four wives and we live together with our husband. Come share our communal tenderness. Our children are still young, they will never know which of us is their mother and their filial piety will surround all five of us.

"Come with me, oh young girl, I too, one day, came from Europe. I had lost my only love. And this is the city without love. And what joy can be compared to that of satisfied flesh when the spirit can no longer know jealousy?

"On Union Square, Brigham Young had raised up his hands and all men, Mormons and Gentiles, removed their hats. Then the prophet spoke. He praised the nobility of the new religion, saying that it was open to all truths little by little as they appeared. He rejoiced that the gods had sent the angels to the sacred nation. He ordered the rich to distribute their surplus among the poor. He glorified polygamy, praising the work of the flesh.

"It is the immense joy of man to be able to procreate like the divinity. And they want to limit the creative power of man to the belly of only one woman! Is that not an insult to generation? Does man's creative power cease while his wife is pregnant? And why, for as long as it lasts, should the husband be forbidden to procreate? Be fruitful and multiply, children of God! Sensual pleasure makes us divine, we climb to paradise when we experience it. Be born, be born, sons and daughters of the Saints, be fruitful and multiply in the name of Merer, by Odiroth, Merevors, Marinikambinissim.

"Ils roulaient par milliers et le prophète chantait toujours jusqu'au moment où le soleil étant à son declin, faisant de sa redingote un fouet, il les en cinglait ces cerceaux humains pour les chasser dans les rues avoisinantes où ils se détendaient en poussant un cri terrible et restaient immmobiles tout couverts de poussière et de bave sanguinolente."

"Enterprises de Brigham Young qui était un homme fort entendu aux affaires. C'est lui qui fonda le premier ces énormes magasins comme on en voit aujourd'hui dans toutes les grandes villes et où l'on vend de tout.

"Et lui qui voulait parler au Prophète qui arrivait à son rang dans le cortège auprès du patriarche et parmi les apôtres, fit un faux pas et tomba devant la troupe auguste.

"Le président s'arrêta et avec lui le cortège tout entier et, tandis que se prolongeaient les sonneries de trompettes, le nègre criait:

"J'ai vu d'un ciel orange Christ-Adam descendre avec ses femmes et des dieux à l'infini traversaient les espaces pour annoncer la rédemption des noirs."

"Mais Brigham Young demanda à son voisin Kimball qui riait bruyamment:

"Quel esprit maudit et menteur habite pour ses péchés au tabernacle de ce nègre?

"Et de la troupe des Septante qui venait ensuite sortirent quatre hommes qui prirent à la Française Paméla, sans lui demander, l'écharpe qu'elle avait posée sur son bras; ils tordirent cette bande de soie comme un cordage, firent un nœud coulant qu'ils lancèrent par-dessus le nègre qui se débattait et criait désespérément:

"C'est moi Esu Claudland, un fils de Missouri."
ou encore:

"Je suis un Yankee!"

"Ils le pendirent aux applaudissements de tous ceux qui assistaient à ce spectacle et aux rires en cascades des Américaines dont les yeux brillaient de la joie qu'elles éprouvaient à avoir été promptement vengées.

"Le pendu se débattait encore, ses pieds dansant la gigue avec l'agilité à laquelle il les avait accoutumés et dans son visage sombre il semblait qu'il y eut à la place des yeux deux grands scorpions blancs qui marchaient l'un contre l'autre et la joie fut à son comble lorsque de la bouche du pendu un jet de salive étant sorti, un des musiciens de l'orchestre de Nauvoo, qui avait été baleinier, cria:

"Elle souffle là!"

"Comme fait, lorsqu'il aperçoit la baleine, le matelot qui interroge la mer du haut du mat.

"They rolled, by the thousands, and the prophet kept on singing until the moment when the sun went down and, using his coat as a whip, he lashed these human hoops hunting them in the neighboring streets where they were relaxing, gave a terrible cry and remained immobile all covered in dust and bloody slaver."

"Enterprises of Brigham Young who was a man respected in matters of business. It was he who founded the first of the enormous stores that sell everything one sees today in all big cities.

"And he who wished to talk to the Prophet, who was arriving in his row in the retinue, close to the patriarch, and among the apostles, slipped and fell in front of the august group.

"The president stopped and with him the entire retinue and, while the ringing of the trumpets went on, the black man cried:

"I saw an orange sky Christ-Adam descend with his wives, and infinite gods crossed space to announce the redemption of black people."

"But Brigham Young asked his neighbor Kimball who laughed loudly:

"What wicked and lying spirit is confined for his sins to the tabernacle of this black man?

"And of the group of the Seventy that was on its way, four men took from the Frenchwoman Pamela, without asking her, the scarf on her arm; they twisted this silk ribbon into a rope, making a flowing knot that they threw around the black man who struggled and cried desperately:

"It is I, Esu Claudland, Missouri's son."
or again:

"I'm a Yankee!"

"They hanged him to the applause of all those who attended the spectacle and to the cascading laughter of American women whose eyes shone with the joy that they felt at having been promptly avenged.

"The hanged man still struggled, his feet dancing the agile jig that they were accustomed to, and in his dark face it seemed that in the place of eyes he had two big white scorpions that walked one alongside the other and joy was at its peak when, a stream of saliva coming from the hanged man's mouth, one of the musicians of the Nauvoo orchestra, who once had been a whaler cried:

"Thar she blows!"

"As was done when he saw a whale, the sailor who looks out over the sea from the top of the mast.

"Puis après les derniers soubresauts du nègre missourien, le cortège reprit sa marche devant le regard fixe du mort rigide comme un mangeur d'opium.

"Avant tout passa un grand mannequin représentant une femme assise et couronnée d'étoiles et d'invisibles roues, dissimulées dans le socle, étaient poussées par deux hommes qu'on ne pouvait voir, tandis qu'un troisième faisait tourner la tête comme si elle avait appartenu à une femme vivante et, de temps en temps le prodigieux simulacre parlait et c'était ces hommes qui criaient à l'intérieur de la machine:

"*Je suis la Démocratie de l'Amérique, terre des femmes grandes et des hommes turbulents qui procréeront des géants plus grands que les énormes séquoises!*"

"Quel âge peut avoir aujourd'hui le Napoléon dont il s'agit?"

"Je l'ignore, mon enfant, et peut-être n'est-il appelé ici Napoléon que par manière de parler et symbolise-t-il tout simplement le nouvel astre impérial qui se prépare à rayonner sur le monde, l'Impérialisme civilisateur né de l'adroite solution des problèmes qui se posent encore aujourd'hui dans la Méditérranée orientale."

"Et tout le reste de la nuit elle entendit Pablo Canouris tambouriner aux volets du rez-de-chaussée en criant: "Elbirre, écoute-moi, oubrre-moi, je te aime, je te adore, et si tu né m'obéis pas, jé té touérrai avec mon rebolber. Elbirre, jé té jourre qué jé raconté à Nicolas et à sa sœur. Oubrre-moi Elbirre: L'amour c'est moi; l'amourr c'est la paix, et je souis l'amourr puisqué jé souis neuttre, et lui c'est la guerre. La guerre c'est pas l'amour, c'est la haine. Donque tou lé détestes et tou me aimes, ma petite Elbirre, oubrre-moi, oubrre à ton Pablo qui té adores."[45]

> Seul je pouvais chanter ainsi
> Mes chants tombent comme des graines
> Taisez-vous tous vous qui chantez
> Ne mêlez pas l'ivraie au blé.[46]

"Rameau central de combat Contact par l'écoute on tire dans la direction "des bruits entendus" Les jeunes de la classe 1915 Et ces fils de fer électrisé ne pleurez donc pas sur les horreurs de la guerre avant elle nous n'avions que la surface de la terre et des mers après elle nous aurons

---

45. *La Femme assise.*
46. "Les Collines," *Calligrammes.*

"Then after the black Missourian's last twitches, the retinue took up its march again before the fixed gaze of the dead man, rigid like an opium eater.

"Before all a tall mannequin representing a seated woman crowned with stars, invisible wheels concealed in its base, was pushed by two unseen men, while a third made the head turn as if it belonged to a living woman, and, from time to time, the incredible simulacrum spoke, and it was these men who called out from inside the machine:

"I am the Democracy of America, land of tall women and boisterous men who will procreate giants taller than the enormous sequoias!"

"How old can Napoleon be today?"

"I don't know, my child, and maybe he's only called Napoleon here as a manner of speaking and he simply symbolizes the new imperial star that is preparing to shine on the world, the civilizing Imperialism born of the skillful solution of problems still found today on the eastern shores of the Mediterranean."

"And for the rest of the night, she heard Pablo Canouris drumming on the shades of the ground floor yelling: "Elbirre, listen to me, oven up, I luf you, I adores you and if you don't obeys me, I kill you with my rebolber. Elbirre, I swear that I tell everyting to Nicolas and his sister. Oven up, Elbirre: I am luf, luf is peace, and I am luf because I am neutral, and him, he's war. War is no luf, is hate. So you hate it and you luf me, my little Elbirre, oven up, oven up for Pablo who adore you."[45]

> Only I could sing this way
> My songs fall like seeds
> Be quiet all of you who sing
> Do not mix the wheat with the chaff.[46]

"Central branch of combat Contact by listening fire in the direction of "noises heard" The boys of the class of 1915 And these electrified barbed wires don't cry over the horrors of war before it we had only the surface of the earth and the oceans afterward we'll have abysses

45. *La Femme assise.*
46. "Les Collines," *Calligrammes.*

les abîmes Le sous-sol et l'espace aviatique maîtres du timon Après après nous prendrons toutes les Industries Agriculture Métal Feu Cristal Vitesse Voix Regard Tact à part Et ensemble dans le tact venu de loin plus loin encore l'au-delà de cette terre.[47]

Un Dernier Chapitre

"Tout le peuple se précipita sur la place publique Il vint des hommes blancs des nègres des jaunes et quelques rouges Il vint des ouvriers des usines dont les hautes cheminées ne fumaient plus à cause de la grève Il vint des maçons aux vêtements maculés de plâtre Il vint des garçons bouchers aux bras teints de sang Des mitrons pâles de la farine qui les saupoudrait Et des commis de commerçants de toutes sortes Il vint des femmes terribles et portant des enfants ou en ayant d'autres accrochés à leur jupes Il vint des femmes pauvres mais effrontées plâtrées maquillées Aux gestes étranges Il vint des estropiés des aveugles des culs de jatte des manchots des boiteux Il vint même des prêtres et quelques hommes mis avec élégance Et hors la place la ville semblait morte ne tressaillant même pas.[48]

Afin que la beauté ne perde pas ses droits.[49]
surgissent trois par trois.[50]
Ta langue le poisson rouge dans le bocal de ta voix.[51]

47. "Guerre," *Calligrammes*.
48. "Quelconqueries," *Reflets de l'incendie*.
49. "Chant de l'honneur," *Calligrammes*.
50. "Arbre," *Calligrammes*.
51. "Fusée-Signal," *Il y a*.

The underground and the aerial space masters of the yoke After after we will take up all the Industries Agriculture Metal Fire Crystal Speed Voice Gaze Touch separately And together in touch come from far away further still beyond this earth.[47]

A Final Chapter

"The whole populace ran to the public square White men came and black and yellow and a few red Workers came from the factories whose tall chimneys smoked no more because of the strike Masons came in clothes spattered with plaster Butcher boys came with their blood-stained arms Bakers' boys dusted pale with flour And merchants' assistants of all kinds Terrifying women came carrying children or with others clinging to their skirts Poor women came brazen plastered painted With strange gestures The crippled the blind the amputees the one-armed the lame Even priests came and a few elegantly dressed men And outside of the square the seemingly dead city didn't even stir.[48]

> That beauty might not lose its privileges.[49]
> arise three by three.[50]
> Your tongue, the red fish in the jar of your voice.[51]

47. "Guerre," *Calligrammes*.
48. "Quelconqueries," *Reflets de l'incendie*.
49. "Chant de l'honneur," *Calligrammes*.
50. "Arbre," *Calligrammes*.
51. "Fusée-Signal," *Il y a.*

& Cie

Writing—the choice of words—(1) the composition as action—of the process—(2) the composition as passion—as felt.[1] The composition as action proceeds with implicit judgment. The composition as passion attests (if sometimes tacitly) the recipience of judgment and the repayment (if sometimes tacitly) of a judgment.

His (Apollinaire's) writing reads its implicit self-criticism (vide chapter 2 of this book as an illustration). *Reading* (recipience) speaking this self-criticism (properly Apollinaire's), and following upon the composition as action, proceeds merely as the discourse of passion (recipience); becomes in the nature of et cetera.

The best language will be suited to the best thoughts. But the best thoughts cannot exist except where knowledge and genius are found; therefore the best language is only suitable in those in whom knowledge and genius are found.[2] Compatibility, which reading sometimes discovers.

The choice of words: poetry seems to remain a pattern to prose writers, and not the converse, which things appear to confer a certain supremacy.[3] It follows that writing—the composition as action—poetry remaining a pattern for prose, prose—proceeds, proceed—with implicit judgment.

Also, judgment may go under the name of a dialectic, an esthetic, a criticism. Following the expression of the best thoughts in the best language, there is third removed from the order of expression (the best thoughts being second removed from expression), perhaps an art of judgment, or an art of criticism.

---

1. Cf. Dante, *De Vulgari Eloquentia*, book 2, chapter 8.
2. Ibid. book 2, chapter 1.
3. Ibid. book 2, chapter 1.

And Co.

L'écriture—ou choix des mots—(1) est composition considérée comme action ou—(2) composition considérée comme chose éprouvée—passion.[1] La composition-action procède par le jugement implicite. La composition-passion atteste (parfois tacitement) la réception d'un jugement et (parfois tacitement) son remboursement.

L'écriture d'Apollinaire lit en elle-même son auto-critique implicite (comme l'illustre le chapitre II de ce livre). Cette auto-critique lui devient une espèce d'*et cœtera* qui s'attache à la composition considérée comme acte et n'est plus que le déploiement de la composition considérée comme chose éprouvée.

La langue la plus belle conviendra aux plus belles pensées; or la beauté des pensées ne se trouve que là où se trouvent savoir et génie. Donc la langue la plus belle ne peut convenir qu'à ceux chez qui on trouve savoir et génie.[2] Cette compatibilité, est parfois révélée à la lecture.

Sous le rapport du choix des mots: la poésie semble rester un modèle pour les prosateurs, et ce n'est pas l'inverse qui est vrai; d'où résulte pour elle certaines prérogatives.[3] Il découle de ces affirmations que l'écriture—composition considérée comme action—(soit poésie qui demeure un modèle pour la prose, soit prose) procède par le jugement implicite.

Or, le jugement peut s'inscrire dans une dialectique, une esthétique, une critique. A la suite de l'expression des plus belles pensées dans la plus belle langue, à un troisième rang (le deuxième étant pris par les plus belles pensées elles-mêmes), on trouve peut-être un art du jugement, ou un art de la critique.

1. Cf. Dante: *De Vulgari Eloquentia,* book 2, chapter 8.
2. Cf. Dante, *De Vulgari Eloquentia,* book 2, chapter 1.
3. Cf. Dante, *De Vulgari Eloquentia,* book 2, chapter 1.

The implicit self-criticism of *language expressed* is, however, not a shadow, the inference of the shadow is still one with the substance of expression. It follows that this chapter, following upon the composition as action and the self-critical inference (Apollinaire's) still implicit, becomes in the nature of et cetera.

The self-criticism of Apollinaire's choice of words and their expression offers gratuitous inference. Apollinaire's criticism of painting and of literature other than his own is self-criticism as expression, third removed, however, from the object discussed (a painting, a composition not his own), and indicating the third order of an art of criticism.

An aesthetic, then, is justified only if its expression is inclusive enough in its terminology to be potentially the guidance properly of the first order of expression, to which the esthetic leads; or, conversely, if its expression is inclusive enough never to specifically stray from the detailed applications of the first order of expression which manifest is composition as action. In his criticism of Picasso, for example, Apollinaire satisfies this measure of an art of criticism: "Si nous savions, tous les dieux s'éveilleraient." "Car les enfants seuls méditent." "Il s'est vu plus latin moralement; plus arabe rythmiquement."[4]

Dealing successively with three different objects of Picasso's painting—with the seeming light of reflection of his portraits, with the contemplative diminutiveness of the children of his groups, with the implied history of painting in the feeling derived from his linear constructions—Apollinaire has done an approximation in words of the objects of painting, an approximation of a third order after the objects of painting; since what follows second upon these is the passion of these objects felt as thoughts previous to verbal expression.

Among the reversals of his comment on literature, Apollinaire noticed that "La publicité devient bien littéraire."[5] An art of criticism being in all senses, except in the sense of its own verbal arrangement, an advertisement of another object is thus in a sense a publicity. But, as verbal expression, the publicity can show in its choice of words an art of writing in which every descriptive term is not only like the defined term of a syllogism, but like the completion itself of the art of the first order discussed and like the sufficiency (since it exists) of the natural or conceptual thing itself.

4. "La Plume," May 15, 1905, *Picasso, peintre.*
5. *Anecdotiques,* p. 167.

L'auto-critique implicite du langage *quand elle s'exprime* n'est pourtant pas une ombre; ou l'apparition de cette ombre est la fonction même de la substance de l'expression. Il s'ensuit que ce chapitre, venant après la composition considérée comme action et l'apparition de l'auto-critique, toujours implicite, doit être accepté comme une sorte d'*et cœtera*.

L'auto-critique du choix des mots d'Apollinaire et de leur expression est une apparition gratuite. Quand Apollinaire critique la peinture et la littérature des autres, il fait de l'auto-critique qui, en tant qu'expression, est placée pourtant au troisième rang, à partir de l'objet discuté (le tableau étant une composition qui n'est pas la sienne), et appartient au troisième ordre d'un art de la critique.

Une esthétique ne se justifie donc que si son expression est assez serrée dans sa terminologie pour mener spécifiquement au premier ordre de l'expression, le rang auquel conduit l'esthétique, ou, différemment, si son expression est assez serrée pour ne jamais s'égarer spécifiquement hors des applications détaillées du premier ordre d'expression lequel manifestement est composition-action. Dans sa critique de Picasso, par exemple, Apollinaire satisfait à cette ambition d'un art de la critique: "If we knew, all the gods would awake." "For only children meditate." "He saw himself as morally more Latin; rhythmically more Arab."[4]

Abordant successivement trois objets différents dans la peinture de Picasso—l'apparente lumière de la réflexion de ses portraits, la petitesse contemplative des enfants dans ses groupes, les implications d'une histoire de la peinture (sentiment que donnent ses constructions linéaires), Apollinaire a donné une approximation du troisième ordre, car ce qui vient en second à partir des objets, c'est la passion de ces objets éprouvés comme des pensées précédant l'expression verbale.

Parmi ses renversements de jugements sur la littérature, Apollinaire remarque que "Advertisements are becoming quite literary."[5] Un art de la critique étant par tous ses aspects, à l'exception de l'arrangement verbal qui lui est propre, une réclame faite pour un autre objet est, d'une certaine manière, de la publicité. Mais, considérée comme expression verbale, la publicité peut présenter dans son choix des mots un art de l'écriture où chaque terme descriptif est non seulement semblable aux termes d'un syllogisme, mais aussi à la réalisation de l'art du premier ordre et, puisque la chose naturelle ou imaginée elle-même existe à sa contenance.

4. "La Plume," May 15, 1905, *Picasso, peintre.*

5. *Anecdotiques*, 167.

An art of criticism has been broached here because this chapter will become in the nature of et cetera; and because Apollinaire's actual critical example presented more than the discourse of verbal approximation which is verbal expression evolving out of criticism. Munificence demands men of great resources.[6] The munificence resulting from criticism would seem to be among the resources of the art of writing, which would seem to demand the special excellence of a man devoted to a particular craft.

To return to writing—the choice of words—the craft of composition as action; but as a prelude, the following written some time ago may serve and also as the exemplar of an aesthetic: "Weight, grandeur and energy in writing are very largely produced, dear pupil, by the use of images. (That at least is what some people call the actual mental pictures.) For the term Imagination is applied in general to an idea which enters the mind from any source and engenders speech, but the word has now come to be used of passages where, inspired by strong emotion, you seem to see what you describe and bring it vividly before the eyes of your audience. That imagination means one thing in oratory and another in poetry you will yourself detect, and also that the object of poetry is to enthrall, of prose writing to present ideas clearly, though both indeed aim at this latter and at excited feeling."[7]

The last clause saves a chapter, which will become in the nature of et cetera, anachronistic expatiation on an already rendered distinction.

In as much as writing—the choice of words—aims at presenting ideas clearly and at excited feeling, there is construction and the utterance of construction.[8] And, if by construction is meant the arranged sentences, and by the utterance of construction the sounding of their grammatical and typographical morphology by the voice, Apollinaire's chapter on the Mormons in *La Femme assise*,[9] if sounded aloud or read in the ear, would indicate: that there is no preestablished law by which internal rhymes (the surrounding print making them so) destroy the movement of prose, but that there is an actual law, which endures with the reading and sounding, showing that internal rhymes may enhance the arrangement of prose and "hide" to reveal its singular movement. So that prose and poetry have

6. Cf. Dante, *De Vulgari Eloquentia*, book 2, chapter 1.

7. Longinus, *On the Sublime*, xv, 2.

8. Cf. Dante, *De Vulgari Eloquentia*, book 1, chapter 6, l. 45.

9. *La Femme Assise*, 79ff.

On a ébauché ici un art de la critique parce que ce chapitre deviendra une manière d'*et cœtera*: et parce que l'exemple critique d'Apollinaire offrait plus que le déploiement d'une approximation verbale émergeant de la critique. La Munificence demande des hommes de grandes ressources.[6] La Munificence qui résulte de la critique semblerait être parmi les ressources de l'art d'écrire, qui semblerait demander le génie spécial d'un homme consacré à un métier particulier.

Pour en revenir à l'écriture—choix des mots—ou technique de la composition-action; cette citation pourra servir de prélude en présentant un modèle d'esthétique qui fut écrit il y a déjà pas mal de temps: "Weight, grandeur and energy in writing are very largely produced, dear pupil, by the use of images. (At the very least it has to do with what some might call true mental images.) For the word Imagination is generally applied to the idea that arrives in the mind and gives rise to speech, but the word is now understood as the transition where, inspired by a strong emotion, you seem to see what you describe and to present it to the reader's eyes in full light. That the imagination has one meaning in oratory art and another meaning in poetry, you will discover on your own and also that poetry's object is to captivate, that of prose is to present ideas clearly, though in fact both are directed at this second goal as well as at the excitement of feeling."[7]

Cette dernière phrase nous épargne un chapitre qui sera, développement anachronique d'une distinction déjà faite, manière d'*et cœtera*.

En tant que l'écriture—choix des mots—vise à présenter des idées clairement et à l'excitation du sentiment, on doit distinguer la construction et la sonorité de la construction.[8] Et si par construction on entend l'arrangement des phrases et par sonorité de la construction, le retentissement vocal de la morphologie grammaticale et typographique, le chapitre d'Apollinaire sur les Mormons dans *La Femme assise*,[9] quand on le fait résonner aux oreilles, indiquerait: qu'il n'y a pas de loi préétablie par laquelle les rimes internes (ce sont les caractères imprimés qui les rendent telles) détruisent le mouvement de la prose. Mais qu'il y a une règle qui persiste à travers lecture et retentissement vocal, montrant que les rimes intérieures peuvent rehausser l'arrangement de la prose et se "dissimuler" pour révéler son mouvement particulier. Ce qui fait que la prose et la

---

6. Cf. Dante, *De Vulgari Eloquentia*, book 2, chapter 1.

7. Longin, *Du Sublime*, xv, 2.

8. Cf. Dante, *De Vulgari Eloquentia*, book 1, chapter 6, l. 45.

9. *La Femme assise*, pp. 79ff.

been so called; and as to the actual matter of "images," which are the choice of words, there are differences of heard and printed accelerations in the composition as action.

The aural, oral—as well as visual, banquet served in the meaning of the ode—received by early natural analysis as tho it were three and not one—by virtue of the syntax, which pertained to grammarians; by virtue of the ordering of the discourse which pertained to rhetoricians; by virtue of the numbers in its parts which pertained to musicians;[10]—may, in the modern extension of verbal expression evolving out of criticism, become as one banquet: grammar, rhetoric and music subsumed under the single absolute of all three, which early natural critical synthesis also knew as construction and the utterance of construction. So that poetry and prose remain so called.

Taking an example or two of each:

Grammar—Apollinaire's o, 50[11]

> As-tu pris la pièce de dix sous
> Je l'ai prise

The choice of words reveals the sounded succession of images in a simple grammatical exercise, which orders implicitly a rhetoric, the discourse of which deals with doubt and belief, which in turn, as a whole construction, sound in words the music of the coin. Grammar used here as a form of duration to transmit feeling rather than to inculcate exercise in the use of the object pronoun before the auxiliary, attests suggestion quite complete as a poem, if still pending as drama.

From *Le Tabac à Priser*

> J'ai du bon tabac
> Dans ma tabatière
> J'ai du bon tabac
> Tu n'en auras pas

A grammatical negative future has been subsumed as music under the absolute of construction.

10. Dante, *The Convivio*, second treatise, chapter 12.
11. "Banalités," "Reflets de l'incendie."

poésie sont ainsi nommées; et quant à la question propre des "images"; choix des mots encore, il y a des différences d'accélération entendues et imprimées dans la composition-action.

Le régal auditif aussi bien que visuel servi dans la signification d'une ode et que l'analyse d'un âge élémentaire considérait sous un triple aspect—selon la syntaxe, qui était le domaine du grammairien, selon l'ordonnance du discours, celui du rhétoricien, selon l'arrangement numérique des vers en strophes, celui du musicien[10] —peut, dans l'extension moderne de l'expression verbale émergeant de la critique, devenir un régal unique: grammaire, rhétorique et musique entrant dans une unité absolue, que la synthèse de ces temps élémentaires reconnaîssait aussi comme construction et sonorité de la construction. De telle sorte que prose et poésie restent ainsi nommées.

On peut prendre un ou deux exemples:

Grammaire—o, 50 d'Apollinaire[11]

Did you take the ten-sous piece
I took it

Le choix des mots révèle la succession sonore d'images dans un simple exercice grammatical, qui ordonne implicitement une rhétorique dont le développement tourne autour du doute et de la croyance, lesquels font résonner par des mots la musique de la pièce de monnaie. La grammaire employée ici comme forme de la durée, pour transmettre le sentiment plutôt que pour exhiber un exercice dans l'emploi du pronom complément devant l'auxiliaire, atteste une évocation complète comme poème, bien qu'en suspens comme drame.

De *Le Tabac à Priser*

I've got some fine tobacco
In my tobacco pouch
I've got some fine tobacco
And nothing for you

Le futur négatif est entré comme musique dans l'absolu de la construction.

10. Dante, *Convivio*, second treatise, chapter 12.
11. "Banalités," "Reflets de l'incendie."

Rhetoric (Also from *Le Tabac à Priser*)
Music

"Mets y pour deux sous de tabac mais du fin"

The simplicity of conversation has become rhetoric, a simple naïve ordering of discourse by mouth.

Besides the examples given under Grammar and Rhetoric,—*Les chants des oliveuses sous les oliviers*—the presence of the musical adornment of the initial rhyme making for the parallelism of rhetoric.

(From his criticism in *Les Marges* 1909—Tome 3) "Les qui, que, quels, les qui, qui, les que, que, que dont son style est farci, ne font pas supposer qu'il ait appris à écrire" his rhetorical and grammatical capabilities irritated by the lack of, and impatiently full of convictions about, certain essentials, amusingly subsumed under verbal dissonance.

The meaning of these examples is that the drive of writing which is an order the vehemence of which makes for regulation as little as it does for relegation, will not be impeded by the third order of an art of criticism. And these examples are not among Apollinaire's best poems. Poetry and prose being so called, criticism must, it cannot help itself, become what has been called critical poetry. And so recently there have also been the poetry of the novel, the poetry of the theater and graphic poetry.

Which means merely that writing today proceeds less by explicit division and more by its own implicit criticism of expression necessarily implying the natural (since words are themselves nature) and because of this implication vehement with ubiquitous intelligence. Concretely: Apollinaire was a historian (or more specifically an anthropologist) in the sense that the American Henry Adams was a poet; in the writing, nature itself, becoming or dispersing, formed in relation to the words and their expression a first order of composition as action as against the composition of words rendering this action as passion; yet, being of the nature of the criticism of an object, the expression itself took an objectivity and was thus nature.

It is easy to see now why design (for example, the graphic) can, so to speak, "partake" of poetry; because it partakes of an order of vehement intelligence, which is nature, and as expression it is only another form of writing of that intelligence. It is also easy to see why writing proceeding

Rhétorique (Aussi du *Tabac à Priser*)
Musique

"For two sous put some of that finest tobacco here"

La simplicité de la conversation est devenue de la rhétorique, simple et naïve ordonnance du développement oral.

Pour ne pas se resservir des exemples donnés pour la grammaire et la rhétorique—dans *Les chants des oliveuses sous les oliviers*—la présence de l'ornement musical de la rime initiale rattrape le parallélisme de la rhétorique.

"The who, what, which, the who, who the what, what, what whose style is stuffed, only make you think that he hadn't learned how to write" (critique dans *Les Marges* [1909], vol. 3). Ici, ses dons oratoires et grammaticaux irrités par le manque de certains principes essentiels qu'ils possédaient avec une sureté exaspérée, s'étaient plaisamment installés dans la dissonance verbale.

La signification de ces exemples est que le flux de l'écriture qui est un ordre, ne sera pas arrêté par le troisième ordre d'un art de la critique. Et ces exemples ne sont pas empruntés aux meilleurs poèmes d'Apollinaire. La prose et la poésie étant ainsi artificiellement nommées, la critique doit inéluctablement, devenir ce qu'on a appelé la poésie critique (Cocteau, *Poésie critique*, etc.,). Et ainsi nous avons eu récemment la poésie romanesque, théâtrale et même la poésie graphique.

Ce qui veut dire qu'aujourd'hui l'écriture procède moins par division explicite et davantage par sa propre et implicite critique de l'expression impliquant le naturel (puisque les mots sont eux-mêmes la nature) et pour cette implication même assurée de la véhémence d'une intelligence omniprésente. Au concret: Apollinaire était un historien (plus exactement un anthropologue) de la même façon que l'Américain Henry Adams était poète; dans l'écriture, la nature même, concentrante ou diffusante, formait par rapport aux mots et leur expression un premier ordre de composition-action opposé à la composition des mots rendant cette action comme passion, pourtant, étant de la nature de la critique d'un objet, l'impression même revêtait une objectivité et était ainsi la nature.

Il est facile de voir maintenant pourquoi le dessin (par exemple, le dessin graphique) peut "participer" à la poésie; parce qu'il participe à un ordre de l'intelligence véhémente qui est la nature, et en tant qu'expression n'est qu'une autre forme de l'écriture de cette intelligence. Il est

as such relegates (if implicitly) a division of prose and poetry to the so called; and why the tendency of writing has been to telescope the old time, the new, and the potential new (if), the old place and extension, the old relativities and the undeveloped mechanisms of rote books into the particular (i.e. as opposed to the old partiality) of simultaneously received construction; because the construction proceeds from nature and is part of it. This fusing aspect of construction may be called "curial."[12]

Language, too, being of the construction, is more and more deservedly styled "curial," because "curiality" is nothing else but the justly balanced rule of things which have to be done. In this sense, the fusing simultaneity of language is an aspect of writing or of composition as action attempting influence over the society of various nationals and internationals interested, and even dialects, argot and foreign languages (tho it has been thought) do not stray from "curiality."

Apollinaire has made several observations in this respect:

" 'Cintième. Dites cinquième.' Et je découvris qu'après cent ans les Français font les mêmes fautes en parlant, et comme, en fait de langues, l'usage est un grand maître, on est forcé d'admettre que dans la plupart des cas la faute est la véritable façon de s'exprimer.

"En 1810, il était de mode de réagir, contre l'orthographe de Voltaire et les décisions du grammairien Urbain Domergue étaient sans appel.

"Cet académicien, aujourd'hui complètement oublié venait de mourir et l'on élut à son fauteuil le poète Saint-Ange, dont personne ne se souvient.

"Détail piquant: Saint-Ange avait été une des victimes de Domergue qui s'était donné la peine de relever dans ses vers des fautes contre la grammaire. Saint-Ange égaya fort l'assemblée, lorsque, le 5 septembre 1810, dans son discours de réception, il raconta qu'un jour M. Domergue avait confié à Beauzée que Voltaire ignorait la grammaire: "Vous me faites plaisir de m'en avertir, répondit Beauzée, cela prouve qu'on peut s'en passer."[13]

"C'était tant pis pour le hareng, dit Mia en riant, il était pas trop bête. Moi, je veux bien qu'on me dise que je suis jolie, mais pas pour rire, pour que nous se fiançions . . .

---

12. Dante, *De Vulgari Eloquentia*, book I, chapter 18.
13. *Anecdotiques*, p. 23.

aussi facile de voir pourquoi l'écriture dans son propre processus distingue les noms particuliers de prose et de poésie; et pourquoi la tendance de l'écriture a été de télescoper l'ancien temps, le nouveau (et sa potentialité), le lieu ancien et l'extension, les anciennes relativités et les mécanismes avortés des livres rabachés dans le foyer central (et non plus l'ancienne partialité) de la construction simultanée; parce que la construction joue le rôle de la nature dont elle fait partie. Cet aspect incorporateur de la construction peut être nommé curial.[12]

Le langage, aussi faisant partie de la construction a droit toujours plus légitimement au titre de "curial"; car le "curial" n'est que la bonne application de la règle des choses à faire. Dans ce sens, la simultanéité incorporante du langage est un aspect de l'écriture ou de la composition-action s'essayant à une influence sur la société de nationaux ou même d'internationaux intéressés, et même l'argot et les langues étrangères ne tournent pas le dos à la "curialité."

Apollinaire a fait plusieurs remarques à ce sujet:

" 'Fith. Say fifth.' And I discovered that one hundred years later French people still make the same mistakes in speaking, and as, in language, usage is a great master, we are forced to admit that in most cases the mistake is the true method of self-expression.

"In 1810, it was the fashion to react against Voltaire's spelling and the grammarian Urbain Domegue's decisions were beyond appeal.

"This academic, now completely forgotten, had just died and the poet Saint-Ange, remembered by none, was elected to his chair.

"Piquant detail: Saint-Ange had been one of Domergue's victims, a man who had taken pains to remove grammatical errors from his verse. Saint-Ange greatly amused the assembly, when, on September 5, 1810, in his acceptance speech, he recounted that one day Mr. Domergue had confided in Beauzée that Voltaire did not know grammar: "I am glad you've warned me, responded Beauzée, that proves that it's not the only thing that counts."[13]

"It was too bad for the herring, said Mia laughing, he wasn't that silly. I want someone to tell me I'm pretty, but not just to be funny, to gets engaged . . .

12. Dante, *De Vulgari Eloquentia*, book 1, chapter 18.

13. *Anecdotiques*, 23.

"Et François des Ygrées remarqua pour la noter cette curieuse particularité de syntaxe qui fait conjuguer le pluriel des verbes pronominaux avec le concours unique, à chaque personne, du pronom réfléchi de la troisième personne; nous se fiançons, vous se fiancez. . . . Et il pensait encore:

"Elle ne m'aime pas. Macarée morte. Mia indifférente. Allons, je suis malheureux en amour."[14]

"Le langage du fantassin est riche en synonymes, par exemple, le même engin de tranchées, l'horrible bombe qui naguère venait en se lamentant . . . se nomme, selon les secteurs, yon-yon, fléchette ou queue de rat.[15]

"D'autre part, il se peut que cette mode de mêler au français des termes étrangers soit un moyen de renouveler le langage, de lui infuser une vertu nouvelle. Les *aficionados* du midi ne feraient pas autre chose que d'enrichir la langue.[16]

(*Fantômas*): "Les descriptions y sont presque toujours exactes et, plus tard ce sera, pour l'argot contemporain, une mine de documents inappréciables."[17]

" . . . mais j'ai fui ses baisers en me réfugiant dans mon ou ma bedroom du ou de la family-house où j'étais descendue."[18]

Tho it has been recorded that the only English Apollinaire spoke was Old Irish.[19]

There is, also, the special linguistic scholarship of his poem "La Victoire":

On veut des consonnes sans voyelles
. . . .
Faites claquer votre langue
Servez-vous de bruit sourd de celui qui mange sans civilité
Le raclement aspiré du crachement ferait aussi une belle consonne
etc.

14. *Le Poète assassiné.*

15. *Anecdotiques*, p. 161.

16. *Le Poète assassiné.*

17. *Calligrammes.*

18. *La Femme assise.*

19. *Anecdotiques*, p. 176.

"And François des Ygrées remarked upon this curious syntactical particularity that had plural pronomial verbs conjugated with the competition unique to each person of the reflexive pronoun of the third person: we gets engaged, you gets engaged . . .
And again he thought:
"She doesn't love me. Macarée dead. Mia indifferent. All right then, I'm unhappy in love."[14]

"The language of infantrymen is rich in synonyms, for example, the same machine of the trenches, the horrible bomb that not so long ago came lamenting . . . is called, according to the area, you—you, little arrow, or rat's tail.[15]

"On the other hand, it is possible that this fashion of mixing foreign terms in with French is a way of renewing the language, of infusing it with a new virtue. The *aficionados* of the south do nothing but enrich the language.[16]

(*Fantômas*): "The descriptions therein are almost always exact and, in time it will be, for contemporary slang, a trove of invaluable documents."[17]

" . . . but I fled her kisses by hiding in mine or in my bedroom from or the family house where I stayed."[18]

Bien qu'on ait noté que le seul anglais qu'Apollinaire parlât était le vieil irlandais.[19]

Il y a aussi l'érudition linguistique spécialisée de son poème "La Victoire":

We want consonants without vowels
. . . .
Cluck your tongue
Use the deaf sound of the uncivil eater
The inhaled throat-clearing spit would also make a lovely consonant
etc.

14. *Le Poète assassiné.*

15. *Anecdotiques,* p. 161.

16. *Le Poète assassiné.*

17. *Calligrammes.*

18. *La Femme assise.*

19. *Anecdotiques,* p. 176.

"Finir. Il faut en *finir*. dites il faut *finir* ou *terminer* cette *affaire*, cette *chose*." Les puristes même ne voudraient pas renoncer à cette expression."[20]

In the *curiality* of language—i.e. in the justly balanced rule of things which had to be done to it in modern times—Apollinaire was as in the development of the undeveloped mechanisms of rote books into simultaneously conceived and received construction, what, in the nature of et cetera, is termed here a good anthropologist. One whose practice of composition as action would indicate he knew: that in every case the formal element that characterizes the style is older than the particular type of representation. This does not signify that early representations do not occur, it means that the method of representation was always controlled by formal elements of distinctive origin. The fixity of the pattern does not permit the artist to apply natural forms unmodified to decorative purposes. His imagination is limited by the pattern. In cases of greater freedom the representative value may not be seriously encroached upon. Such is the case, for instance, with the oriental palmetto and the ear ornaments of the Marquesas Islands, on which in olden times two deities were represented, back to back, while nowadays two girls in a swing are carved, in exactly the same special arrangement. — The style of a dominant industry may be imposed upon work made by other processes (weaving patterns, for instance, imitated in painting and pottery).

It is quite possible that in different industries, particularly when carried along by different parts of the population, quite distinctive styles may prevail — when the two sexes carry on different industries they may develop distinctive styles.[21]—A comparison of the fundamental elements that are found in the graphic and plastic arts—in the arts of space—as contrasted with those of poetry, music, and dance,—the arts of time,—brings out certain differences and similarities. Common to both are rhythm and it seems likely that the rhythm of technique is merely a spatial expression of the rhythm of time, in so far as the rhythmic movements result in rhythmic forms when applied to technical pursuits. We may perhaps also speak in both types of art of attempts to emphasize

20. *Anecdotiques*, p. 27.

21. Cf. Apollinaire's application of these with reference to Louise Lalanne, and the clause "Féminisme intégral ou différenciation innombrable des sexes," in his manifesto *L'Antitradition futuriste* (chapter 1 of this book).

"To finish. One must *finish*. Say one must *finish* or *end* this *business*, this *thing*." Even the purists wouldn't want to give up that expression."[20]

Dans la *curialité* de la langue—c'est-à-dire le juste équilibre de la règle des choses qui étaient à faire de cette langue dans les temps modernes—Apollinaire était—développement des mécanismes avortés des livres ressassés vers une construction simultanément conçue et reçue—un homme qui, manière d'*et cœtera*, est désigné ici comme un bon anthropologiste. Un homme dont la pratique de la composition comme action indiquerait qu'il savait: que dans tous les cas l'élément formel caractérisant le style est plus ancien que le type particulier de représentation. Ce qui ne veut pas dire que des représentations ne se présentent pas dès le début mais seulement que la méthode de représentation a toujours été contrôlée par des éléments formels d'origine marquée. La fixité du dessin ne permet pas à l'artiste d'appliquer des formes naturelles sans modification à des fins décoratives. Son imagination est limitée par le dessin. Dans les cas de plus grande liberté on peut ne pas trop empiéter sur la valeur représentative. Ainsi c'est le cas du palmiste oriental et des boucles d'oreilles des Iles Marquises sur lesquels autrefois deux divinités étaient figurées dos à dos tandis qu'aujourd'hui ce sont deux jeunes filles disposées de la même manière. . . . Le style d'une industrie prédominante peut s'imposer à un ouvrage fait par d'autres procédés (des dessins de tissage peuvent ainsi être imités en peinture ou en poterie).

Il se peut fort bien que dans de différentes industries, et particulièrement quand elles sont pratiquées par des parties différentes de la population, des styles tout à fait distincts s'imposent . . . que lorsque les deux sexes pratiquent des industries différentes ils engendrent des styles différents . . . [21] Une comparaison des éléments fondamentaux que l'on trouve dans les arts plastiques et graphiques d'une part (art de l'espace) et d'autre part les arts de la poésie, de la musique, de la danse (art du temps)—apporte certaines différences et certaines similitudes. Le rythme est commun aux uns et aux autres et il semble probable que le rythme de la technique n'est qu'une expression spatiale du rythme du temps, pour autant que les mouvements rythmiques ont pour aboutissements des formes rythmiques quand ils s'appliquent à des recherches techniques. On peut probablement parler aussi de l'existence dans les

20. *Anecdotiques*, p. 27.

21. Cf. l'application qu'Apollinaire a faite de ce principe au sujet de Louise Lalanne et la phrase: "Integral feminism or innumerable differentiation of the sexes." dans son manifeste *L'Antitradition futuriste* (chapitre 1 de ce livre).

closed forms, for often we find musical phrases, and single ideas in poetry closed by what might be called a decorative end, consisting of bur-
dens or of codas. Similar elements may also appear as introductions in
the beginning. Completely lacking in the pure arts of time is symmetry, because an inverted time order does not convey the impression of
symmetry, as is the case in the arts of space. It occurs only in symmet-
rical arrangement of phrases. —Representative and symbolic values of
form (the latter's ulterior significance related to religions or philosophical ideas).

What distinguishes modern aesthetic feeling from that of primitive
people is the manifold character of its manifestations. We are not so
much bound by a fixed style. The complexity of our social structure
and our more varied interests allow us to see beauties that are closed
to the senses of people living in a narrower culture. It is the quality of
their experience, not a difference in mental make-up that determines the
difference between modern and primitive art production and art appreciation. Art arises from two sources, from technical pursuits and from the
expression of emotions and thought, as soon as these take fixed forms —
fundamental sameness of mental process in all races and cultural forms
in the present day; —every cultural phenomenon the result of historic
processes.[22]

Inevitably as well as consciously having to partake of the simultaneously conceived and received construction of the esthetic feeling of his
culture (his time's), Apollinaire infused the contemporary principles of a
dominant (if not the dominant) industry of the arts—painting—into the
implicit judgment of his compositions as action—poetry and prose being
so called.

Notes:[23] "On connaît les recherches de peinture pure faites par
Robert Delaunay.

"Réalité, Peinture-Pure. —Tout récemment, montrant ses dernières
œuvres où la réalité est aussi mouvementée que la lumière vivante, il
expliquait son point de vue sur ces découvertes et l'on a pensé qu'il serait
utile de noter ses déclarations esthétiques sur la construction de la réalité
dans la peinture pure.

22. Franz Boas, *Primitive Art* (Cambridge, 1927), pp. 354, 349, introduction.
23. Included in *Il y a*.

deux groupes d'arts d'efforts pour accentuer les formes fermées, car c'est souvent qu'on trouve des formes musicales et des idées isolées en poésie fermées par une sorte de terminaison décorative: refrains et codas. Des éléments similaires peuvent aussi se présenter comme introduction, au commencement. Ce qui manque complètement dans les purs arts du temps, c'est la symétrie, car en ce qui concerne le temps, un ordre renversé ne donne pas l'impression de symétrie, comme c'est le cas dans les arts de l'espace. Un équivalent de la symétrie n'apparaît que dans l'arrangement symétrique des phrases. . . . Des valeurs formelles, représentative ou symbolique (cette dernière est un sens surajouté par des idées religieuses ou philosophiques).

Ce qui distingue le sens artistique des modernes de celui des primitifs, c'est la multiplicité des manifestations de celui-là. Nous ne sommes pas autant retenus par un style fixe. La complexité de notre structure sociale et nos intérêts plus variés nous permettent de voir des beautés qui sont fermées aux sens de peuples vivants dans une culture plus étroite. C'est la qualité de leur expérience, non une différence de forme mentale, qui détermine la différence entre les manifestations et les plaisirs artistiques. . . . L'art naît de deux sources: des recherches techniques et de l'expression des émotions et des pensées, dès que celles-ci prennent des formes fixes. . . . On remarque l'identité fondamentale des processus mentaux dans toutes les races et toutes les formes culturelles actuelles. . . . Chaque phénomène culturel est le résultat de processus historiques.[22]

Parce que aussi bien fatalement que consciemment, il devait participer à la construction simultanément conçue et reçue du sentiment esthétique de sa culture: (son époque), Apollinaire infuse les principes contemporains d'une industrie artistique prédominante (sinon dominante) (la peinture) dans le jugement implicite de ses compositions-actions—la prose et la poésie restant ainsi nommées.

Notes:[23] "We know of Robert Delaunay's research into pure painting.

"Reality, Pure-Painting. —Quite recently, showing his latest works where reality is as turbulent as the living light, he explained his point of view on these discoveries and it seemed that it would be useful to take note of his aesthetic declarations on the construction of reality in pure painting.

22. Franz Boas, *Primitive Art* (Cambridge, 1927), p. 354, 349, introduction.
23. Dans *Il y a.*

"Le *réalisme* est pour tous les arts la qualité éternelle qui doit décider de la beauté de sa durée et qui lui est adéquate.

"Dans le domaine de la peinture, recherchons la pureté des moyens, *l'expression* de la beauté la plus *pure*.

"*L'impressionnisme* nous mettait devant la nature immédiate, loin des styles.

"Ce fut une grande époque de préparation, la recherche de la seule réalité.

"Le *fonctionnement de la lumière* nécessaire à toute expression *vitale* de la beauté est resté le problème de la peinture moderne. De la lumière Seurat a dégagé le contraste des complémentaires.

"Ce peintre fut un des premiers théoriciens de la lumière. Le contraste devint *moyen* d'expression; la mort prématurée de Seurat a peut-être intérrompu la suite de ses découvertes.

"Sa *création* reste le *contraste de couleurs complémentaires* (le mélange optique par points, n'étant que technique, n'a pas l'importance du contraste, moyen de construction à l'expression pure).

"Ce premier moyen lui servait dans la traduction scénique de la nature; les tableaux qu'il peint sont des sortes d'*images fugaces*.

"Le *contraste simultané* n'a pas été découvert, c'est-à-dire réalisé, par les plus audacieux des impressionnistes, et cependant il est la seule base de toute expression *pure* en peinture actuelle.

"Le *contraste simultané* assure le dynamisme des couleurs et leur *construction*, c'est-à-dire leur profondeur, leurs limites dans le tableau, et il est le moyen le plus fort d'*expression de la réalité*.

"La simultanéité des couleurs, par le contraste simultané et toutes les mesures (impaires) issues des couleurs selon leur expresssion dans leur mouvement représentatif, voilà la seule réalité pour construire en peinture.

"Nous arrivons à un *art* de peinture purement expressive.

"La *lumière* n'est pas un procédé et elle nous vient de la sensibilité essentielle entre la nature et notre *âme*. C'est dans nos yeux que se passe le *présent* et par conséquent notre *sensibilité*.

"Nous ne pouvons rien sans la sensibilité, donc sans lumière. Par conséquent, notre âme maintient sa vie dans *l'harmonie* et *l'harmonie* ne s'engendre que de la simultanéité où les *mesures* et *proportions* de lumière arrivant à *l'âme*, sens suprême, par nos yeux.

"*Realism* is for all of the arts an eternal quality that must decide beauty, its duration, and that it is adequate for it.

"In the domaine of painting let us seek out the purity of means, the *purest expression* of beauty.

"*Impressionism* placed us before immediate nature, far from styles.

"It was a great era of preparation, the search for the only reality.

"The *functioning of light* necessary to all *vital* expression of beauty has remained the problem of modern painting. From light, Seurat emphasized the contrast of complementarities.

"This painter was one of the first theoreticians of light. Contrast became the *means* of expression; the premature death of Seurat may have interrupted the progression of his discoveries.

"His *creation* remains the *contrast of complementary colors* (the optical mixture of points being only technique, doesn't have the importance of contrast, means of construction of pure expression).

"This first option helped him in the scenic translation of nature; the canvases he painted are sorts of *fleeting images*.

"*Simultaneous contrast* had not been discovered, that is to say, realized, by the most audacious of impressionists, and even so it is the sole basis of all *pure* expression in contemporary painting.

"*Simultaneous contrast* assures the dynamism of colors and their *construction*, that is to say, their depth; their limits on the canvas, and that represents a strong means of the *expression of reality*.

"The simultaneity of colors, by the simultaneous contrast and of all their measures (odd numbers) stemming from colors according to their expression in their representative movement, here is the only reality in constructing a painting.

"We arrive at an *art* of purely expressive painting.

"*Light* is not a process and it comes to us through the essential sensitivity between nature and our *soul*. It is in our eyes that the *present* happens and therefore our *sensitivity*.

"We can do nothing without sensitivity, and therefore without light. As a result, our soul maintains its life in *harmony* and *harmony* only comes into being in simultaneity or *measures* and *proportions* of light reaching the *soul*, supreme sense, through our eyes.

"Et l'âme juge les figures de l'œuvre naturelle en comparaison (critique pure) avec la *nature* et commande à *l'inventeur*. L'inventeur tient compte de ce qui est dans *l'univers* par essence, fréquence, imagination et simultanéité.

"La nature engendre donc la *science de la peinture*.

"Les premières peintures furent seulement une ligne qui entourait l'ombre d'un homme faite par le soleil sur le sol.

"Mais combien sommes-nous loin, par les moyens actuels de ces *simulacres*, puisque nous avons la lumière (couleurs claires, couleurs foncées, leurs compléments, leurs intervalles et leurs simultanéités) et toutes les mesures de couleurs issues de l'intelligence à créer l'harmonie.

"*L'harmonie en peinture c'est le sujet*, c'est-à-dire la proportion harmonique; cette proportion est composée de divers membres simultanés dans une action.

"Cette proportion harmonique est créée d'un côté par la *sensibilité*; de l'autre elle est ordonnée par le créateur qui doit s'évertuer à donner le plus d'*expression réaliste*.

"Le sujet est 'éternel' dans l'œuvre d'art et doit apparaître à l'*initié* dans tout son *ordre* et dans toute sa *science*. Le sujet est tout plastique dans la peinture et ressort de la *vision* et doit être l'*expression pure de la nature* humaine, l'éternel sujet est trouvé dans la nature même; l'inspiration et la claire vision appartiennent à celui qui découvre les limites les plus belles et les plus fortes" (1912).

And among Apollinaire's last poems integrated by color schemes, evolving out of an older decade's thematic symbols (*symbolisme*) may be found his simultaneous cubistic abstractions in words; tending to another decade in which the emphasis was to be: "sur la croyance à la réalité supérieure de certains formes d'association négligées jusqu'à lui, à la toute puissance du rêve, au jeu désintéressé de la pensée. Il tend à ruiner définitivement tous les autres mécanismes psychiques et à se substituer à eux dans la résolution des principaux problèmes de la vie."[24]

24. André Breton, *Manifeste du surréalisme*.

"And the soul judges the figures of the natural work in comparison (pure criticism) with *nature* and commands the *inventor*. The inventor takes account of that which is in the *universe* by essence, frequency, imagination, and simultaneity.

"Nature then gives rise to the *science of painting*.

"The first paintings were only a line that surrounded the shadow of a man made by the sun on the earth.

"But how far are we, by current means, from these *simulacrae*, since we have light (light colors, dark colors, their complements, their intervals, and their simultaneity) and all the measures of colors given rise to by intelligence to create harmony.

"*Harmony in painting is the subject*; that is, the harmonic proportion: this proportion is composed of diverse simultaneous members in an action.

"This harmonic proportion is created on the one hand by *sensitivity*; on the other it is ordered by the creator who must struggle for the most *realistic expression*.

"The *subject* is 'eternal' in the work of art and must appear to the *initiate* in all its *order* and in all its *science*. The subject is all plastic in painting and comes from *vision* and must be the *pure expression of human nature,* the eternal subject is found in nature itself; the inspiration and clear vision belong to he who discovers the most beautiful and the strongest limits." (1912)

Et parmi les derniers poèmes d'Apollinaire que réintègrent des schémas de couleurs dérivant des symboles thématiques d'une décade antérieure (*symbolisme*) on trouve dans le champ des mots, ses abstractions cubistes simultanées. Elles mènent à une autre décade où l'accent fort devait être mis "on the belief in the superior reality of certain forms of association neglected until then, in the all-powerfulness of the dream, in the disinterested play of thought. It tends to definitively ruin all of the other psychic mechanisms and to substitute itself for them in the resolution of the principal problems of life."[24]

24. André Breton, *Manifeste du surréalisme*.

Bouche ouverte sur un harmonium
C'était une voix faite d'yeux
Tandis qu'il traîne de petites gens

Une toute petite vieille au nez pointu
J'admire la bouillotte d'émail bleu
Mais le rat pénètre dans le cadavre et y demeure[25]

La fontaine n'a pas tari
Pas plus que l'or de la paille ne s'est terni
Regardons l'abeille
Et ne songeons pas à l'avenir

Regardons nos mains
Qui sont la neige
La rose et l'abeille
Ainsi que l'avenir[26]

Mes tapis de la saveur
moussons des sons
obscurs et ta bouche
au souffle azur[27]

"Ainsi, la littérature dont si peu de peintres se sont passés, disparaît—, mais non la poésie."[28]

Apollinaire's calligrammes making the choice of words and the graphic mutual thus reveal writing the composition as action, which proceeds, in turn, with implicit judgment not only of a life suggested between the space of words (rhythm) but with the judgment of the graphic (tonality) luminously opposed to brooding over prolixity, and filling the order of words with simultaneous complementary values, so that the words as the case may be, simulate threads of rain, or hair over the ankle of a horse, or a fan suggestive of savours.[29] Yet since they remain words of their time deriving from other times their style balances the

25. "Souvenirs," *Calligrammes*.

26. "L'avenir," *Calligrammes*.

27. "Eventail des saveurs," *Calligrammes*.

28. *Peintres cubistes* (on Marcel Duchamp).

29. "Il pleut"—Calligram for an Exhibition—*L'Esprit nouveau*, October 1924, "Evantail des saveurs," *Calligrammes*.

Open-mouthed on a harmonium
It was a voice made up of eyes
While little people followed after

A little old woman with a pointed nose
I admire the blue enamel hot water bottle
But the rat crawls inside the corpse and lives there[25]

The fountain has not run dry
Any more than the golden straw has tarnished
Let's look at the bee
And not dream of the future

Let's look at our hands
Which are snow
The rose and the bee
And then the future[26]

My monsoon flavoured carpets
of obscure sounds
and your mouth
purple breath.[27]

"Thus the literature that so few painters have done without disappears . . . , but not poetry."[28]

Les calligrammes d'Apollinaire établissant la mutualité entre le choix de mots et la graphie révèlent ainsi dans l'écriture la composition-action, qui procède par jugement implicite non seulement d'une vie qu'évoque l'espace entre les mots (rythme), mais aussi par le jugement du graphique (tonalité) lumineusement à la rêverie prolixe, tout en comblant l'ordre des mots à l'aide de valeurs complémentaires simultanées; de telle sorte que les mots, selon les cas, simulent les raies de la pluie, ou les poils sur la cheville d'un cheval, ou un évantail évocateur des saveurs.[29] Pourtant, puisqu'ils demeurent mots de leur époque dérivant d'autres époques, leur style équilibre l'élément de représentation, et la composition-action

25. "Souvenirs," Calligrammes.

26. "L'avenir." *Calligrammes.*

27. "Evantail des saveurs," *Calligrammes.*

28. *Peintres cubistes* (sur Marcel Duchamp).

29. "Il pleut"—Calligram for an Exhibition—*L'Esprit nouveau*, October 1924. "Eventail des saveurs," *Calligrammes.*

element of representation and the composition as action escapes what mature critics are in great haste to call "imitation." For if the page is considered, it is obvious that the rain is of, and not on, the page, that the hair of the horse "imitated" is print, and that it is the composition as passion—the composition as action received in the reading—which is suggestive of savours, and but for an original passion's repayment of a state of things into a choice of words, the graphic fan would not exist even as print.

So that again poetry and prose are proved so called, and there remains instead writing which, if the supremacy of poetry deferred to by the old criticism (that is criticism of an established standing) be deferred to may be called poetry. And if it is realized that the supremacy the old criticism deferred to was the intuition that (the best) writing proceeds less by explicit division and more by its own explicit criticism of expression, the modern extension of this writing may, without intimidation or the imperiling of a just payment of passion in return for a composition as action, be named poetry.

The canzone was said to embrace the whole theme and the stanza the whole art, and in works of art that was considered noblest which embraced the whole art.[30] In Apollinaire, the whole art would seem to be the telescoping, into the choice of words, of times, existences and their thoughts composing into the dominant arts (writing, painting, music) of his era—the intelligence moved by passion and repaying by composition as action. This is not the process, for example, of an art in which a corporeal cerebellum dispenses from a mountain. Apollinaire's whole art (the journalistic sections, products of an inferior specialty set aside) would seem to be a dialectical sensibility the simultaneous comprehension of which is telescoped into a choice of words without the accretion of rendered corpulence or logical cracking.[31] There are thus left his books, their names, and writing. An implied aesthetic it is true results from the necessary trial by intelligence of all forms to attain a definition of them. But in Apollinaire the definition is not a division into Song, Talk, Novel, Drama, Criticism, Epic, etc., because the intelligence has foreshortened times, existences and their thoughts to define each of these once-isolated forms by all the others.

30. Cf. *De Vulgari Eloquentia*, book 2, chapters 3 and 9.

31. Technical sense: A process of distillation of petroleum or some other oil composed of volatile elements, by which the components are separated under heat in accordance with their respective volatilities.

échappe à ce que les critiques ne peuvent manquer d'appeler l'"imitation." Car si on considère la page, il est sûr que la pluie appartient à la page, mais n'est pas sur elle, que le poil du cheval "imité" est caractères d'imprimerie et que c'est la composition-passion—composition-action reçue à la lecture—qui est évocatrice des saveurs, et, n'était un remboursement original par la passion d'un état de choses en un choix de mots, l'éventail graphique n'existerait même pas comme caractères imprimés.

De sorte qu'encore une fois prose et poésie sont des noms, et ils restent à leur place l'écriture qui (si la suprématie de la poésie reconnue par l'ancienne critique, qui est la seule critique bien fondée, est respectée) peut-être appelée poésie. Et si l'on comprend que la croyance à cette suprématie venait de l'intuition que l'écriture (la vraie) procède moins par division explicite et davantage par sa propre critique explicite de l'expression, l'extension moderne de cette écriture peut, sans intimidation ou la mise en péril d'un juste paiement de la passion en retour d'une composition-action, s'appeler poésie.

La canzone—(disait-on)—embrassait le thème entier et la strophe tout l'art, et parmi les œuvres d'art celle-là était considérée la plus noble qui embrassait l'art tout entier.[30] Chez Apollinaire, l'art tout entier semblerait se télescoper dans le choix de mots, les temps, les existences et les pensées se réintégrant ainsi dans les arts dominants (littérature, peinture, musique) de son époque — l'intelligence mue par la passion et remboursssant par la composition-action. Cela n'est pas l'art d'un Goethe qui pontifie du haut des Alpes italiennes. Tout l'art d'Apollinaire (laissant de côté ses pages de journalisme, produits d'un ordre inférieur) semblerait être une sensibilité dialectique dont la compréhension simultanée est télescopée dans un choix de mots. Ce n'est pas ici une opération de raffinage logique, mais on ne nous présente pas, non plus une masse brute.[31] Restent ses livres, leurs noms, leur écriture. Une esthétique impliquée il est vrai résulte de l'examen nécessaire que fait l'intelligence de toutes les formes afin d'en atteindre une définition. Mais chez Apollinaire la définition n'est pas une division en chanson, conversation, roman, drame, critique, épopée, etc . . . car l'intelligence a raccourci les temps, existences et leurs pensées, pour définir chacune de ces formes jadis isolées par toutes les autres.

30. Cf. *De Vulgari Eloquentia*, book 2, chapters 3 and 9.

31. Dans le sens technique: procédé de distillation du pétrole ou de quelqu'autre huile composée d'éléments volatiles, par lequel les composants sont séparés par la chaleur selon leurs volatilités respectives.

1890
l'X

"Toutes les femmes de 45 à 50 ans se souviennent
d'avoir été amoureuses de Capoul."

M. Capus

Et de bien d'autres

As epos what could be more like an era, yet the narrative could not
be more epigrammatic.

A chapter which will become in the nature of et cetera might continue then with his books and refer to an occasional chronology: for his
intelligence matured early, he had to wait only for his data and the facts
to fill out the dialectic implicitly proceeding from his compositions as
actions. That is: the writing.

Et cetera:

L'Hérésiarque & Cie (1899–1910)
Dédication: A Thadée Natanson
ces
Philtres de Phantaisie

"Le Passant de Prague": Isaac Laquedem, l'Éternel Juif, le Juif Errant, of this *story* (merely a convenient term, poetry and prose being
so-called) is an excellent antiquary, bibliographer, and more in the same
line. Apollinaire, in his writing, it may be assumed, was not all these
things for fun, or for the sake of erudition, but so that his work which
was the periphery of his Life might be. Himself, like old Isaac Laquedem,
he had to absorb, in several ways, all the life which had been: "Le Spectateur de l'Humanité, qui me procure de merveilleux divertissements"
(the pseudo self-isolation of humor which qualifies the first part of this
sentence).

"la marche excite l'appetit et je suis un gros mangeur."

"C'est un juif. Il va mourir": the words a rite for the last vestiges of
an ethnography.

1890
X

"All the women between the ages of 45 and 50 remember
having been in love with Capoul."

Mr. Capus

And with many others

Rien ne peut égaler davantage l'étendue d'une époque que ce récit
(épique), pourtant on ne peut plus épigrammatique.

Un chapitre qui serait une manière d'*et cœtera* pourrait poursuivre
par ses livres et en référer à l'occasion à la chronologie; car son intelligence trouva une maturité précoce et il ne dut atteindre que ses données
et les faits pour remplir la dialectique procédant implicitement de ses
compositions-actions; c'est-à-dire l'écriture.

Et cetera:

> *L'Hérésiarque & C*ie (1899–1910)
> To Thadée Natanson
> I dedicate these
> Philters of Phantasy

"Le Passant de Prague": Isaac Laquedem, l'Eternel Juif, le Juif Errant, de cette *histoire* (mot employé par commodité, prose et poésie étant
ainsi nommées) est un excellent antiquaire, bibliographe et autres personnages de ce genre. Apollinaire, dans ces écrits, peut-on supposer, n'était
pas tous ces gens-là, pour rire, ou par amour de l'érudition, mais pour
que son œuvre qui était la périphérie de sa Vie, pût exister. Lui-même,
comme Isaac Laquedem dut absorber de plusieurs façons toute la vie,
lui qui avait été: "the onlooker of Humanity, who brings me marvelous
distractions" (le pseudo isolement de soi-même par l'humour justifie la
première partie de cette phrase).

"walking whets the appetite and I eat a lot."

"He's a Jew. He's going to die:" les mots sont un rite pour les derniers
vestiges d'une éthnographie.

"Le Juif latin": "Comme Fernisoun fut baptisé non loin d'une station de voitures, l'avocat du diable insinuera que cette eau ne fut peut-être que du pissat de cheval. Si cette opinion prévaut, il sera avéré que Gabriel Fernisoun n'a jamais été baptisé et, en ce cas, mon Dieu! nous savons tous que l'enfer est pavé de bonnes intentions." A not definitely formulated heresy of this kind is to be expected of Apollinaire's dialectic.

"L'Infaillibilité": Lors de son premier voyage *ad limina* cet évêque ayant proposé au Saint-Siège l'érection en dogme de la croyance à la mission divine de la France, le cardinal Porporelli, quand il l'apprit, s'écria:

"Pur gallicanisme! Mais l'administration gallo-romaine, quel bienfait pour les Gaules! Elle est nécessaire pour dompter la turbulence des Français. Et que de peine pour les civiliser! . . ." The uses Infallibility might be put to—Apollinaire's dialectic (his judgment and judgment's implicit reversal of ideas); he *played* with the idea!

With this play of dialectic on religion might be collated Apollinaire's apostrophe to Marinetti: "Fondateur de religion! vous êtes le premier du XXe siècle. Et au XIXe je n'en connais qu'un seul: Joseph Smith, fondateur du mormonisme, sorte de paganisme idéaliste, tiré des superstitions des Indiens peaux-rouges et que caractérise la polygamie anthume et posthume des fidèles.

"Vous, dans le but d'honorer 'la beauté de la vélocité,' vous faites naître 'la nouvelle religion morale de la vélocité' de votre 'grande guerre libératrice' " (*Anecdotiques* pp. 216–217).

" 'Que Vlo-ve?' où le surnaturalisme trouve sa formule."[32] The same critic, evidently aware that Apollinaire's writing possessed in *suggestion* the style of former and subsequent "schools" and their extension, touchingly declined to speak of Apollinaire's spoiled future reputation, and preferred to fill the gaps of self-admitted ignorance by considering Apollinaire's best work, which somehow seemed to withstand the zeal of new movements in "literary history."

Compare: (*Le Temps,* October 14, 1913) what Apollinaire says on negro sculpture: "avec quel art . . . dans ces œuvres grotesques et grossièrement mystique . . . les imagiers de la Guinée et du Congo arrivaient à reproduire la figure humaine en n'utilisant aucun élément emprunté à la vision directe."

32. André Breton, *Les Pas perdus.*

"Le Juif latin": "As Fernisoun was baptised near a carriage station, the devil's advocate will suggest that this water may actually have been horse piss. If this opinion prevails, it will be said that Gabriel Fernisoun was never baptized and, in this case, my God! we all know that hell is paved with good intentions." Une hérésie de cette espèce, non définitivement formulée, était à prévoir de la dialectique d'Apollinaire.

"L'Infaillibilité": "When he made his first voyage *ad limina* this bishop proposed to the Holy See that the belief in the divine mission of France should be made dogma. When Cardinal Porporelli learned of it, he cried:

"Pure Gallicanism! But the Gallo-Roman administration is so good for the Gauls! They need it to tame the French. And how difficult to civilize them! . . ." Il *joue* avec l'idée: les emplois possibles de l'Infaillibilité (dialectique d'Apollinaire: le jugement et les renversements implicites d'idées).

A ce jeu de la dialectique avec la religion, on pourrait comparer l'apostrophe d'Apollinaire à Marinetti: "Founder of religion! you are the first of the 20th century. And in the 19th I know of only one: Joseph Smith, founder of Mormonism, a sort of idealistic paganism, taken from the superstitions of the redskins and that are characterized by the anthumous and posthumous polygamy of the faithful.

"You, in order to honor 'the beauty of speed' you give birth to 'the new moral religion of speed' with your 'great liberating war' " (*Anecdotiques,* pp. 216–217).

" 'Que Vlo-ve?' where supernaturalism finds expression."[32] Le même critique, sachant évidemment que l'écriture d'Apollinaire possédait en *suggestion* le style d'"écoles" précédentes et postérieures et leur extension, s'est discrètement interdit de parler de la réputation plus tard gâtée d'Apollinaire, et a préféré excuser sa négligence en l'avouant et en considérant les meilleures œuvres d'Apollinaire, qui, d'une façon ou d'une autre, semblaient résister au zèle de nouveaux mouvements dans l' "histoire littéraire."

Comparez: (*Le Temps,* 14 octobre 1913) ce que dit Apollinaire de la sculpture nègre "with what art . . . in these grotesque and crudely mystical works . . . the image-makers of Guinea and the Congo had managed to represent the human figure without using elements of direct vision."

32. André Breton, *Les Pas perdus.*

The criticism "spontaneity of the sensibility," applied to Picasso, may be applied to Apollinaire's extension of writing absorbing painting. This writing, in the different particular cases, subsumed the principles of contemporary styles of painting: cubism and expressionism or futurism. For definitions: see Guillaume Janneau, *L'Art cubiste*, Paris, 1929; "Tandis que le futurisme s'appliquait à manifester la complexité chaotique des sensations primaires, le cubisme, constraint, pour se distinguer de lui, à préciser ses conceptions particulières, s'applique à saisir les lois d'un ordre nouveau. Il va définir un point de vue devant l'impressionisme, devant Cézanne. Opérant à la fois un travail de déblaiement et de construction, il établit un ensemble de principe, les uns techniques, les autres spirituels, qu'il convient de dégager du verbiage incontinent et souvent fumeux qui les enveloppe" (p. 31). Futurism: multiple, simultaneous projection of the object, according with the states of soul or experience— dynamic sensation—; the particular rhythm and interior force of the object projected, in the painting, a synthesis recalling the dynamics of sight, or the object as it might be successively seen.

Collate: with these styles of painting and writing in Apollinaire's time, these 2 facts determining the general morphology of culture: 1- the period of hunting 2- the period of gardening and agriculture 3- the period of cities and manual crafts. These 3 periods of mutation radiate their respective representations (or criticism of themselves—the world) in expression dealing respectively with 1- Animals 2- The souls of the dead men 3- The Solar Gods.[33]

Apollinaire's time, of the period of cities and manual crafts, seems to have *radiated, in his writing*, the solar gods of velocity.

Le Poète assassiné—1916 (*including the pieces at the end of the volume*): see Dante, *De Vulgari Eloquentia*, book 1, chapter 10, 1.19: *The exquisite legends of King Arthur, and very many other works of history and learning.* The word translates "legends" (ambages) means "turnings" or "windings," and figuratively "digressions," and was a kind of technical expression for novels of adventure.

33. Cf. Frobenius, *Paideuma*.

L'expression critique: "spontaneity of sensitivity," appliquée à Picasso, peut s'appliquer à Apollinaire et à l'extension qu'il donne à l'écriture pour lui faire absorber jusqu'à la peinture. Cette écriture, dans les différents cas particuliers, englobait les principes des styles contemporains de la peinture: cubisme et expressionisme ou futurisme. —Pour les définitions, V. Guillaume Janneau, *L'Art cubiste*, Paris, 1929: "while futurism manifests the chaotic complexity of primary sensations, cubism, constrained, in order to distinguish itself from it, to specify its particular conceptions, seizes the laws of a new order. It will define a point of view after impressionism, often light color, after nature, after expressionism, after Cézanne. Working to clear and to build at once, it establishes an ensemble of principles, some technical, others spiritual, which it uses to release them from the incontinent and often hazy verbiage surrounding them (p. 31)." Le futurisme: projection, multiple, spontanée, de l'objet, selon les états d'âme ou les expériences—sensation dynamique—; le rythme particulier et la force intérieure de l'objet projeté, en peinture, une synthèse rappelant la dynamique de la vue, ou l'objet tel qu'il pourrait être vu successivement.

Comparez avec les styles de la peinture et de l'écriture à l'époque d'Apollinaire, ces deux faits déterminant la morphologie générale de la culture: (1) le climat; (2) la parenté renouvelée telle que le mariage et la transmigration. Il est aussi possible et souhaitable d'observer les changements de la culture selon ces divisions successives du temps: (1) période de la chasse; (2) période du jardinage et de l'agriculture; (3) période des villes et arts manuels. Ces trois périodes du changement font rayonner leurs représentations respectives (ou critiques d'elles-mêmes—le monde) dans une expression traitant respectivement: (1) des animaux; (2) des âmes des morts; (3) des dieux solaires.[33]

L'époque d'Apollinaire appartenant à l'époque des villes et des arts manuels, semble avoir fait *rayonner, dans son écriture,* les dieux solaires de la vitesse.

Le Poète assassiné (1916), y compris les morceaux de la fin: V. Dante, *De Vulgari Eloquentia*, Livre 1, Ch. 10, l. 19, *Les charmantes légendes du Roi Arthur, et beaucoup d'autres œuvres d'histoire et d'érudition.* Le mot traduit "légendes" (ambages) signifie "tournants" ou "tournoiements," et au figuré "digression," et était une espèce d'expression technique désignant les romans d'aventures.

33. Cf. Frobenius, *Paideuma.*

Apollinaire's subsequence after Cervantes and Sterne made for the addition of brevity.

The insistence on the constant display and play of language would recall Lewis Carroll, without the English logic and the sweetener of the bedtime story. And therefore Apollinaire's book is involved in the time. The author took his subject's risk of being assassinated, which action Carroll did not to take.

However, the grotesqueness in Apollinaire's writing, the laughter provoked by the human spasms, does not make for the least tragedy to grieve over. The upcropping of primitive myth in this book persists only as irony, as jest—the rumor of a great wind gurgling in a vial.

With Laforgue as an index—the section *Dramaturgie* might be compared with the players' scene in *Hamlet*, for the records of two different intelligences reacting to their respective contemporary histrionisms.

Of the love of man and woman in this book and in *La Femme assise*: Love is fitted into the objective symbolism of l'enchanteur pourrissant of Apollinaire's first book (1909) as of 1916 to 1918, the physical side of love rotting, post-, if resembling the pre-Christian. The rotting is more a replete presence than a denial of love. So are even the women who deny the male heroes. For the rest, these books are what happened when certain individuals who loved between 1916 and 1918, the priapic ghostliness of all the race, many races, confirmed on the scene of the rotting. So that the irony of the female speech is dressed with conscious cloyingness, the implied opposite of which is perhaps a free breath of air which does not exist as a book or literature: a breath of air which would exist pure if unbreathed even by Apollinaire's sensible and sensuous dialectic.

(p. 75, *Le Poète assassiné*): "Un grand couturier médite de lancer les costumes tailleurs en dos de vieux livres, reliés en veau. C'est charmant. Toutes les femmes de lettres voudront en porter, et l'on pourra s'approcher d'elles et leur parler à l'oreille sous prétexte de lire les titres. Les arêtes de poisson se portent beaucoup sur les chapeaux."[34] Which really happened, if not exactly as described in these details. The poet studied his race as tho it were "primitive."

34. *Le Poète assassiné*, p. 75.

Après Cervantès et Sterne, Apollinaire apparaît apportant la brièveté.

Son insistance à jouer avec le langage et à exhiber constamment ce jeu rappellerait Lewis Carroll, moins la logique anglaise et moins l'adoucissement qui couvre le goût amer aux enfants dans leurs contes. Et donc ouvertement le livre d'Apollinaire est pris dans l'époque. L'auteur a couru le risque d'être assassiné, ce que Carroll n'a pas fait.

Pourtant, le grotesque d'Apollinaire, le rire provoqué par les spasmes humains, n'amène pas la moindre tragédie sur laquelle s'apitoyer. La croissance du mythe primitif dans ce livre ne persiste que comme ironie, comme plaisanterie—la rumeur d'un grand vent sifflant dans une fiole abandonnée.

Prenant Laforgue pour index—la partie de la *Dramaturgie* pourrait se comparer avec la scène des acteurs dans *Hamlet*, comme documents de deux intelligences différant dans leurs réactions à l'égard de leurs respectifs histrionismes contemporains.

Quant à l'amour de l'homme et de la femme, dans ce livre et dans *La Femme assise* (1916 à 1918), il se replonge dans le symbolisme objectif de l'enchanteur pourrissant du premier livre d'Apollinaire (1909): le côté physique de l'amour pourrissant, époque post-chrétienne même si elle ressemble à une époque pré-chrétienne (la période 1916–1918). Cette putréfaction est plutôt la présence envahissante de l'amour qu'une négation de l'amour. Il en est de même des femmes qui nient les héros mâles. Par ailleurs, ces livres racontent ce qui est arrivé quand certains individus aimèrent entre 1916 et 1918, le priapisme fantômatique de toute la race, beaucoup de races, est confirmé dans la scène de la putréfaction. De telle sorte que l'ironie du discours des femmes s'enveloppe dans une satiété consciente, dont l'opposé impliqué est peut-être l'air d'une haleine libre qui n'existe pas comme livre ou comme littérature; une haleine qui existerait dans sa pureté si elle n'était pas respirée, même par la dialectique sensuelle et sensible d'Apollinaire.

(p. 75, *Le Poète assassiné*): "A famous fashion designer is considering launching a line of women's suits made out of old book covers bound in calfskin. It's charming. All women of letters will want to wear them, and you'll be able to walk up to them and whisper in their ears under the pretext of reading the titles. Fish bones are being worn a lot on hats."[34] Ce qui est arrivé dans la réalité si non exactement comme dans cette description détaillée. Le poète a étudié sa race comme si elle était "primitive."

34. *Le Poète assassiné*, 75.

(p. 82, *Le Poète assassiné*): the discussions of aesthetics rendered in a contemporary imaginary conversation: "Croniamantal regretta que ce passant fut mort. Mais rien ne s'oppose à ce qu'on parle avec un mort, et la rencontre était agréable.

"Allons, se dit Croniamantal, pour un passant c'est un passant, et l'auteur même du *Passant*. C'est un rimeur habile et spirituel, ayant le sentiment de la réalité. Parlons avec lui de la rime."

"Le poète du *Passant* fumait une cigarette noire. Il était vêtu de noir, son visage était noir; il se tenait bizarrement sur une pierre de taille, et Croniamantal vit bien, à son air pensif, qu'il faisait des vers. Il l'aborda, et après l'avoir salué lui dit à brûle-pourpoint:

"Cher maître, comme vous voilà sombre."
"Il répondit courtoisement:
"C'est que ma statue est de bronze. Elle m'expose constamment à des méprises. Ainsi, l'autre jour,

> Passant auprès de moi le nègre Sam MacVea
> Voyant que j'étais plus noir que lui s'affligea

"Voyez comme ces vers sont adroits. Je suis en train de perfectionner la rime. Avez-vous remarqué comme ce distique que je vous ai déclamé rime bien pour l'œil.

"En effet, dit Croniamantal, car on prononce Sam MacVi, comme on dit Shakspire.

"Voici quelque chose qui fera mieux votre affaire, continua la statue:

> Passant auprès de moi le nègre Sam MacVea
> Sur le socle aussitôt ces trois noms écrivit

"Il y a là un raffinement qui doit vous séduire, c'est la rime riche pour l'oreille.

"Vous m'éclairez sur la rime, dit Croniamantal. Et je suis bien heureux, cher maître, de vous avoir rencontré en passant.

"C'est mon premier succès, répondit le poète métallique. Toutefois je viens de composer un petit poème portant le même titre: c'est un monsieur qui passe, le *Passant*, à travers un couloir de wagon de chemin de fer; il distingue une charmante personne avec laquelle, au lieu d'aller simplement jusqu'à Bruxelles, il s'arrête à la frontière hollandaise.

(p. 82, *Le Pòete assassiné*): Les discussions esthétiques rendues dans une conversation imaginaire contemporaine: "Croniamantal was sorry that this passerby was dead. But there's nothing to prevent you from talking with a corpse and the meeting was pleasant.

"All right, said Croniamantal, for a passerby, he's really quite a passerby, and he's even the author of *The Passerby*. He's a clever and spiritual rhymer who has a feeling for reality. Let's talk about rhyme with him."

"The poet of *The Passerby* was smoking a black cigarette. He was dressed in black, his face was black; he was perched bizarrely on a carving stone, and Croniamantal saw perfectly well, in his pensive air, that he was composing verse. He approached him, and, after greeting him said frankly:

"Dear Master, how gloomy you are."

"He answered courteously:

"It's that my statue is made of bronze. It exposes me to constant contempt. Thus the other day,

> The black man Sam MacVea passing near me
> Was distressed to see how much darker I was than he

"See how deft these verses are. I am now perfecting the rhyme. Have you noticed how the distich I declaimed for you rhymes for the eye as well.

"Quite, said Croniamantal, for Sam MacVi is pronounced like Shakspire.

"Here's something better for you, continued the statue:

> The black man Sam MacVae passing near me
> Wrote on the base the names of three

"There's a charming refinement, it's a rich rhyme for the ear.

"You're clarifying rhyme for me, said Croniamantal. And I am quite pleased, dear Master, to have passed near you.

"It's my first success, answered the metallic poet. However, I've just composed a little poem with the same title: it's a man passing, the *Passerby*, through the aisle of a railroad car; he notices a charming lady, with whom, instead of simply going to Brussels, he stops at the Dutch frontier.

Ils passèrent au moins huit jours à Rosendael
Il goûtait l'idéal elle aimait le réel
En toutes choses d'elle il était différent
Par conséquent ce fut bien l'amour qu'ils connûrent.

"Je vous signale ces deux derniers vers, bien que rimant richement, ils contiennent une dissonance qui fait contraster délicatement le son plein des rimes masculines avec la morbidesse des féminines.

"Cher maître, reprit Croniamantal, plus haut, parlez-moi du vers libre.

"Vive la liberté! cria la statue de bronze.

"Et après l'avoir saluée, Croniamantal s'en alla plus loin dans l'espoir de rencontrer Tristouse."[35]

Continued (or perhaps by way of postscript to contemporary aesthetic controversy—i.e. of G. A.'s time): "Croniamantal, se récriant sur la nouveauté du sujet, comprit aussitôt combien il prêtait à mettre en valeur la sensibilité de l'auteur.

"Croniamantal s'en fuit. . . . Une dame lui marcha sur les pieds. Elle était auteur et ne manqua point d'affirmer que cette rencontre ou collision lui fournirait un sujet de nouvelle délicate.

"Croniamantal prit ses jambes à son cou et arriva auprès du pont des Saints-Pères où trois personnes qui discutaient un sujet de roman le prièrent de juger leur cas; il s'agissait d'écrire l'histoire d'un officier.

"Beau sujet," s'écria Croniamantal.

"Attendez," dit le voisin, un homme barbu, "je prétends que le sujet est encore trop neuf et trop rare pour le public actuel."

"Et le troisième expliqua qu'il s'agissait d'un officier de restaurant, l'homme de l'office, celui qui essuie la vaisselle . . .

"Mais Croniamantal ne leur répondit pas et s'en fut visiter une ancienne cuisinière qui faisait des vers, chez laquelle il espérait rencontrer Tristouse, à l'heure du thé. Tristouse n'était pas là, mais Croniamantal s'entretint avec la maîtresse de maison qui lui déclama quelques poèmes.

"C'était une poésie pleine de profondeur où tous les mots avaient un sens nouveau. C'est ainsi qu'*archipel* n'était employé par elle que dans le sens de *papier buvard*.

35. *Le Poète assassiné*, p. 82.

They passed at least eight days in Rosendael
He appreciated the ideal she loved the real
They thought of everything differently
And so it was love that they knew, certainly.

"I'll tell you, those last two lines, though they have a rich rhyme, contain a dissonance that makes the full sound of the masculine rhymes contrast delicately with the morbidity of the feminine ones.

"Dear Master, Croniamantal said again louder, talk to me about free verse.

"Long live freedom!" cried the bronze statue.

"And after taking his leave, Croniamantal went off in hopes of meeting Tristouse.[35]

"Et, en manière de postcriptum aux controverses esthétiques de l'époque: "Croniamantal, exclaiming over the subject's novelty, understood immediately how it lent itself to setting off the author's sensitivity.

"Croniamantal left. . . . A lady stepped on his toes. She was an author and she didn't fail to let him know that this encounter or collision provided her with a subject for a delicate short story.

"Croniamantal took off and arrived near the Saints-Pères bridge where three people were discussing the topic of a novel. They begged him to judge their case; it had to do with writing the story of an officer.

"Great subject!" cried Croniamantal.

"Wait," said his neighbor, a bearded man, "I maintain that the subject is still too new and unusual for today's public."

"And the third explained that it was a restaurant officer, the pantry man, the fellow who wipes the plates . . .

"But Croniamantal did not answer and went off to visit a retired lady chef who wrote verse, in whose home he hoped to meet Tristouse, at teatime. Tristouse was not there but Croniamantal spoke with the lady of the house who recited several poems for him.

"It was a poetry full of depth where each word had a new meaning. And so she used the word *archipelago* only in the sense of *blotting paper*.

35. *Le Poète assassiné*, 82.

"Le Roi-Lune": However emphasized the bizarre dialectic is in this piece, its human connections are clear, sympathetically. The magic and the rites are the bizarre dialectic made concrete for sensible consumption.

"Giovanni Moroni": Judgment at work even in this simple piece of childhood. The necessity of naming things: "une fois, je vis un poisson sur la table de la cuisine. J'y pensai longtemps, me le désignant du nom de Bionoulor." The father (the narrator of this piece) leaves his boy and his wife and Italy forever to see a marionette show in Paris. Evidently in his time, the marionettes were a greater attraction than domesticity.

"Le Départ de l'ombre": The magic hold, on Apollinaire, of Hebraic superstition.

"Saint Adorata": The rites of asceticism foiled on the martydom of natural love.

"Les Souvenirs bavards": of ventriloquy, the voice and necromancy—the mannequin hope of human isolation in the England of Apollinaire's time.

"La Rencontre au cercle mixte": A concise rendition of the theme of Thomas Mann's *Death in Venice,* done before 1910; emphasis on quick horror rather than on moral expatiation and sombre baroque.

"Arthur Roi Passé Roi Futur": The art of writing telling a "story" so that the dead live in the telling: cf. the Tuschimini of Frobenius' Africans. King Arthur lives just as Apollinaire's contemporaries live. The magic of the telling is that Arthur seems to have been and never really to have disappeared—tho other events—George V, for instance,— are taking their usual course. The present tense of the telling dispenses with extra explanation of the mysteries of resurrection and immortality. Arthur is part of the future, because the "story" is being told.

"L'Ami Méritarte": Secular rites can be as special as rites of other days and the special rites of esoteric religion: a piece about the art of cooking can achieve the contemplation of comedy, the horror of tragedy and the religiousness of fatality. Writers by the mere force of composition and verbal carpentry have achieved dignity and distinction and an effect of grandeur.[36]

36. Longinus, *On the Sublime*, xl, iv.

"Le Roi-Lune": Quelque soulignée que soit ici la dialectique étrangère, ses attachements humains deviennent clairs par la force de la sympathie. La magie et les rites sont cette dialectique elle-même dans son étrangeté et rendue concrète pour leur acceptation par les sens.

"Giovanni Moroni": Le jugement est à l'œuvre jusque dans cette simple composition d'enfance. La nécessité de nommer les choses: "once, I saw a fish on the kitchen table. I thought about it for a long time, calling it by the name of Bionoulor." Le père (le narrateur de cette histoire) quitte à jamais la mère du petit garçon et l'Italie pour aller voir des marionnettes à Paris. Evidemment à son époque les marionnettes avaient plus d'attrait que les soins domestiques.

"Le Départ de l'ombre": L'emprise magique des superstitions hébraïques sur Apollinaire.

"Saint Adorata": les rites de l'ascétisme s'empalant sur le martyre de l'amour naturel.

"Les Souvenirs bavards": de la ventriloquie, voix et nécromancie. C'est le mannequin de l'espoir de l'isolement humain dans l'Angleterre de l'époque d'Apollinaire.

"La Rencontre au cercle mixte": traitement concis du thème de *La mort à Venise*, de Thomas Mann, fait avant 1910; recherche de l'horreur vivante plutôt que du développement moral ou du baroque sombre.

"Arthur Roi Passé Roi Futur": L'art de l'écriture raconte une "histoire" pour faire vivre les morts dans le récit: cf. les Tuschimini des Africains de Frobenius. Le roi Arthur vit tout à fait comme vivent les contemporains d'Apollinaire. La magie du récit est qu'Arthur semble avoir été et n'avoir jamais disparu, bien que d'autres événements (George V par exemple) suivent leur cours habituel. Le présent historique dispense d'explication supplémentaire sur les mystères de la résurrection et de l'immortalité. Arthur fait partie du futur, parce que le "conte" est raconté.

"L'Ami Méritarte": les rites séculiers peuvent être aussi spéciaux que les rites des temps passés et les rites spéciaux de la religion ésotérique: un passage sur l'art culinaire peut arriver à la contemplation de la comédie, l'horreur de la tragédie et de la religiosité de la fatalité. Les écrivains par la simple force de la composition et la charpente verbale ont atteint la dignité et la distinction et un effet majestueux.[36]

---

36. Longin, *Du Sublime*, xi, iv.

A hint as to the affiliations of *Le Poète assassiné* and the pieces in the same volume: "Le Merveilleux Dumas père, la poétique de Paul Féval, inventeur de chansons imprévues et touchantes comme celles que nous a conservées le riche folklore de la Bretagne, les épopées populaires américaines: *Nick Carter*, et Buffalo Bill, ces deux éloges de l'énergie contre lesquels s'élèvant vient mal à propos certains moralistes . . ." (*Anecdotiques*, p. 176)

Collate: "le sujet (poésie) qui est l'essence des arts plastiques (on Francis Picabia, *Les Peintres cubistes*)." Also: "Marcel Duchamp oppose, à la composition concrète de ses tableaux, un titre intellectuel à l'extrême. En ce sens, il va aussi loin que possible et ne craint pas d'encourir le reproche de faire une peinture ésotérique, sinon obscure." And: "Tous les hommes, tous les êtres qui ont passé près de nous ont laissé des traces dans notre souvenir et ces traces de la vie ont une réalité, dont on peut scruter, dont on peut copier les détails. Ces traces acquièrent ainsi toutes ensemble une personnalité dont on peut indiquer plastiquement les caractères individuels, par une opération purement intellectuelle." And: "Un art qui se donnerait pour but de dégager de la nature, non des généralisations intellectuelles mais des formes et des couleurs collectives dont la perception n'est pas encore devenue notion est très concevable."[37] And: "C'est un narrateur de l'école de Marcel Schwob."[38]

The two plays—*Les Mamelles de Tirésias* (but for the last scene and prologue, finished in 1903, first presented in 1916) and *Couleur du temps* (posthumous, 1920): with the decline of their emotional power great writers and poets give way to character study which cannot be said of the respective exuberance and monolithic inevitableness of the first and second play.

Les Mamelles de Tirésias: (from the preface) — "le théâtre n'est pas plus la vie qu'il interprète que la roue est une jambe. Par conséquent, il est légitime à mon sens, de porter au théâtre des esthétiques nouvelles et frappantes qui accentuent le caractère scénique des personnages et augmentent la pompe de la mise en scène, sans modifier toutefois le pathétique ou le comique des sitations qui doivent se suffire à elles-mêmes.

37. Marcel Duchamp, *Les Peintres cubistes*.
38. André Billy, *La Littérature Française contemporaine*, 1927.

Voici qui indique les affiliations du *Poète assassiné* et les autres morceaux du volume: "The marvelous Dumas père, the poetic of Paul Féval, inventor of those unexpected and touching songs that preserve the rich folklore of Brittany for us, the popular American epics: *Nick Carter* and Buffalo Bill, these two stages of energy against which certain moralists raise their voices quite nastily . . ." (*Anecdotiques* p. 176).

Comparez cela et ceci: "The subject (poetry) which is the essence of the plastic arts (on Francis Picabia, *Les Peintres cubistes*)." Et aussi: "Marcel Duchamp is opposed, in the concrete composition of his paintings, to an extreme intellectual title. In this sense, he goes as far as possible and is not afraid to incur the reproach of making an esoteric, if not obscure, painting." Et puis: "All men, all beings who have passed near to us have left their traces in our memory and these traces of life have a reality, which can be examined, whose details can be copied. All of these traces together thus acquire a personality whose individual characteristics can be shown in the plastic arts by a purely intellectual operation." Et puis: "An art whose goal is the release from nature, not from intellectual generalisations but from forms and from collective colors whose perception has not yet become a notion, that art is very conceivable."[37] Et enfin: "It's a narrator imitating the style of Marcel Schwob."[38]

Les deux pièces: *Les Mamelles de Tirésias* (à l'exception de la dernière scène et du prologue, finies en 1903, et présentées en 1916 pour la première fois) et *Couleur du temps* (posthume, 1920); avec le déclin de leur pouvoir émotif, de grands écrivains se donnent aux études de caractères mais on ne peut pas en dire autant à propos de l'exubérance de la première pièce et de l'inévitabilité monolithe de la deuxième.

Les Mamelles de Tirésias: (préface) "The theater is no more the life it interprets than a wheel is a leg. Thus, it is legitimate to bring to the theater new and striking aesthetics that accentuate the scenic nature of the characters and add to the pomp of the setting, without modifying the pathetic or the comic elements of situations that should be enough in themselves.

37. On Marcel Duchamp, *Les Peintres cubistes*.
38. André Billy, *La Littérature Française contemporaine*, 1927.

"J'ajoute que, dégageant des velléités littéraires contemporaines une certaine tendance qui est la mienne, je ne prétends nullement fonder une école, mais avant tout protester contre ce théâtre en trompe-l'œil qui forme le plus clair de l'art théâtral d'aujourd'hui. Ce trompe-l'œil qui convient, sans doute, au cinéma est, je crois, ce qu'il y a de plus contraire à l'art dramatique.

"J'ajoute qu'à mon avis, le vers qui seul convient au théâtre, est un vers souple, fondé sur le rythme, le sujet, le souffle et pouvant s'adapter à toutes les nécessités théâtrales. Le dramaturge ne dédaignera pas la musique de la rime, qui ne doit pas être une sujétion dont l'auteur et l'auditeur se fatiguent vite désormais, mais peut ajouter quelque beauté au pathétique, au comique dans les chœurs, dans certaines répliques, à la fin de certaines tirades, ou pour clore dignement un acte."

"Le vers qui seul convient au théâtre"—at least his theater—he seems to have perfected in *Couleur du temps*:

Madame Giraume

C'est ici qu'a eu lieu la bataille
Il est tombé frappé à la tête.

(*Elle trouve la croix sous laquelle repose son fils*)

Mon fils te voilà sous cette croix
Te voici mon joyau précieux
Te voici mon fruit blanc et vermeil
C'est mon fils c'est mon enfant c'est lui
Fils tu n'es plus rien que cette croix
C'est mons fils c'est mon enfant c'est toi
O très belle fontaine vermeille
Te voilà taire à tout jamais
O toi dont la source était en moi
C'est mon fils c'est mon enfant c'est toi
Tu dors dans la pourpre impériale
Teinte du sang que je t'ai donné
O fils beau lys issue de ma chair
Floraison exquise de mon cœur
Mon fils mon fils te voilà donc mort

"Let me add that, releasing my own tendency from contemporary literature's vague impulses, I do not attempt to found a school, but above all to protest against this *trompe-l'œil* theater that is the most evident in today's theatrical arts. This *trompe-l'œil,* which certainly suits the cinema, is, I believe, most opposed to dramatic art.

"Let me further add that, in my opinion, the only verse that suits the theater is a flexible verse, based on rhythm, the subject, the breath, and that can adapt itself to all theatrical necessities. The dramaturge does not hold the music of rhyme in contempt, which must not be a constraint that quickly bores the author and the listener, but that can add some beauty to the pathetic, to the comic, in choruses, in certain replies, at the end of certain tirades, or to close an act with dignity."

"The only verse that suits the theater"—du moins à son théâtre—il semble l'avoir atteint dans *Couleur du temps*:

Madame Giraume

This is where the battle was
He fell with a blow to his head.

(*She finds the cross that marks her son's grave*)

Here you are my son beneath this cross
Here you are my precious jewel
Here you are my white vermillion fruit
It's my son it's my child it is he
Son now you are no more than this cross
It's my son it's my child it is you
Oh very lovely vermillion fountain
Here you will run dry forever
Oh you who flowed from me
It's my son it's my child it is you
You sleep in imperial purple
Stained with the blood that I gave you
Oh son lovely lily of my flesh
Exquisite flowering of my heart
My son my son here you lie dead

A ton front une bouche nouvelle
Rit de tout ce que ce soir j'endure
Parle sous terre bouche nouvelle
Que dis-tu bouche toujours ouverte
Tu es muette bouche trop rouge

Mavise
Sa mère est près de son tombeau
O Fiancé si beau si fort
Toi qui mourus vêtu de bleu
Un morceau de ciel enterré
Il était adroit et habile
il était fort j'étais savante
Lui le travail moi la pensée
La vie et l'ordre en un seul couple
Lui le travail moi la pensée
Il était fort j'étais savante

Madame Giraume
Et comme ton corps doit être lourd
Déjà je plie sous ton souvenir
O mon fils je t'ai porté jadis
Lorsque tu ne pesais presque rien
Et je n'ai plus de lait pour nourrir
Ta mort comme j'ai nourri ta vie
J'ai fait des démarches incroyables
Pour atteindre ce lieu prohibé
Et le voilà mort mon cher enfant
Qu'ont-ils fait de toi ils t'ont tué
Ils s'y sont mis tous pour te tuer
Et puisqu'ils en voulaient à mon sang
Pourquoi donc pour en tarir la source
N'ont-ils pas pris ma vie o mon fils
Pourquoi ta vie et non pas la mienne

A new mouth on your forehead
Laughs at all that I endure tonight
Speak below ground new mouth
What are you saying mouth forever open
You are mute too red a mouth

Mavise

His mother is by his tomb
Oh Fiancé so handsome so strong
You who died wearing blue
A bit of buried sky
He was skillful and deft
He was strong and I was wise
His was the work and mine the thought
Life and order in a single couple
His was the work and mine the thought
He was strong and I was wise

Madame Giraume

And as your body must be heavy
I already bend beneath your memory
Oh my son I carried you in olden days
When you weighed next to nothing
And I no longer have milk to feed
Your death as I fed your life
I took incredible steps
To reach this forbidden place
And here you are dead my dear child
What have they done to you they've killed you
They all came here to kill you
And since it was my blood they wanted
Why didn't they come to dry up the source
Why didn't they take my life oh my son
Why your life and why not mine

And

> Là-bas d'où nous venons un homme n'est plus rien
> Là-bas l'individu n'est qu'une particule
> D'êtres au corps énorme anciens ou nouveaux
> L'homme n'est qu'une goutte au sang des capitales
> Un tout petit peu de salive dans la bouche
> Des assemblés brin d'herbe au champ qu'est un pays
> C'est un simple coup d'œil jeté dans un musée
> La pièce de billon dans la caisse des banques
> C'est un peu de buée aux vitres d'un café.
> . . . .

And

> O nuit ô splendide nuit où rampent
> Les célèstes bêtes de phosphore
> Belles musiques agonisant
> Dans la rondeur de l'immensité
> Je jouis pleinement de la paix
> De ces splendeurs et de ces blancheurs
> Et l'éternité qui les fit naître
> Ne les verra jamais mourir

And

> Nous n'avons pas le droit
> D'abandonner ainsi
> Les morts et les vivants

These lines spoken by the young woman, Mavise, suggests comparison with a fine recent rearrangement of *Antigone*.[39] But Apollinaire did not rearrange, and the cleanness may be granted *Couleur du temps*, it weighs more than cleanness.

---

39. By Jean Cocteau.

Et

> Where we come from a man is nothing now
> The individual is but a particle
> Of the enormous bodies of ancient or new beings
> Man is nothing but a drop of the capital blood
> A tiny drop of saliva in the mouth
> Assemblies blade of grass in a field that is a country
> It's just a glance tossed in a museum
> The coin in a bank deposit
> It's a bit of steam in a café window.
> . . . .

Et

> Oh night oh splendid night where slither
> The celestial phosphorous beasts
> Beautiful music dying
> In immensity's roundness
> I enjoy the fullness of peace
> Its splendors and its whiteness
> And eternity that gives birth to them
> Will never see them die

Et

> We do not have the right
> To abandon thus
> The dead and the living

Ces vers dits par la jeune femme, Mavise, appellent un rapprochement avec un réarrangement récent d'*Antigone*,[39] du reste ingénieux. Mais Apollinaire n'a pas réarrangé, et bien qu'on puisse accorder à *Couleur du temps* l'ingénuité aussi bien que l'ingéniosité, la pièce a une portée qui dépasse bien celle de l'ingénuité et même de l'ingéniosité.

39. Par Jean Cocteau.

Alcools (Poèmes 1898–1913)

Prosody: "Et de tout ce que l'on a tenté, en ce sens, au XIXe siècle, que reste-t-il?" André Van Hasselt,[40] poète belge assez médiocre et complètement oublié, était parvenu à mesurer le vers rimé, sans imiter le vers Baïffin. Et certes, l'effort dépassait celui de Baïf qui pliait servilement son langage à la prosodie grecque et latine. Avec un talent digne de plus de renommée, Laurent Evrard a renouvelé une forme intéressante de la poésie française: la rime enrimée qui jusqu'alors n'avait été considérée que comme une des innombrables complications poétiques, un des mille jeux de versification auxquels se plaisent les poètes marotiques. Mais, ces nouveautés et quelques autres n'ont généralement pas plu. Le vers libre seul a réussi. Toutefois, si on le regarde parfois comme le but de la prosodie française, on l'envisage trop souvent comme sa négation. De là des malentendus, et bien des poètes écrivent en alexandrins incomplets ou prolongés. Le "ragoût" de beaucoup de poèmes modernes réside, il faut l'avouer, dans les fautes imprévues de versification. Les licences poétiques sont aujourd'hui au rebours des anciennes qui modifiaient l'orthographe au profit de la prosodie. Le vers boiteux qui rebutait autrefois et semblait rude comme Vulcain, se pare aujourd'hui des grâces tremblantes d'une fille dont une jambe est plus courte que l'autre et, qui ne sait que les boiteuses sont les plus aimables et les plus aimées des femmes! Bref, à cette heure, la prosodie en vogue est l'ancienne dont certains transgressent les règles au hasard. Mais il se trompent: le vers libre n'est pas une simplification prosaïque de la poésie. Et, si l'on cherche dans l' œuvre de chaque poète une personnalité, on ne s'étonnera pas de rencontrer des prosodies personnelles. Les moins relâchés d'entre les poètes s'honoreront par des efforts qui ennobliront leur lyrisme sans choquer la métrique traditionnelle et en la dépassant (1908).[41]

---

40. "D'autre part, pour mieux organiser la musique intérieure, le rythme du vers, surtout de celui destiné à être chanté, il songea à adopter une prosodie basée sur la distinction des syllabes toniques et atones. Il fit ainsi des vers français sur le modèle des vers néerlandais et allemands, où le membre rythmique est mesuré à l'intervalle compris entre deux accents, et qui réalisent une grande souplesse de mouvement harmonique." préface to André Van Hasselt—*Poems*—Bruxelles 1906, by Arthur Daxhalt. Van Hasselt's *Etudes rythmiques* first appeared in 1862.

41. Jean Royère, *Il y a.*

Alcools (Poems 1898–1913)

Prosodie: "And of all that we have tried, in this sense, in the nine-teenth century, what remains?" André Van Hasselt,[40] a fairly mediocre and completely forgotten Belgian poet, had succeeded in measuring the rhymed verse without imitating Baïffin verse. And admittedly, the effort surpassed that of Baïf who submissively bent his language to match that of Greek and Latin prosody. With a talent worthy of more renown, Laurent Evrard renewed an interesting form of French poetry: the en-rhymed rhyme that until then had only been considered as one of the innumerable poetic complications, one of a thousand games of versifi-cation to amuse *marotique* poets. But these novelties and a few others were not generally pleasing. Free verse was the only success. However, if you occasionally look at it as the goal of French prosody, you will too often envision it as its negative. There misunderstandings arise with quite a few poets writing in incomplete or overlong alexandrine. The "stew" of many modern poems resides, one must admit, in unforeseen errors in versification. Today poetic license is the opposite of that of the ancients who changed their spelling for the benefit of prosody. The clumsy verse that put one off in the past and seemed stiff like Vulcan adorns itself with trembling graces like a girl with one leg shorter than the other. And who knows, but that the clumsy are not the most lovable and the most loved of women! Anyway, nowadays ancient prosody is fashionable and its rules are broken at random. But they are mistaken: free verse is not a prosaic simplification of poetry. And if you are looking for a personality in each poet's work then you won't be surprised to find personal prosodies. The least relaxed of the poets will honor himself with efforts to ennoble his lyricism without shocking traditional meter while surpassing it. (1908)[41]

40. "Otherwise to better organize the internal music, the rhythm of the verse, above all of that, meant to be sung; he dreamt of adopting a prosody based on the distinction of tonal and atonal syllables. He thus made French verses on the model of Dutch and German models, where the rhythmic member is measured at the interval understood between two accents, and who realize a great flexibility of harmonious movement." Préface aux *Poèmes* d'André van Hasselt (Bruxelles, 1906), par Arthur Daxhalt. Les *Etudes rythmiques* de Van Hasselt avaient parues pour la première fois en 1862.

41. Jean Royère, *Il y a.*

"Zone": Never shocks the traditional metric and has its own metric. Le vers libre; but not a simplification of prosody. The mechanism of the verse describes itself in the avoidance of useless equivocation which, had it been present, would have detracted from the theme. From a mixture of smooth and rough rhymes the tragedy itself gains in brilliancy.[42]

"Le Pont Mirabeau": A French prosody based on the distinction between tonics and atonics, the intervals between two accents measure the rhythm. Written to be sung. Perhaps the kind of thing Guillaume composed for, extempore, at the piano at the outset of his career—extempore from which Salmon dissuaded him.

"La Chanson du Mal-Aimé": To be read, as part task of a study of the concision of fluency, with Corbière's "La Rapsodie Foraine" and "Le Pardon De Sainte-Anne" and Villon.

> Un soir de demi-brume à Londres[43]
> Un voyou qui ressemblait à
> Mon amour vint à ma rencontre
> Et le regard qu'il me jeta
> Me fit baisser les yeux de honte
>
> . . . .
>
> Beaucoup de ces dieux ont péri
> C'est sur eux que pleurent les saules
> Le grand Pan l'amour Jésus-Christ
> Sont bien morts et les chats miaulent
> Dans la cour je pleure à Paris

The dialectic, like the versification, shuttles between the contemporary and the classic (the French medieval Villon)—the enjambment (giving the feeling of an expanded prose rhythm), the unaccented rhyming of a preposition with the hovering accent of a propelled verb of the first stanza given here; and the rhythmic repeats of the rise, fall and rise of the end-stopped lines emotionally flowing over the full, old rhymes of the second stanza given. The poem is a series of modulations of an absorbed personal ritual become impersonal—presented as periphery. Compare Villon's Paris and the city of this poem, "Soirs de Paris ivres du gin:"

---

42. Cf. Dante, *De Vulgari Eloquentia*, book 2, chapter 8.
43. The rhyming of final consonants already present in Rimbaud.

"Zone": Ne bouscule pas la métrique traditionnelle et a sa métrique propre, le vers libre n'y est pas une simplification de la prosodie. Le mécanisme du vers se décrit en évitant une équivoque inutile qui, eût-elle été présente, aurait enlevé beaucoup au thème. A un mélange de rimes coulantes et heurtées la tragédie elle-même gagne en éclat.[42]

"Le Pont Mirabeau": la prosodie française basée sur une distinction des toniques et atones; l'interval entre deux accents mesure le rythme. C'est écrit pour être chanté. C'est peut-être une de ces choses que Guillaume improvisait, au piano, au début de sa carrière. On sait que Salmon le dissuada de ces improvisations.

"La Chanson du Mal-Aimé": A lire pour une étude de la concision du style bien-coulant, en même temps que "La Rapsodie foraine" et "Le Pardon Sainte-Anne" de Corbière et Villon.

> One foggy night in London[43]
> An urchin who looked like
> My beloved came to meet me
> And the look that he gave me
> Made me lower my eyes with shame
> . . . .
> Many of these gods have perished
> It is for them the willows weep
> Great Pan love Jesus Christ
> Are all dead and the cats howl
> In the yard I weep in Paris

La dialectique, comme la versification est un va et vient entre le contemporain et le classique (Moyen-âge français et Villon). C'est, en effet, d'une part, l'enjambement, qui donne l'impression d'un rythme de la prose s'étirant, au moyen d'une syllabe non-accentuée d'une préposition rimant avec l'accent indécis d'un verbe dans la première strophe; d'autre part, les répétitions rythmiques d'une ascension des vers s'arrêtant à la fin de ceux-ci, reprenant, et débordant d'émotions lorsqu'on atteint les rimes anciennes et pleines de la deuxième strophe. Le poème est une série de modulations d'un rituel personnel absorbé et devenu impersonnel— présenté comme périphérie. Comparez le Paris de Villon à la ville de

---

42. Cf. Dante, *De Vulgari Eloquentia*, Livre 2, chapter 8.

43. De semblables rimes se trouvent déjà dans Rimbaud.

there is less autobiography in Apollinaire than in Villon, i.e. autobiography which might have disturbed the objectivity of the poem and made the rendition of the objective a sharper struggle. There is then more of the ornament of prolixity in Apollinaire than in Villon: i.e. it happens that we sing sometimes persuasively, sometimes dissuasively, sometimes in congratulation, sometimes in irony, sometimes in praise, sometimes in contempt, let those words whose tendency is unfavorable always hasten to the end, and the others gradually advance to the end with a becoming prolixity.[44]

The total absence of punctuation in Apollinaire's poems, especially those published after Jan 2, 1915[45]—natural after Mallarmé. The explanation which follows, is not quite correct: "En supprimant la ponctuation le poète (Apollinaire) invite à lire ses vers sans exclamations et sans fioritures, d'une voix monotone, comme on lit les cantiques et les psaumes, c'est l'application d'usage religieux à la vie profane." Nor is this correct: " . . . part of his revolt against the logical articulation of the phrase." "Comme on lit les cantiques et les psaumes, l'application d'usage religieux à la vie profane" no doubt, but it would seem to be an impossibility to read the verses of *La Chanson du Mal-Aimé* without exclamations or flourishes, unless they be murmured, and at that the exclamation and flourishes would be different murmurs. The voice articulating is logical hence the phrase must take on the logic of the voice. The logical articulation of *La Chanson du Mal-Aimé* is its use of vast and replete vocables of the canticle become secular *poésie*.

Diction (as in all the poems of *Alcools*—*Calligrammes* seems persistently close to actual speech): a fluent blend of the rare, aureoled word— "argyraspides," "chibriap"—and the resurrection of the common epithets, as in all great poetry, thru the vigor of the movement and the force of the sensible disposition and contiguity of the words—"C'est l'ami aux si douces mains," "Une femme une rose morte."

The syntax is nearly always popular, never trammeling the reading, notwithstanding the absence of punctuation.

44. Dante, *De Vulgari Eloquentia*, chapter 14.

45. A considerable loss to American scholarship, since it has often given the most careful attention to misprints of punctuation.

ce poème. "Paris nights drunk on gin." Il y a moins d'autobiographie dans Apollinaire que dans Villon; l'autobiographie aurait pu nuire à l'objectivité du poème et rendre le traitement de l'objectif un effort plus ardu. L'ornementation de la prolixité est plus grande chez Apollinaire que chez Villon; c'est-à-dire qu'il nous arrive de chanter parfois persuasivement, parfois disuasivement, parfois en congratulation, parfois par ironie, parfois pour des louanges, parfois par mépris, mais les mots dont la tendance n'est pas favorable se pressent vers la fin et les autres graduellement avancent vers la fin avec une prolixité convenable . . . [44]

L'absence complète de ponctuation dans les poèmes d'Apollinaire (particulièrement dans ceux parus après le 2 janvier 1915)[45] est naturelle après Mallarmé. L'explication qui suit n'est pas tout à fait correcte: "In deleting punctuation, the poet (Apollinaire) invites his lines to be read without exclamations and without flourishes, in monotone, as hymns and psalms are read, it's the application of religious usage to profane life." Et ceci n'est pas juste: "[this behavior] . . . makes up a part of his revolt against the logical articulation of the sentence." "As one reads hymns and psalms, it is the application of religious usage to profane life," sans doute, mais il semble bien qu'il soit impossible de lire les vers de *La Chanson du Mal-Aimé* sans exclamations ni fioritures, à moins qu'on ne les murmure et même ainsi s'accuseraient exclamations et fioritures dans des différences de murmures. La voix qui articule est logique, d'où résulte que la phrase doit prendre la logique de la voix. L'articulation logique de *La Chanson du Mal-Aimé* consiste dans l'emploi de vocables vastes et pleins du cantique devenu poésie séculière.

La diction (dans tous les poèmes d'*Alcools*; les *Calligrammes* paraissant constamment fermés à la vraie parole) est amalgame coulant du mot rare, auréolé—"argyraspides," "chibriap"—et la résurrection des épithètes connues, comme dans toute vraie poésie, par la vigueur du mouvement et la force de la disposition sensible et la contiguïté des mots—"It is the friend with such soft hands," "a woman a dead rose."

La syntaxe est presque toujours populaire, ne se mettant jamais en travers de la lecture, malgré l'absence de ponctuation.

---

44. Dante, *De Vulgari Eloquentia*, chapitre 14.

45. Une perte considérable pour les chercheurs américains, car ils ont souvent été très attentifs aux erreurs de ponctuation.

> De fausses femmes dans vos lits
> Aux déserts que l'histoire accable
> . . . .
> Face tournée au ciel changeant

indicate concretely the shuttling rhythm of the poem's implicit dialectic.

"Les Colchiques": "Pour toujours ce grand pré mal fleuri par l'automne"—perhaps an extrasensible symbol of contemporary mutation—a pastoral version of "Zone": Christianity on the ill-flowered field of contemporary autumn.

"Palais": The art of verse telling.

> Dame de mes pensées au cul de perle fine
> Dont ni perle ni cul n'égale l'orient

These lines are not the indulgence of the amorous anthologies, as the second line taking up the first, in antiphon would show.

> Or ces pensées mortes depuis des millénaires
> Avaient le fade goût des grands mammouths gelés
> Les os ou songe-creux venaient des ossuaires
> En danse macabre aux plis de mon cervelet

These images of pagan and Christian vestiges not later touched upon in *Calligrammes* are intimate but not personal,—the vestiges already made impersonal by the objective sounding of his intimacy. His dilemma in this early poem (and in the other allegories like it) is occasioned by the difference of a desire for an approved mode determined by the current tradition, and socially deferred to by the artist, and the desire for innovation with which he intuited and already experimented. The difference at least made for clarity. What the symbolists made a haze of, he had the sense to use not only according to their mode, but with the rich decor of elegiac (classic sense) satire.

> False women in your beds
> To the deserts overburdened by history
> . . . .
> Face turned to the changing sky

indiquent concrètement le va et vient de la dialectique.

"Les Colchiques": "Forever autumn great unflowering meadow"—peut être un symbole dégagé de la sensibilité d'un changement contemporain—version pastorale de "Zone": Christianisme dans le champ mal-fleuri de l'automne contemporain.

"Palais": L'art de conter:

> Perlescent-assed lady of my thoughts
> Neither pearl nor ass are matched by the orient.

Ces vers ne peuvent pas être une perle d'anthologie galante, comme le montre le deuxième vers reprenant le premier en antiphone.

> Yet these thoughts dead for millennia
> Had the bland taste of the great frozen mammoths
> The bones or hollow bones coming from the bone piles
> To the macabre dance in the folds of my cerebellum

Ces images de vestiges païens et chrétiens que les *Calligrammes* ne cultivent plus sont intimes, mais non pas personnelles, — les vestiges étant déjà rendus impersonnels par la résonnance objective de l'intimité d'Apollinaire. Son dilemme dans ce poème du début (en même temps que dans d'autres allégories semblables) est occasionné par les différences d'un désir d'un mode approuvé déterminé par la tradition courante, et auquel l'artiste socialement s'en remet, et le désir d'une innovation manifesté déjà par des intuitions et même des expériences. Au moins les différences rendaient de la clarté. Ce que les symbolistes faisaient passer en brouillard, il eut l'intelligence de l'employer non seulement selon leur mode, mais avec le riche décor de la satire élégiaque (sens classique).

Dedication: To Max Jacob.[46]
"Chantre": the image of the single line the entire poem.

Et l'unique cordeau des trompettes marines

Presentation blending the senses is not always felicitous, since the suggestion is not finitely full but infinite and not quite clear. *But:* Apollinaire has presented and integrated sound thru sight (the printed words), at the same time the sounded words take the place of sight—this entire process is an art in itself.

Collate: " . . . l'Art tactile."

Je l'avais imaginé, l'an dernier (1917) dans un petit conte intitulé *Mon ami Ludovic*, qui fut publié dans *l'Almanach des lettres et des arts* édité par Martine.

En voici les traits principaux précisés dans mon conte.

"C'est mon cher Ludovic, disais-je, qui a inventé l'art du tact du contact du toucher.

"Je ne donnerai point le détail des effleurements, chatouillis, coups de toute sorte et de toute force dont mon cher Ludovic fit sur nous l'expérience et que nous avions la patience de subir . . . .

"Toutefois, il entre dans mon plan de vous dire que cet art, dont les règles et la technique sont aujourd'hui dans tout leur développement, est fondé sur la façon différente dont, selon leur nature, les objets affectueux le sens de toucher, le sec, l'humide, le mouillé, tous les degrés du froid et du chaud, le gluant, l'épais, le tendre, le mou, le dur, l'élastique, l'huileux, le soyeux, le velouté, le rêche, le grenu, etc. . . . etc., mariés, rapprochés de façon inattendue, forment la riche matière où mon ami Ludovic puise les combinaisons subtiles et sublimes de l'art tactile, musique muette qui exacerbait nos nerfs . . . .

46. Converti au christianisme en 1918, Max Jacob est devenu un poète catholique. Il a lui-même raconté l'histoire de sa conversion d'abord dans *Le Christ à Montparnasse*, examen de conscience et confession, puis dans *La Défense de Tartuffe*, extases, remords, visions, prières, poèmes et méditations d'un Juif converti. A. Billy, *La Littérature Française contemporaine* (1927). A. Billy (with Moïse Twersky) is the author of *L'Épopée de Ménaché*, Foïgel (1927).

Dédié à Max Jacob.[46]
"Chantre": l'image du vers unique c'est le poème tout entier.

And the only line of marine trumpets

Cette présentation mêlant les différents sens n'est pas toujours heureuse. Car l'évocation ne fournit pas une plénitude finie, mais infinie et pas tout à fait claire. *Mais:* Apollinaire a présenté et intégré l'entendu dans le vu (le mot imprimé); en même temps les résonances des mots prennent la place de la vision, ce qui est un art qui a ses droits.
Comparez: " . . . Tactile art."
I had imagined it, last year (1917) in a short story called *My Friend Ludovic*, that was published in the *Almanac des lettres et des arts*, edited by Martine.
En voici les traits principaux précisés dans mon conte.
"I said it was my dear Ludovic who invented the art of tact, of contact, of touch.
"I will not give any detail of the light touches, tickles, blows of all sorts and of all strengths bestowed upon us by my dear Ludovic to which we patiently submitted. . . .
"However, my plan is to tell you that this art whose rules and technique are developing today is based on the different ways that objects of different consistencies appear to the sense of touch. Dry, moist, wet, all the degrees of cold and hot, sticky, thick, tender, soft, hard, elastic, oily, silky, velvety, rough, grainy, etc . . . , etc . . . , married, brought together in an unexpected manner, forming the rich material from which my friend Ludovic draws the subtle and sublime combinations of tactile art, mute music that excites our nerves. . . .

46. Converted to Catholicism in 1918, Max Jacob became a Catholic poet. He told the story of his conversion first in *Le Christ à Moutparnase*, self-examination and confession, then in *La Défense de Tartuffe*, ecstasies, remorses, visions, prayers, poems and meditations of a Converted Jew. *La Littérature Française contemporaine* (1927). A. Billy (with Moïse Twersky) is the author of *L'Epopie de Ménaché*, Förgel, 1927.

"Mon cher Ludovic professait que tous les genres de contact, ressentis simultanément, procureraient la sensation du vide, car, ajoutait-il, on ne l'ignore plus depuis longtemps, *la nature a horreur du vide*, et ce que l'on prend pour la vie, c'est le solide même."[47]

In any case, the criticism which follows, does not apply to "Chantre:" "vers de certains prosateurs qui gongorisent sans mallarmiser le moins du monde."[48]

"Crépuscule": the dedication gives the key to this poem's technique.

"Annie": Sur la côte du Texas

> . . . .
> Comme cette femme est mennonite
> Ses rosiers et ses vêtements n'ont pas de boutons
> Il en manque deux à mon veston
> La dame et moi suivons presque le même rite

Probably written very early, despite its finished simplicity: about 1903 when he wrote the chapter on the Mormons later included in *La Femme assise*?

"La Maison des morts":

> Et tous bras dessus bras dessous
> Frédonnant des airs militaires

"Clotilde": For want of the voice of Blake in French, this might be read as one of his *Songs of Experience*.

"Cortège": "Ou bien encore à cause du vocabulaire et non de l'écriture."

All of Guillaume's passionate vocabulary—his reaction to the world seen as composition as action—is in this poem. "Oiseau tranquille au vol inverse oiseau," présente tout ensemble et l'effort et l'effet: invocation and the discursive sound less tenuous in Apollinaire's French than they might in Shelleyan or Wordsworthian English.

"Marizibill": "Elle s'appelait Marie-Sybille ou Marizibill, pour parler comme les gens de Cologne, sa ville natale."

47. *Anecdotiques*, p. 253.
48. *Anecdotiques*, p. 289.

"My dear Ludovic claims that all types of contact, sensed simultaneously, would give the sensation of the void, because, he would add, we've known for some time that *nature abhors a vacuum* and that what we take for a vacuum is solidity itself."[47]

En tout cas, cette critique ne peut pas s'appliquer à "Chantre:" "verse of certain prosodists who gongorize without mallarmizing at all."[48]

"Crépuscule": la dédicace donne la clef de la technique de ce poème.

"Annie": On the Texas coast

> . . . .
> Because this woman is a Mennonite
> She has no buttons on her roses or her clothes
> On my jacket I am missing two of those
> This lady and myself almost follow the same rite

Cela écrit probablement très tôt malgré le fini de la simplicité: vers 1903, quand il écrivait le chapitre sur les Mormons qu'il a plus tard incorporé dans *La Femme assise* (?)

"La Maison des morts":

> And all were arm in arm
> Humming military tunes

"Clotilde": La voix de Blake manquant en français, ceci pourrait être lu au lieu de l'un de ses *Songs of Experience*.

"Cortège": "Because of the vocabulary and not the writing."

Tout le vocabulaire passionné de Guillaume Apollinaire—sa réaction au monde vu comme composition-action—est dans ce poème. "Tranquil bird in flight inverted bird," presented all together and the effort and the effect: L'invocation et la discursivité sont moins ténues dans ce français qu'elles ne le seraient dans l'anglais des romantiques Wordsworth ou Shelley.

"Marizibill": "She was called Marie-Sybille or Marizibill in the accent of Cologne, her native city."

47. *Anecdotiques*, 253.

48. *Anecdotiques*, 289.

> C'était un juif il sentait l'ail
> Et l'avait venant de Formose
> Tirée d'un bordel de Changaï
> ·
> Je connais gens de toutes sortes
> Ils n'égalent pas leurs destins
> Indécis comme feuilles mortes
> Leurs yeux sont des feux mal éteints
> Leurs cœurs bougent commes leurs portes.

The classicism of T.S. Eliot; on the whole, warmer, if somewhat sentimental.

"Le Voyageur": The "Bateau ivre" of intimacy and friendship. The catalog of things remembered seen is not Whitmannian, but proceeds with continuous concrete change of value belonging to variables—(nautical meaning: a shifting of wind or winds; also, places where such winds are common).

"Te souviens-tu des banlieus et du troupeau plaintif des paysages": Apollinaire's technique of offsetting the conversational noun (banlieu) against the cliché of traditional idyllic poetry.

"Marie": To be read with Robert Burns' "To Mary Morrison."

"La Blanche Neige":

> Les anges les anges dans le ciel
> L'un est vêtu en officier
> L'un est vêtu en cuisinier
> Et les autres chantent
> · · · · · · · · · · · · · · · · ·
> Le cuisinier plume les oies
>   Ah! tombe neige
>   Tomb et que n'ai-je
> Ma bien-aimée entre mes bras.

Degas and Picasso's early period, in poetry. The conceit might also be Cocteau's.

"Poème Lu Au Mariage d'André Salmon Le 13 juillet 1909."—"À travers les rues à travers les contrées à travers la raison."

"L'Adieu": Not since Charles D'Orléans . . . . etc.,

"Salomé": The historic heroic soliloquy, not at all important.

He was a Jew he smelled of garlic
He came from Formosa
Taken from a Shanghai bordello
· ·
I know people of all kinds
They are not equal to their fates
Wavering like dead leaves
Eyes like dimming fires
Their hearts swing like doors.

Le classicisme de T.S. Eliot est là; pourtant cela est sans doute plus enflammé malgré la sentimentalité.

"Le Voyageur": C'est "le Bateau ivre" de l'intimité et de l'amitié. Le catalogue des choses vues par la mémoire ne sera pas whitmanien, mais procèdera par le changement de valeur propre au *variable* (ce mot est employé ici dans le sens qu'on lui donne dans l'expression: *temps variable*).

"Do you remember the suburbs and the plaintive herds of the countryside": la technique d'Apollinaire renversant le nom commun (banlieue) est à opposer à la forme-cliché de la poésie idyllique traditionelle.

"Marie": A lire à côté du poème de Robert Burns: "To Mary Morrison."

"La Blanche Neige":

Angels angels in the sky
One dressed as an officer
One dressed as a cook
And the others singing
· · · · · · · · · · · · · · · · · ·
The cook plucks geese
            Ah! falls the snow
            Falls and what don't I have
My beloved in my arms.

Les Degas et les Picasso des débuts, en poésie Cocteau a aussi des préciosités semblables.

"Poème lu au Mariage d'André Salmon, le 13 juillet 1909": "Crossing streets, crossing regions, crossing reason."

"L'Adieu": jamais depuis Charles d'Orléans . . . etc. . . .

"Salomé": le soliloque héroïque; très peu important.

"La Porte": The sentimental verse colloquy, again not important. But both these last poems probably get translated quickly into foreign anthologies.

"Merlin et la vieille femme": The material of *L'Enchanteur pourrissant*—

> Puis Merlin s'en alla vers l'est disant Qu'il monte
> Le fils de la Mémoire égale de l'Amour

As for Apollinaire's use of the alexandrine, it is described in the poem:

> Mes tournoîments exprimaient les béatitudes
> Qui toutes ne sont rien qu'un pur effet de l'art

"Saltimbanques": Of the nature of Picasso's creations.

"Le Larron": These verses have been given as a defense for the alexandrine.[49]

Symbolism of this kind is hardly ever thoroughly resolved,—since the ideal emanation of the texture does not always coincide with the "interior"intention. The chorus of this poem, for example, seems at once confusingly the counterpart and the opposite spiritual principle of the "Larron." Maybe that was the intended point. In that case, the drama is at fault, the technique related to uncertainty.

"Le Vent nocturne":

> Attys Attys Attys charmant et débraillé
> C'est ton nom qu'en la nuit les elfes ont raillé
> Parce qu'un de tes pins s'abat au vent gothique
> La forêt fuit au loin comme une armée antique
> Dont les lances ô pins s'agitent au tournant
> Les villages éteints méditent maintenant

The last line separates the past (the previous lines) from all comers by the implicitness of the new technique suddenly shifting the scene; the past is thus saved from becoming a curiosity of anachronistic sensibility.

---

49. André Breton, *Les Pas perdus*.

"La Porte": Le colloque sentimental, très peu important. (A remarquer avec quelle facilité ces deux poèmes passent dans les traductions des anthologies étrangères).

"Merlin et la vieille femme": La matière de *l'Enchanteur pourrissant*:

> Then Merlin left for the east saying Let him climb
> Memory's thread is none other than Love.

Quant à l'alexandrin d'Apollinaire, il est décrit dans le poème:

> My whirling arms recited beatitudes
> Which are nothing but the purest effect of art

"Saltimbanques": De la nature des créations de Picasso.

"Le Larron": On s'est servi de ces vers pour justifier l'alexandrin.[49]

Du symbolisme de cette espèce n'est presque jamais complètement résolu — car l'émanation textuelle idéale ne coïncide pas toujours avec l'intention "interne." Le chœur accompagnant ce poème, par exemple, semble être à la fois la reproduction confuse et l'opposition spirituelle du "Larron." Peut-être était-ce là l'intention. Dans ce cas, le drame a un défaut, la technique est basée sur une incertitude.

"Le Vent nocturne":

> Attys Attys Attys charming and untidy
> Yours is the name that elves mocked nightly
> Because one of your pines falls in the gothic wind
> Trees flee in the distance like an ancient army
> Whose lances oh pines wave at the road's bend
> Now burned-out villages meditate

Le dernier vers absout le passé mythologique des vers précédents de toute vulgaire déclamation perrichonesque par une nouvelle technique implicite qui tout à coup déplace la scène; le passé évite ainsi de devenir une curiosité de la sensibilité anachronique.

---

49. André Breton, *Les Pas perdus*.

"Lul de Faltenin": Already quoted in chapter 2.
"La Tzigane":

> L'amour lourd comme un ours privé
> Dansa debout quand nous voulûmes
> Et l'oiseau bleu perdit ses plumes
> Et les mendiants leurs Avé.

The narrative past tense of this poem detracts from the logical play of the words. Not up to "Marizibill."

"L'Ermite": As good technically as "Le Larron." Still, this criticism is true of the general effect: "Au reste son fabuleux savoir prosodique n'est plus à vanter. Non content d'innover dans l'expression, il a entrepris de doter la technique de son art. Tout en admettant le principe d'une distinction des rimes et masculines et féminines, c'est ainsi qu'il tente de définir leur genre à nouveau."[50]

"Automne": Again unimportant, but clear.

"L'Emigrant de Landor Road": "Seuls des bateaux d'enfant tremblaient à l'horizon," better in Rimbaud. But this is not in Rimbaud:

> Les mannequins pour lui s'étant déshabillés
> Battirent leurs habits puis les lui essayèrent
> Le vêtement d'un lord mort sans avoir payé
> Au rabais l'habilla comme un millionaire
>
> > Au dehors les années
> > Regardaient la vitrine
> > Les mannequins victimes
> > Et passaient enchaînées.

"Rosemonde": A sweeter "Marizibill."
"Le Brasier":

> Le galop soudain des étoiles
> N'étant que ce qui deviendra
> Se mêle au hennissement mâle

50. André Breton, *Les Pas perdus.*

"Lul de Faltenin": Déjà cité au chapitre 2.
"La Tzigane":

> Love was heavy as a bear
> Who danced when we desired
> The blue bird lost its feathers
> The beggars their prayers.

Le passé historique: "dansa" réfreine la danse logique des mots. Cela ne vaut pas "Marizibill."

"L'Ermite": réussite technique aussi belle que celle du "Larron." Cette critique est vraie de l'effet général: "There's no more need to praise his fabulous kowledge of prosody. Not happy with innovating expression, he went on to inform technique with his art. All the while recognizing the distinction between masculine and feminine rhymes—that was his way of renewing the definition of the genre."[50]

"Automne": sans importance mais clair.

"L'Emigrant de Landor Road": "Only children's boats trembled on the horizon." Rimbaud a mieux écrit cela; pourtant il n'a pas écrit:

> The mannequins undressed for him
> Gathered their suits then gave them to him
> The borrowed costume of a dead lord
> Cheaply dressed him like a millionaire
>
> The years outside
> Looked in the window
> At the mannequin victims
> And passed in chains.

"Rosemonde": "Marizibill" avec un "charme particulier."
"Le Brasier":

> The sudden gallop of the stars
> Was nothing but the future
> Mixed with the male neighing

---

50. André Breton, *Les Pas perdus.*

Des centaures dans leurs haras
Et des grandes plaintes végétales
· ·
Et les serpents ne sont-ils que les cous des cygnes
· ·
Jardins roulant plus haut que tous les ciels mobiles
· ·
Quand bleuira sur l'horizon la Désirade
· ·
Et le troupeau de sphinx regagne la sphingerie

"Rhénanes": "Nous transportâmes le *Festin* à Neuilly. Non sans faire halte à la synagogue de la rue Jacques-Dulud." Les chœurs mâles incitaient Guillaume à des variations héroïcomiques sur telle pièce du "Vent du Rhin" ("Rhénanes" des *Alcools*) voire à de séduisantes théories gramophonétiques."

"Signe": "Mon Automne éternelle ô ma saison mentale"—exceeded by "O soleil c'est le temps de la Raison ardente" of "La Jolie rousse" (*Calligrammes*).

"Un Soir": "Quand les tramways roulaient jaillissaient des feux pâles."

"La Dame":

Et trotte trotte
Trotte la petite souris.

"Les Fiançailles": 3, 4, and 5 anticipate the rank of *Calligrammes*—The series as a whole is spoiled: "Il vit décapité sa tête est le soleil. Et la lune son cou tranché"—it is easy for one loving "uniquement" to give himself to the expansiveness of Biblical metaphor. In the excellent lines, he imposes mental restrictions—

J'ai tout donné au soleil
Tout sauf mon ombre

"Qu'ai-je fait aux bêtes théologales de l'intelligence" could have been written only by Apollinaire and has something to do with the dedication "A Picasso."

Of centaurs on their stud farm
And the great vegetal groans
. . . .
And snakes are but the necks of swans
. . . .
Rolling gardens higher than the shifting skies
. . . .
When Désirade darkens the horizon
. . . .
And the herd of sphinxes goes back to the sphinxerie

"Rhénanes": "We carried *le Festin* in Neuilly. Not without stopping at the synagogue on rue Jacques-Dulud." Les chœurs mâles incitaient Guillaume à des variations héroïcomiques sur telle pièce du "Vent du Rhin" ("Rhénanes" des *Alcools*) voire à de séduisantes théories gramophonétiques."

"Signe": "My eternal autumn oh my mental season" que surpasse "Oh Sun it is the time of ardent Reason" de "La Jolie rousse" (*Calligrammes*).

"Un Soir": "When the streetcars ran and flashed pale fires."

"La Dame":

And trot trot
Trot the little mouse.

"Les Fiançailles" 3, 4, et 5 anticipent sur les résultats de *Calligrammes*. La série est gâtée dans son ensemble: "He saw decapitated his head is the sun. And the moon his throat slit." Il est facile pour qui aime "uniquement" de se donner à l'expansion de la métaphore biblique. Dans ses meilleurs vers, il impose certaines restrictions mentales:

I gave all to the sun
All but my shadow

"What have I done to the theologale beasts of intelligence" ne pouvaient être écrits que par Apollinaire et ont des rapports étroits avec la dédicace à Picasso.

"Clair de lune": "Les astres assez bien figurent les abeilles"—an intentionally laughable dementia of figure; but not the important, mordant moonlight of Laforgue.

1909:

La dame avait une robe
En ottoman violine
Et sa tunique brodée d'or
Etait composée de deux panneaux
S'attachant sur l'épaule

Les yeux dansent comme des anges
Elle riait elle riait
Elle avait un visage aux couleurs de France
Les yeux bleues les dents blanches et les lèvres très rouges
Elle avait un visage aux couleurs de France

Elle était décolletée en rond
Et coiffée à la Récamier
Avec de beaux bras nus

N'entendra-t-on jamais sonner minuit

La dame en robe d'ottoman violine
Et en tunique brodée d'or
Décolleté en rond
Promenait ses boucles
Son bandeau d'or
Et traînait ses petits souliers à boucles
Elle était si belle
Que tu n'aurais pas osé l'aimer
J'aimais les femmes atroces dans les quartiers énormes
Où naissaient chaque jour quelques êtres nouveaux
Le fer était leur sang la flamme leur cerveau
J'aimais j'aimais le peuple habile des machines
Le luxe et la beauté ne sont que son écume
Cette femme était si belle
Qu'elle me faisait peur

Which would show that the dialectic is not always the property of MM. les philosophes—cf. Marx on the poverty of philosophy.

"Clair de lune": Le vers: "The stars quite resemble bees" contient d'autres métaphores folles (à faire rire); mais est moins important que l'ironie mordante des clairs de lune de Laforgue.

1909:

The lady wore a dress
Of Ottoman design
And her gold embroidered tunic
Was made of two panels
Held at her shoulder

Eyes dancing like angels
She laughed she laughed
Her face wore the colors of France
Blue eyes white teeth and very red lips
Her face wore the colors of France

Her neckline was round
And her hair done like Récamier's
Her arms lovely and bare

Will midnight's bell never ring

The lady in the Ottoman dress
And in the gold embroidered tunic
With the round neckline
Flaunted her curls
Her gold headband
And trailed her little buckled shoes
She was so beautiful
That you wouldn't have dared to love her
I loved wretched women in the slums
Where each day new beings were born
With iron their blood and fire their brains
I loved I loved skilled workers
Luxury and beauty are nothing but her froth
That woman was so beautiful
That she frightened me

Ces vers peuvent bien montrer que la dialectique n'est pas toujours la propriété de MM. les philosophes. V. Marx sur la misère de la philosophie.

"A la Santé": The equivalent in English of these VI poems would be Hardy working with the smoothness of the cavalier poets (an impossibility in English?).

> Non je ne me sens plus là
> Moi-même
> Je suis le quinze de la Onzième (II)
> . . .
> Une mouche sur le papier à pas menus
> Parcourt mes lignes inégales (IV)
> Nous sommes seuls dans ma cellule
> Belle clarté Chère raison (VI)

"Cors de chasse," ("Automne malade" and "Hôtels" preceding this might be skipped). "L'Adieu" given historic latitudes—the lyric dignity of loving and avoiding the pathetic was not in Thomas de Quincey who is inevitably brought into the poem as he passes.

"Vendémiaire": Thru the clutter of histories realized the drunkenness of this poem lives.

Calligrammes—Poèmes de la Paix et de la Guerre (1913—1916)

His best work.

"L'ordre de ces poèmes n'est pas indifférent—"Ondes, Etendards," "Case d'Armons," "Lueurs des tirs" et "Obus couleur de lune," "La Tête étoilée." N'y paraît-il cette variation connue de l'âme de tout combattant qui mène du départ en chant à la halte glorieuse!

. . . .

"Une des pages les plus émues de ce livre est celle de "La Colombe poignardée et le Jet d'eau"—C'est-à-dire l'amour et l'amitié. — Je n'entreprendrai pas d'en justifier la disposition typographique pour ceux qui demandent compte aux poètes de leurs fantaisies. J'ai lu dans La Papesse Jeanne que les Gaulois disposaient leurs chants bachiques en forme de tonneau. Pour ma part je regrette que "l'Horloge de demain," de 391, n'ait pu être reproduite dans Calligrammes. Je crois en effet que cette œuvre, tout en restant dans la tradition populaire des graffitti, aux confins de l'art d'écrire et de l'art de peindre, inaugure une série d'expériences."[51]

51. André Breton, Les Pas perdus.

"A La Santé": L'équivalent anglais de ces VI poèmes se trouverait dans Hardy s'il avait la fluidité des "poètes cavaliers," ce qu'il n'a pas, ce que l'anglais ne lui permet pas.

> No I am no longer here
> > Myself
> I am the fifteenth of the Eleventh (II)
>
> . . . .
>
> A fly on the paper with delicate steps
> Crosses my uneven lines (IV)
> We are alone in my cell
> Beautiful clarity Dear reason (VI)

"Cors de chasse": ("Automne malade" et "Hôtels" qui précèdent peuvent être laissés de côté). Semblable à "l'Adieu" avec, en plus, le souffle historique; la dignité lyrique obtenue par l'amour du pathétique et par l'art de s'en libérer ne se trouve pas chez Thomas de Quincey que ce poème fatalement arrête au passage.

"Vendémiaire": A travers le fracas des certitudes historiques, l'ivresse de ce poème prend vie.

Calligrammes—Poèmes de la Paix et de la Guerre (1913–1916).

Son œuvre la meilleure.

"The manner in which these poems have been arranged is not by chance: 'Ondes, Etendards,' 'Case d'Armons,' 'Lueurs des tirs,' 'Obus couleur lune,' and 'La Tête étoilé.' It also appears that this variation is well known to the souls of all those who fight and who go forward singing to their next glorious stop!

. . . .

"One of the most moving pages of this book is 'La Colombe poignardée et le Jet d'eau,' that is to say, love and friendship. I'll not presume to justify the typographical disposition for those who wish to have poets justify their fantasies. I've read in 'La Papesse Jeanne' that the Gauls ordered their bachic songs in the shape of a barrel. As for me I regret that 'L'horloge de demain' in 391 has not been reproduced in *Calligrammes*. In fact I believe that this work, all the while faithful to a popular graffiti tradition, at the limits of the art of writing and painting, inaugurates a series of experiences."[51]

51. André Breton, *Les Pas perdus.*

Hurrying past landmarks:

"Les Fenêtres"—At the confines of the art of writing and the art of painting; but he did not need to make this poem a calligramme. He broke up his thoughts into his lines.[52]

"Les Collines"—The volume should be in print,[53] all this poem should be quoted. The poem is an entire art of bordering on rhyme and forcing the dignity of the material to avoid it—i.e. rhymes. But only the training of *La Chanson du Mal-Aimé* could have permitted his attempt, and won for him his ardor.

"Arbre"—"Tu chantes avec les autres tandis que les phonographes galopent"—a long way in temper from the beheaded Catholicism of "Zone." The tree of an anticipated Europe.

"Lundi Rue Christine"—The poet executing his own assassination, with the time.[54] This is all of the events of the year 1913.

"Lettre—Océan"—In which a calligramme covers geography.

"Sur les Prophéties"—"Une cartomancienne cérétane Marguerite je ne sais plus" Cf. T.S. Eliot's *The Waste Land*.

"Le Musicien de Saint-Merry"—"J'ai enfin le droit de saluer des êtres que je ne connais pas:" The promise of *Alcools* realized.

> Passeurs des morts et les mordonnantes mériennes
> . . . .
> Il s'en allait indifférent jouant son air
> Il s'en allait terriblement

"La Cravate et la Montre"—The calligramme hands of a clock say: "Il est—5 enfin Et tout sera fini
"Un Fantôme de nuées":

> Comme c'était la veille du quatorze juillet
> Vers les quatre heures de l'après-midi
> Je descendis dans la rue pour aller voir les saltimbanques

The whole poem becomes an art of expectancy—

52. The legend of its making is given in Billy, *Apollinaire vivant*.

53. 1932.

54. Cf. Breton.

Se hâtant, pour brûler les bornes:

"Les Fenêtres": Aux confins de l'art de l'écriture et de celui de la peinture; mais il n'avait pas besoin de faire un calligramme de ce poème. Il a émiétté ses pensées dans ses vers.[52]

"Les Collines": Tout le poème est à citer.[53] C'est tout l'art de la rime qu'on frôle et que l'on fait éviter à la dignité du sujet. Mais seul l'exercice de *La Chanson du Mal-Aimé* pouvait permettre cette expérience et lui valut cette ardeur.

"Arbre": "You sing with the others while the phonographs gallop"; le poète est bien éloigné par son tempérament du catholicisme coupé de "Zone." L'arbre d'une Europe anticipée.

"Lundi Rue Christine": Le poète exécutant son propre assassinat avec l'époque.[54] Tous les événements de l'année 1913.

"Lettre-Océan": Un calligramme circonscrit la géographie.

"Sur les Prophéties": "A Ceretan fortune-teller, was her name Marguerite?" Cf. T.S. Eliot: *The Waste Land*.

"Le Musicien de Saint-Merry": "Finally I have the right to greet those I do not know:" la promesse d'*Alcools* est réalisée.

> Ferryman of the dead and humming Saint Merryians
> . . . .
> He went indifferently on his way playing his tune
> He went terribly on his way

"La Cravate et la Montre": Les aiguilles calligrammes de la pendule disent:

"It is—five at last And all will end."

"Un Fantôme de nuées":

> On the eve of the fourteenth of July
> Around four o'clock in the afternoon
> I went down to the street to see the acrobats

Le poème tout entier devient un art de l'attente:

52. La légende de sa composition est donnée par Billy dans *Apollinaire vivant*.
53. 1932.
54. Cf. Breton.

Son corps mince devint une musique si délicate que nul
    parmi les spectateurs n'y fut insensible
Un petit esprit sans aucune humanité
Pensa chacun
Et cette musique des formes
Détruisit celle de l'orgue mécanique
Que moulait l'homme au visage couvert d'ancêtres

Le petit saltimbanque fit la roue
Avec tant d'harmonie
Que l'orgue cessa de jouer
Et que l'organiste se cacha le visage dans les mains
Aux doigts semblables aux descendants de son destin
Fœtus minuscules qui lui sortaient de la barbe
Nouveaux cris de Peau-Rouge
Musique angélique des arbres
Disparition de l'enfant
. . . .
Mais chaque spectateur cherchait en soi l'enfant miraculeux
Siècle ô siècle des nuages

Had there been no Picasso, the poem might perhaps never have been done. But then there is the first and lesser "Saltimbanques" in *Alcools*: the century of clouds was at the root of both.

    "Tour":

Au Nord au Sud
Zénith Nadir
Et les grands cris de l'Est
L'Océan se gonfle à l'Ouest
La Tour à la Roue
S'adresse

Which, in the poem at least, it does.

    "Voyage":

Adieu amour nuage qui
Fuis Refais le Voyage de Dante

or specifically:

His thin body became such delicate music that
    all spectators were touched by it
A little inhuman spirit
Each one thought
And this music of forms
Destroyed that of the mechanical organ
Molding the man whose face was covered with ancestors

The little acrobat did a cartwheel
With such harmony
That the organ stopped playing
And the organ player hid his face in his hands
His fingers like descendants of his destiny
Miniscule foetuses coming out of his beard
New cries of the Red-Skin
Angelic music of the trees
Disappearance of the child
. . . .
But each spectator searched inside himself for the miraculous child
Century oh century of clouds

Sans Picasso le poème n'aurait peut-être jamais été écrit. Il est vrai qu'il y a, moins importants, dans *Alcools*: "Les Saltimbanques:" le siècle des nuages est à la base des deux.
    "Tour":

        To the North to the South
        Zenith Nadir
        And the great cries of the East
        The Ocean swells in the West
        The Tower to the Wheel
        Speaks

Ce qu'elle fait réellement, du moins dans le poème.
"Voyage":

        Goodbye love cloud
        Fleeing Double Dante's Voyage

ou spécifiquement:

"A Travers l'Europe": The dream is not necessary for the journey. Not automatism, but the facts: "90 ou 324 un homme en l'air un veau qui regarde à travers le ventre de sa mère." The internal rhymes are passed over in the ease of the poem as a journey.

Continued in:

"La Petite auto": which ends as a calligramme: a flat tire.

"La Mandoline l'Œillet et le Bambou"—3 calligrammes—"Traverse la vérité car la Raison c'est ton Art."

"Fumées": an art of smell in words.

> Et tandis que la guerre
> Ensanglante la terre
> Je hausse les odeurs
> Près des couleurs-saveurs.

"A Nîmes": The seeming haphazard of seeming disorder under the control of the verse (arranged as heroic couplets) gives the order of military life.

"2e Canonnier conducteur": A poem in which the usual typography alternates with several calligrammes. The procedure: it is enough to enumerate the things seen in peace as the war goes on, for the war to go on and for poems to live by seemingly accidental contrasts.

"Ombre":

> Et qui danse au soleil sans faire de poussière
> Ombre encre du soleil

"Oracles": Prophecy is cryptic, yet concretely, in all objects:

> Le sifflet me fait plus plaisir
> Qu'un palais égyptien
> Le sifflet des tranchées
> Tu sais

The soldier is expectant, isolate, and yet unchanged, in love.

"Vers le Sud":

"Les Soupirs du servant de Dakar": the exotic as part of the color of war.

"A Travers l'Europe": Le rêve n'est pas nécessaire au voyage. Ce n'est pas de l'automatisme mais les faits: "90 or 324 a man in the air a calf that looks through its mother's stomach." Les rimes internes sont survolées dans l'aisance du poème-voyage.

Suite dans:

"La Petite auto": qui finit par un calligramme: un pneu crevé.

"La Mandoline L'Œillet et Le Bambou": 3 calligrammes. "Cross the truth for Reason is your Art."

"Fumées": art de l'odorat dans les mots.

> And while the war
> Bloodies the earth
> I raise odors
> Close to colors-flavors.

"A Nîmes": L'apparence accidentelle d'un apparent désordre sous le contrôle du vers (le rhythme épique) donne l'ordre de la vie militaire.

"2e Canonnier conducteur": Poème dans lequel la typographie ordinaire alterne avec divers calligrammes. La méthode: il suffit d'énumérer les choses vues dans la paix tandis que la guerre continue, pour que la guerre continue et pour que les poèmes vivent par des contrastes en apparence accidentels.

"Ombre":

> And who dances in the sun without raising dust
> Shadow ink of the sun

"Oracles": La Prophétie est cryptique, et pourtant d'une façon concrète, dans tous les objets:

> Whistling makes me happier
> Than an Egyptian palace
> The whistling of the trenches
> You know

Le soldat est dans l'attente, isolé, et pourtant immuable dans l'amour.

"Vers le Sud":

"Les Soupirs du Servant de Dakar": L'exotisme qui fait partie des couleurs de la guerre.

"Fête":

> L'air est plein d'un terrible alcool
> Filtre des étoiles mi-closes
> Les obus caressent le mol

A day in the life of the writer of *Alcools*.

"Les Grenadines répentantes"—Recalls "Clotilde" in *Alcools*; more like Blake than like Mallarmé.

"Le Palais du Tonnerre": Quotation may as well stop here for there are yet "Le Chant d'Amour," "Du coton dans les oreilles" (the most intense and varied use of the calligramme in literature), "Le Départ," "Le Vigneron champenois" (recalling the battles in Shakespeare), "Océan de terre" (the war given as a surrealist painter might give it), "Chevaux de Frise" (Non chevaux barbes mais barbelés Et je les anime tout soudain); "Tristesse d'une étoile," "La Victoire," "La Jolie rousse" (His Grand Testament).

Par l'issue ouverte sur le boyau dans la craie
En regardant la paroi adverse qui semble en nougat
On voit à gauche et à droite fuir l'humide couloir désert
Où meurt étendue une pelle à la face effrayante à deux yeux réglementaires
    qui servent à l'attacher sous les caissons
Un rat y recule en hâte tandis que j'avance en hâte
Et le boyau s'en va couronne de craie semée de branches
Comme un fantôme creux qui met du vide où il passe blanchâtre
Et là-haut le toit est bleu et couvre bien le regard fermé par quelques lignes
    droites
Mais en deçà de l'issue c'est le palais bien nouveau et qui paraît ancien
Le plafond est fait de traverses de chemin de fer
Entre lesquelles il y a des morceaux de craie et des touffes d'aiguilles de
    sapin
Et de temps en temps des débris de craie tombent comme des morceaux de
    vieillesse
A côté de l'issue que ferme un tissu lâche d'une espèce qui sert généralement
    aux emballages
Il y a un trou qui tient lieu d'âtre et ce qui y brûle est un feu semblable à
    l'âme
Tant il tourbillonne et tant il est inséparable de ce qu'il dévore et fugitif

"Fête":

> The air is full of a terrible alcohol
> Filtered by half-closed stars
> The shells caress the soft

Voyage dans la vie de l'auteur d'*Alcools*.

"Les Grenadines répentantes": Rappelle la "Clotilde" d'*Alcools*, plus près de Blake que de Mallarmé.

"Le Palais du Tonnerre": Autant vaut arrêter ici les citations. Restent encore: "Le Chant d'Amour," "Du Coton dans les oreilles" (l'usage le plus intensif et varié fait du calligramme en littérature), "Le Départ," "Le Vigneron champenois" (rappelant les batailles de Shakespeare), "Océan de terre" (la guerre présentée comme un peintre surréaliste pourrait la présenter), "Chevaux de Frise" (Not Barbary horses but barbed wire And I give them sudden life), "Tristesse d'une étoile," "La Victoire," "La Jolie rousse" (Son *Grand Testament*).

By the exit to the narrow chalky passage
Facing the opposite wall that looks like nougat
one sees left and right the damp deserted hallway fleeing
Where a tossed shovel dies with a terrifying face with two regulation eyes
    that attach it under the caissons
A rat hastily draws back while I hastily go forth
And the trench goes on crowned in chalk bristling with branches
Like a hollow ghost who leaves emptiness where he passes in white
And above the roof is blue and covers the gaze closed in with straight lines
But on this side of the exit the palace is quite new and looks ancient
The roof is made of railroad ties
Between them are bits of chalk and pine-needle tufts
And from time to time fragments of chalk fall like bits of old age
Next to the exit covered by a loose cloth of the kind generally used for
    packaging
There is a hole where there should be a hearth and what burns there is a
    fire like the soul
It swirls so much and is so inseparable from what it devours and fleeting

Les fils de fer se tendent partout servant de sommier supportant des
    planches
Ils forment aussi des crochets et l'on y suspend mille choses
Comme on fait à la mémoire
Des Musettes bleues des casques bleus des cravates bleues des vareuses
    bleues
Morceaux du ciel tissus des souvenirs les plus purs
Et il flotte parfois en l'air de vagues nuages de craie

Sur la planche brillent des fusées détonateurs joyaux dorés à tête émaillée
Noirs blancs rouges
Funambules qui attendent leur tour de passer sur les trajectoires
Et font un ornement mince et élégant à cette demeure souterraine
Ornée de six lits placés en fer à cheval
Six lits couverts de riches manteaux bleus
Sur le palais il y a un haut tumulus de craie
Et des plaques de tôle ondulée
Fleuve figé de ce domaine idéal
Mais privé d'eau car ici il ne roule que le feu jailli de la mélinite
Le parc aux fleurs de fulminate jaillit des trous penchés
Tas de cloches aux doux sons des douilles rutilantes
Sapins élégants et petits comme en un paysage japonais
Le palais s'éclaire parfois d'une bougie à la flamme aussi petite qu'une
    souris
O palais minuscule comme si on te regardait par le gros bout d'une lunette
Petit palais où tout s'assourdit
Petit palais où tout est neuf rien rien d'ancien
Et où tout est précieux où tout le monde est vêtu comme un roi
Une selle est dans un coin à cheval sur une caisse
Un journal du jour traîne par terre
Et cependant tout paraît vieux dans cette neuve demeure
Si bien qu'on comprend que l'amour de l'antique
Le goût de l'anticaille
Soit venu aux hommes dès le temps des cavernes
Tout y était si précieux et si neuf
Tout y est si précieux et si neuf
Qu'une chose plus ancienne ou qui a déjà servi y apparaît
    plus précieuse
Que ce qu'on a sous la main
Dans ce palais souterrain creusé dans la craie si blanche et si neuve

Iron wires everywhere grow taut in box springs supporting boards
They also form hooks and a thousand things are hung there
As things hang on memory
Blue bags blue helmets blue ties blue peacoats
Bits of sky the purest material of memories
And sometimes vague chalk clouds float through the air
On the board the detonator rockets shine golden jewels for the spangled
    head
Blacks whites reds
Tightrope walkers who wait their turn to pass along trajectories
And make a slim elegant ornament in this underground residence
Decorated with six beds forming a horseshoe
Six beds covered with handsome blue coats
Above the palace there is a high tumulus of chalk

And rippled sheets of steel
Congealed river of this ideal domain
But without water because here only fire flows sprung from melinite
The park with fulminite flowers bursting from tilting holes
Pile of bells of gentle sounds of gleaming cartridges
Small elegant fir trees as in a Japanese landscape
The palace lights up occasionally with a candle whose flame is as small as a
    mouse
Oh miniscule palace as if one looked at you from the large end of a telescope
Little palace where all is muffled
Little palace where all is new nothing nothing old
And where all is precious and everyone is dressed like a king
A saddle is in a corner horseback on a crate
A daily paper lies on the floor
And still all seems old in this new residence
So much so that one understands that the love of the antique
The taste for antiques
Has come down to men from the time of caves
Here all was so precious and so new
Here all is so precious and so new
That one thing that is older or that has already been used here appears
    more precious
Than what one has in hand
In this underground palace cut into the chalk so white and so new

Et deux marches neuves
            Elles n'ont pas deux semaines
Sont si vieilles est si usées dans ce palais qui semble antique sans imiter
    l'antique
Qu'on voit que ce qu'il y a de plus simple de plus neuf est ce qui est
Le plus près de ce que l'on appelle la beauté antique
Et ce qui est surchargé d'ornements
A besoin de vieillir pour avoir la beauté qu'on appelle Antique
Et qui est la noblesse la force l'ardeur l'âme l'usure
De ce qui est neuf et qui sert
Surtout si cela est simple simple
Aussi simple que le petit palais du tonnerre

There would seem to be nothing so unsurcharged with ornament since Rimbaud's "Les Assis:" the verses appear to need no restricted form to have aged them. Simplicity serves even where Rimbaud might imaginably have wrenched it. Comparison is beside the point. "Le Palais du Tonnerre" is a war poem; "Les Assis" is not. Each exists, in its own rite, in different times, and the words of each partake of the composition as action of painting as it appeared in two different cultures. Apollinaire would seem to be the only (not war poet, but) poet who has lived in the time of war. And the art is as always: "un sens complet et relatif comme les lettres d'un livre"—so that the book does not exist. Only two events: the war and the words.

The same poet in the same time reincarnated certain simplicities of the Provençal in French: "Tandis que l'oiseau dit cui-cui . . ." And he sent the bird sounds on post-cards.[55]

55. See André Rouvèyre—*Souvenirs de mon commerce*: "7 avril 1915."

And two new steps
          not yet two weeks old
Are so old and so worn in this palace that seems antique without imitating
   the antique
That you see that What is simplest newest is what is
The closest to what is called antique beauty
And what is heavy with ornaments
Needs to age to have this Antique beauty
Which is nobility strength ardor soul wear tear
Of what is new what serves
Above all if it is simple simple
As simple as the little palace of thunder

Il semble que rien n'ait été écrit d'aussi peu surchargé d'ornements depuis "Les Assis" de Rimbaud; les vers semblent n'avoir demandé les restrictions d'aucune forme pour les vieillir. La simplicité sert même dans les endroits où on pourrait imaginer que Rimbaud l'aurait compromise. Une comparaison n'est pas de mise. "Le Palais du Tonnerre" est un poème de guerre: "Les Assis" n'en sont pas un. L'un et l'autre existe dans son propre rite, dans des époques différentes et les mots de l'un comme de l'autre participent à la composition-action, à la peinture telle qu'elle apparaît dans deux cultures différentes. Apollinaire semble être non le seul poète guerrier, mais le seul à avoir su vivre à l'époque de la guerre. Et l'art, comme toujours est "un sens complet et relatif comme les lettres d'un livre." Si bien que le livre n'existe pas, seuls deux événements existent: la guerre, les mots.

Le même poète à la même époque réincarne certaines simplicités du Provençal en français : "While the bird says tweet tweet . . ." et il envoya les cris de l'oiseau sur des cartes postales.[55]

55. Voir André Rouvèyre, *Souvenirs de mon commerce*: "7 avril 1915."